China with a Cut

 PUBLICATIONS SERIES

General Editor
Paul van der Velde

Publications Officer
Martina van den Haak

Editorial Board
Prasenjit Duara (University of Chicago) / Carol Gluck (Columbia University) / Christophe Jaffrelot (Centre d'Études et de Recherches Internationales-Sciencespo) / Victor T. King (University of Hull) / Yuri Sadoi (Meijo University) / A.B. Shamsul (Institute of Occidental Studies / Universiti Kebangsaan Malaysia) / Henk Schulte Nordholt (Royal Netherlands Institute of Southeast Asian and Caribbean Studies) / Wim Boot (Leiden University)

The *IIAS Publications Series* consists of Monographs and Edited Volumes. The Series publishes results of research projects conducted at the International Institute for Asian Studies. Furthermore, the aim of the Series is to promote interdisciplinary studies on Asia and comparative research on Asia and Europe.

The *International Institute for Asian Studies* (IIAS) is a postdoctoral research centre based in Leiden and Amsterdam, the Netherlands. Its objective is to encourage the interdisciplinary and comparative study of Asia and to promote national and international cooperation. The institute focuses on the humanities and social sciences and, where relevant, on their interaction with other sciences. It stimulates scholarship on Asia and is instrumental in forging research networks among Asia scholars worldwide.
IIAS acts as an international mediator, bringing various parties together, working as a clearinghouse of knowledge and information. This entails activities such as providing information services, hosting academic organisations dealing with Asia, constructing international networks, and setting up international cooperative projects and research programmes. In this way, IIAS functions as a window on Europe for non-European scholars and contributes to the cultural rapprochement between Asia and Europe.

For further information, please visit www.iias.nl.

China with a Cut

Globalisation, Urban Youth and Popular Music

Jeroen de Kloet

AMSTERDAM UNIVERSITY PRESS

PUBLICATIONS SERIES

MONOGRAPHS 3

Cover illustration: Performance artist at the Modern Sky Music Festival of 2008 (photo by the author)

Cover design: Maedium, Utrecht
Layout: The DocWorkers, Almere

ISBN   978 90 8964 162 5
e-ISBN 978 90 4851 114 3
NUR   761

© IIAS / Amsterdam University Press, Amsterdam 2010

Contents

List of Figures and Tables

Figures

Tables

Acknowledgements

In many ways, the completion of this book is a closure. At the same time, I will always remember the making of this book as an opportunity for me to encounter so many people, and so much involvement, tenderness and, indeed, love. First and foremost, I would like to thank the musicians, record company representatives, and young people who responded so openly to my endless questioning and probing into their lives. I want to thank in particular Cui Jian, Feng Jiangzhou, Qiu Ye, Anthony Wong and Zu Zhou for their support, wit, critical views and, indeed, their music which never fails to transport me to Beijing and Hong Kong even when I am firmly back in Amsterdam. Contrary to popular belief, the music industries have been very helpful and inspiring. For that I want to thank Leslie and Louis Chan, Dickson Dee, Niu Jiawei, and Shen Lihui.

In China, many people helped me feel more than at home. In 1992, Jin Hui and Zhou Xinping introduced me to their lives and families. Even now, whenever I am in Beijing, Xinping greets and treats me like I have never left the city. In 1997, Qin Liwen quickly changed from a research assistant into a close companion, with whom I still explore, more than a decade later, the city we have claimed as our own. She showed me so much more about China than, I think, she ever imagined possible. Louis Ho offered invaluable help from Hong Kong. In the Olympic year of 2008, Vincent Zhu accompanied me to see new bands and venues. I admire his fun attitude toward life, and his energy and support in this research. Another research companion of mine in that significant year, Sylvie Luk, offered me not only her critical views, but also her inspiring interest in the trendy and the artistic. Both Vincent and Sylvie attest to the possible openness, energy and criticality of the 1980s generation of China.

Treading further back in time, I want to thank Peter van der Veer, the supervisor of my PhD dissertation which formed the basis of this book; I thank him for his trust in me and his critical readings and comments. Leo Douw was the one to introduce me to China; his teaching left a strong impression on me, forcing me to avoid easy moral judgements. After all these years, I still cherish his advice to think, sometimes, as a Chinese Communist Party member would. More recently, I have been delighted to work closely with Stefan Landsberger; I enjoy his openness, support and our arguments that continue from the corridor to the class-room. I am also grateful to the oral defence committee of my disserta-tion: René Boomkens, Maghiel van Crevel, Arif Dirlik, Joke Hermes, Patricia Spyer and Liesbet van Zoonen. Patricia Spyer was there from the very start, combining a critical perspective with a profoundly perso-nal approach. Liesbet van Zoonen's maternal support in the years after the completion of my PhD meant a lot to me.

My students have compelled me not only to stay tuned to the sonic signs of our times, but also to stay alert in my writing and thinking. I would like to thank in particular Gladys Pak Lei Chong, Bram Hendra-wan, Esmé Meivogel, Melanie Schiller, Leonie Schmidt and Zeng Guo-hua. I thank my colleagues at the Department of Media Studies, Univer-sity of Amsterdam, and the Amsterdam School for Cultural Analysis, for their support and all the discussions: Laura Copier, Sudeep Dasgup-ta, Karel Dibbets, José van Dijck, Joke Hermes, Eloe Kingma, Jaap Kooijman, Erik Laeven, Andrea Meuzelaar, Hester Morssink, Pamela Pattynama, Patricia Pisters, Maarten Reesink, Margriet Schavemaker, Markus Stauff, Wanda Strauven, Hannes Taken, Marijke de Valck, Frank van Vree, Martijn de Waal and Maryn Wilkinson. I especially want to thank Jan Teurlings, hoping that our discussions over politics and Marxism – and our refusal to capitulate – will continue in the years to come. I thank Jacqueline Antonissen, Jobien Kuiper, Maria Romijn, and Dymph Verdriesen for their more than administrative support. I also thank Martina van den Haak, Paul van der Velde and the editorial team at Amsterdam University Press for turning the manuscript into this book.

Discussions with fellow academics in similar research fields have been wonderfully rewarding. For this I want to thank in particular the following friends who share my passion for Chinese music: John Nguyet Erni, Anthony Fung, Jeroen Groenewegen, Andrew Jones, An-dreas Steen, Cynthia Wong, and Basile Zimmerman. With my fellow board members of the Benelux branch of the International Association for the Study of Popular Music (IASPM), I share the mission to pro-mote popular music studies in the Low Countries: Tom ter Bogt, Pedro de Bruyckere, Toon van Veelen, and Koos Zwaan. On a more transna-tional stage, many academics have offered comments, help and inspira-tion. I would like to thank: Marieke Bloembergen, Chen Xiaoming, Woei Lien Chong, Martin Cloonan, David Hesmondhalgh, Ke Huixin, Edwin Jurriëns, Tak-Wing Ngo, Motti Regev, Tony Saich, Lena Scheen, Hyunjoon Shin, Will Straw and Zhang Xudong. Without Tony Mitchell, whose tireless support started at a memorable conference in Sydney in 1999, I don't think I would have had the confidence to finish this book. I owe him a lot. Rey Chow's work has deeply inspired my writing and thinking. Her visit to Amsterdam turned the intellectual bonding to something more personal, palpable, and unforgettable. It is her work I return to when I doubt the pleasures of academic life.

The death of my father, a few months before my very first trip to China in 1992, continues to colour my experiences of China. It still hurts whenever I realise that he has never known of my further exploration of China, and the intricate ways this exploration has reconfigured his son. My mother, aunt, brother and sister have, in their intimate ways, indulged me to follow my curiosity, and my desire to leave The Netherlands regularly.

Talking is an underestimated, and yet indispensible, component of thinking. Countless discussions with my friends have been essential for me. I would like to thank Corné de Jong for our shared pleasure in doing cultural studies; Dineke Koerts and Constance Vos for their successful attempts to make China dance; Helen Hok-sze Leung for being the twin sibling I never had; Kam Wai Kui for his energy and his passion for cinema and ability to share that with his community; Anne Minnema for his support and trust since 1986; Kam Wing Ling for his humour and sharpness; Ijme Woensdregt and Nicolette Hetzler for all the nights in Xiamen, Shanghai and Kloosterburen; and Peter Ho, without whom I may never have gone to China at all – how I cherish our intertwined academic journeys. Song Hwee Lim's friendship, his ironic views and infinite wit help me take the serious things of life light-heartedly (and the light-hearted things seriously). I am grateful to Marcel Vergunst for his inexhaustible readiness to offer an alternative reading, a different perspective, another thought.

Ever since our PhD days, Giselinde Kuipers has always been a lively source of inspiration. What started as debates over modernism and postmodernism has slowly morphed into rhizomic conversations ranging from the attractiveness of Keanu Reeves and the spirituality of Gandalf to the possibility of being political. It is hard to imagine, let alone to live, academic life without such conversations.

To Yiu Fai Chow I owe this book, its arguments, the pleasure of writing, and the fun of doing research. From our very first hours together, he challenged my Beijing-centeredness, as well as my non-reflective preference for rock, to pop. He has challenged so much more over the past decade. Our never-ending discussions, our shared love for art, cinema and music, our mistrust in Chineseness, our equally strong if not stronger doubts about Dutchness, our inescapable entanglements with both – in ways divine and mundane, they contribute to a shared enjoyment of life.

Note on Romanisation and Publication History

This book uses the Hanyu Pinyin system of Romanisation for Chinese words, names and phrases, except in instances when a preferred alternative spelling exists (for example, most Hong Kong and Taiwanese personal names).

Earlier versions of some parts of this book have previously been published elsewhere. All of these texts have been substantially rewritten, updated and reorganised for this book. These texts are:

1. (2000). "Let Him Fuckin' See the Green Smoke Beneath My Groin – The Mythology of Chinese Rock". In: A. Dirlik & X. Zhang (eds.), *Postmodernism and China*. Durham: Duke University Press, 239-274. Reprinted in: (2003). "Marx or Market: Chinese Rock and the Sound of Fury". In: J. K. W. Lau (ed.), *Multiple Modernities – Cinema and Popular Media in Transcultural East Asia*. Philadelphia: Temple University Press, 28-53.
2. (2002). "Commercial Fantasies: China's Music Industry". In: S. H. Donald, M. Keane & Y. Hong (eds.), *Media Futures in China, Consumption, Content and Crisis*. London & Surrey: Routledge / Curzon Press, 93-104.
3. (2003). "Confusing Confucius – Rock in Contemporary China". In: M. Cloonan & R. Garofalo (eds.), *Policing Popular Music*. Philadelphia: Temple University Press, 166-186.
4. (2005a). "Popular Music and Youth in Urban China – The Dakou Generation", *China Quarterly*, 183, 609-626.
5. (2005b). "Sonic Sturdiness – The Globalisation of 'Chinese' Pop and Rock", *Critical Studies in Media Communication*, 22(4), 321-338.
6. (2005c). "Authenticating Geographies and Temporalities: Representations of Chinese Rock in China", *Visual Anthropology*, 18(2-3), 229-256.

Introduction: Global Longings with a Cut

What is found at the historical beginning of things is not the inviolable identity of their origin; it is the dissension of other things. It is disparity.

Michel Foucault (1984 [1971]: 79)

Fuelled (..) by China's immanent ascendance to the status of an economic superpower in the twenty-first century, it is important that the term 'Chinese' not be invoked in such ways as to become, automatically and at all times, the equivalent of the People's Republic.

Rey Chow (2007: 24)

Cosmopolitan Poses and Haunting Questions

Much has changed, I realised, when I attended the Modern Sky music festival in October 2008 in Haidian Park in West Beijing. The crowds that were allowed to gather in a public park, the wide array of music genres ranging from death metal to urban folk, the lyrics now often sung in English, the trendy youth from the 80s generation, all turned the festival into a profoundly cosmopolitan experience. An experience simultaneously saturated with articulations of Chineseness, judging from the Chinese flags people carried with them or painted on their faces. For three days, old stars from the early 1990s like He Yong and Zhang Chu shared the stage with more recent bands like Carsick Cars and Re-establishing the Rights of Statues – whose English band names also attest to the cosmopolitanism of the scene. More than fifteen years since the album's release, audiences could still remember Zhang Chu's lyrics word by word – turning the evening of his performance into a collective ritualised experience. While walking from the main stage, where The New Pants had just performed their last song, entitled *Bye Bye Disco*, to the small stage, I ran into Shen Lihui, organiser of the festival, owner of the Modern Sky label and leading vocalist of the Beijing 'Britpop' band Sober. He plays a pivotal role in the cultural scene of Beijing, and can be seen as the embodiment of the economical, cultural and political changes which have taken place in China since the mid 1990s. In establishing Modern Sky in 1997, he made use of the increased liberties in the Chinese media market (Zhao 2008), and has since then been able to operate at the outer limits of the permissible, playing the political and economic game skilfully.

The changes taking place at the end of the 1990s have paved the way for what may be termed a rebirth of Chinese rock culture. Whereas considerable attention has been given to the earlier generations of Chinese rock (Baranovich 2003; Huang 2001, 2003; Jones 1992, 1994; Steen 1996), this new generation has remained largely invisible. In the 1990s, being marginal was no longer considered a desirable option. 'Plunging into the ocean' (*xiahai*), a popular metaphor for engaging in private business, and 'linking up with the tracks of the world' (*yu shijie jiegui*) became more dominant lifestyle choices (Z. Zhang 2000). This context of commercialisation and globalisation facilitated the rebirth of Chinese rock, epitomised by the emergence of *dakou* culture in the mid-1990s. At that time, the more alternative forms of Western popular music were not freely available on the Chinese domestic market due to political and economic reasons. Illegally imported CDs punched with a cut, the *dakou* CDs, as they soon became known among Chinese youth and musicians, filled in this gap. The *dakou* CDs have inspired many bands and audiences, and stimulated the rise of new independent record companies in Beijing – of which Modern Sky and its subsidiaries like Badhead serve as the prime example. *Dakou* became the label for a new and vibrant urban youth culture emerging in China. This book focuses on the *dakou* generation and its aftermath. It explores a critical period in the development of Chinese youth culture – the 'roaring 1990s,' delving into the socio-cultural transformations in the years up to 2008. These years are, in my view, crucial if we are to understand contemporary China and its position in the world. As Wang argues, 'Without a penetrating analysis of the cultural situation of the 1990s, it is difficult to understand the economic, environmental, and political aspects of a complex culture.' (2003: 600; see also X. Zhang 2008)

My fascination with Chinese popular music started in 1992, when I saw punk-rocker He Yong in a documentary singing out loud how he was living on a garbage dump. I was surprised by the provocative poses apparently allowed in China. This fascination betrayed my double bias at that time; in my reading, music was inherently provocative, and China was ruled by a monolithic totalitarian state without any freedom. Confronted with much more fuzzy and multilayered experiences in China, in the years since 1992, I spent a great deal of energy debunking these interpretations of rock music and the role of the Chinese state. This book will show that if we dig deeper, both sonic as well as political realities in China are more complex and contradictory than we may at first realise, and hence refuse to be essentialised into monolithic meanings or labels like 'rebellious' and 'totalitarian,' or to be contained in fixed dichotomies like official versus unofficial or resistance versus compliance. Neither state nor artist can be pigeonholed that easily. Kraus' debunking of the myth of the rebellious artist is telling. 'The charismatic view of the artist as a heroic figure, locked in constant struggle against repressed and repressive authority, is a product of nineteenth-century Western romantic ideology. But Chinese artists are not so completely innocent; nor is the Chinese state so consistently malevolent.' (Kraus 2004: 2)

More questions started to haunt me after that evening in 1992, when I saw He Yong. Why has it become increasingly difficult to write of *Chinese* popular music? How valid is such a spatial adjective in our current times of globalisation? How can one ever use the idea of China and Chineseness innocently after two decades of fierce critique, deconstruction and queering (Ang 2001; Chow 1998a, 1998b; Chun 1996; Leung 2008; Lim 2007)? This book can be read as an attempt to write on rock and pop in China and Hong Kong without claiming this to be *Chinese* rock or *Chinese* pop. Yet, as the continuous use of parentheses or phrases like 'rock in China' became tedious, I still decided to use the phrase 'Chinese rock.' An anticategorical analysis that refrains from using the prefix 'Chinese' altogether also becomes rather unworkable, explaining my choice to try to challenge and interrogate the idea of 'Chinese' and 'Chineseness' from within. 'The point is not to deny the importance – both material and discursive – of categories but to focus on the process by which they are produced, experienced, reproduced, and resisted in everyday life.' (McCall 2005: 1783) Before probing further into the linguistic lenience and therefore persistence of 'Chinese' as prefix in popular and academic discourse, it is important to grasp first the changes which have taken place since the emergence of rock star Cui Jian.

From *Liumang* to *Dakou* and *Balinghou*

Liumang

In the wake of Cui Jian – still heralded as the Godfather of Chinese rock – a generation of Chinese rockers emerged in the early 1990s, attracting a relatively large audience in Mainland China. He Yong, Zhang Chu, Dou Wei, Tang Dynasty and Hei Bao were among the most popular rockers and bands of these years (see Jones 1992; Steen 1996; Baranovich 2003 for a comprehensive account of this period). The Taiwanese label Magic Stone played an important role in the promotion of this second wave of Chinese rock. Baranovich interprets the popularity of Chinese rock in the early 1990s as a continuation of the assumedly more critical and rebellious spirit of the 1980s. According to him,

> The rock fad began in the euphoric and carnivalistic spring of 1989, during which it rose to the surface and achieved popularity in the most general public sphere. The intensification of the fad during the early 1990s was a continuation of the process that had started just before and during the movement, but it was also a backlash, a popular expression of anger, defiance, and perhaps a kind of compensation for the failure of the movement. (Baranovich 2003: 36)

His equation of rock with anger, defiance and frustration reifies a rather univocal, stereotypical reading of rock as a rebellious and subcultural sound. Also, by interpreting Chinese rock as a fad, Baranovich not only assumes its temporality; he also exaggerates rock's popularity in the early 1990s. Nevertheless, his reading of rock's popularity at the early 1990s as a residue of the cultural spirit of the 1980s remains valid.

The works of Wang Shuo, the renegade writer whose books were bestsellers between 1987 and 1992, paralleled the popularity of rock, and 'represented the spirit of the alienated, semi-criminal fringe of Beijing youth culture and Chinese urban life in general.' (Barmé 1999: 77) The *liumang* was celebrated in the work of Wang Shuo as a person living on the fringes of urban society, someone who plays around, has sex, gets drunk and listens to rock music. However, under the forces of commercialisation which swept over China after Deng Xiaoping's visit to the southern special economic zones in the summer of 1992 – after which a 'socialist market economy (...) quickly mushroomed' (Dai 2002: 217) – both Wang Shuo's and rock music's appeal declined steadily, and with them the *liumang* generation faded away as well.[1] The mid-1990s were subsequently characterised by a crisis in Chinese rock culture (Qian 2007), as critic Zhao Ke puts it (1999: 2-3):

> Even if we are touched by the most pure, the most original rock music, that kind of emotion is still outdated. This era does not belong to those who gather together to scream in one voice. What we need now is individuality, our individual voice. Whether as music, as spirit, or as ideal, rock fulfilled its historical mission in the 1980s.

Rock was considered to be out of touch with the spirit of the 1990s. The rebellious spirit of rock was perceived to be endangered by the forces of commercialism unleashed during the 1990s, with the Party acting as the invisible puppet-master behind the 'gold' screen. As Dai phrases it, in the 1990s 'the commercial displaced the political.' (2002: 216) The crisis made people look back not so much to the early 1990s, but more so the 1980s, when culture fever swept over China (Barmé & Jaivin 1992; Dai 2002; Keane 2007; Wang 1996; Zhang 1997).

Indicative of the perceived crisis of Chinese rock in the mid-1990s are the words of DJ Zhang Youdai, who told me:

> The new generation does not have their own culture, or their own life; it's consumerism. I think the 1980s were the golden years. People ask me why Chinese rock started in the 1980s. I think you should ask why in the 1990s rock died in China. (...) In the 1980s young people concentrated more on culture; right now people concentrate on the economy, on making money.

Baranovich interprets the decline of rock along similar lines. To him, it 'reflects the fact that young people and others lost much of their past idealism and their will to change things.' (2003: 44) Instead, according to Baranovich, 'commercial' pop from Hong Kong and Taiwan gained popularity in the Mainland, and became the urban sound of the 1990s. He enters into the murky grounds of cultural essentialism by suggesting it may well be the significant cultural, political and social differences between the West and China that prevent rock from becoming a mainstream sound. However, changes throughout the second half of the 1990s, during which Chinese rock witnessed a revival still ongoing today, prove that labelling rock in China as a fad is inadequate.[2] Although rock may not reach the same level of popularity as it did in the early 1990s, the rise of the *dakou* generation in the second half of the 1990s does mark the birth of a new generation of Chinese rock music.

Dakou

In 1999, China's most prolific rock critic, artist and entrepreneur Yan Jun published, together with Ou Ning, an overview of the bands he considered emblematic of what they coined as the Beijing New Sound movement (Yan & Ou 1999). Their book is dedicated to the *dakou* generation of China. At about the same time, Fu Chung, manager of the small Beijing record label New Bees, dedicated his first release of pop-punk band The Flowers to the sellers of *dakou* tapes at Zhong Tu Men – one of the spots in Beijing where they are sold. Among many other meanings, *da* stands for strike, break, smash, attack, and *kou* stands for opening, entrance, cut. Together, *dakou* stands for the cut CDs and tapes being sold in urban China, often along with pirated CDs, on a bustling black market (see Figure 0.1).

Figure 0.1   *A Dakou CD*

Dakou CDs are dumped by the West, intended to be recycled, but instead are smuggled into China. *Dakou* CDs and tapes are cut to prevent them from being sold. However, since a CD player reads CDs from the centre back to the margin, only the last part is lost. Not only have these CDs been tremendously nourishing for Chinese rock musicians in the 1990s, as they opened up a musical space that did not officially exist in China, they have also come to signify a whole urban generation. As rock critic Dundee explained (Dundee 1999: 28):

> This plastic rubbish dumped by foreign record companies becomes a major source of pleasure for those discontented youths after they switch off their TV. When this plastic rubbish started flowing from the south to Beijing, it actually heralded a new rock era. All the new rock musicians in Beijing have grown up with *dakou* tapes.

It is remarkable that an urban generation chooses to name itself after an illegal product dumped by the West. On one Internet discussion site, You Dali presents a description of the *dakou* generation that is worth quoting at length. He writes:

> *Dakou* cassette tape, *dakou* CD, *dakou* video, *dakou* MD, *dakou* vendors, *dakou* consumers, *dakou* musicians, *dakou* music critics, *dakou* magazines, *dakou* photo books; this is a *dakou* world, a new life where you don't even have to leave the country to realise your spiritual adventure. When Americans fiercely give themselves a cut, they also give the world a possibility of communism and unity. The Government doesn't encourage 1.3 bil-

lion people to listen to rock and roll. A small bunch of them therefore secretly look for offerings to their ears, to their eyes, to their brains, and to their generation. If you can't do it openly, do it secretly! (...) It enables not only part of the population to become rich first, but also another part of the population to become poor first, and it also enables part of the population to become spiritually strong! *Dakou* products have ushered 1 million Chinese youths into a new wave, a new listening sensibility, a new awareness, a new mind and a new set of values. Whether the *dakou* generation is a *jinkou* [import] generation or a *chukou* [export] generation confuses quite a few social observers. [3]

This is a parody of propaganda talk, such as the reference to Deng Xiaoping's famous defence of his reform policy, in which he declared that one part of the population should be allowed to become rich first. There is a certain critical irony toward the US, which 'gives itself a cut' and thereby supports a communist world. At the same time there is a critique of the Chinese state, which, according to this author, restricts the sound of rock. Also, the text evokes feelings of excitement and energy. The idea of being *dakou* seems empowering enough to build one's life upon. It is not just a cut in a CD, but an identity bordering on the permissible.

According to Yan Jun, the *dakou* generation 'represents a generation that refuses to be suppressed, that seeks unseeingly, that connects to the underground, that creates marginal culture and lifestyle, that grows stubbornly, that resists and struggles.' (Yan 2004: 176) His reading presents one side of being *dakou*, as it celebrates the rebellious. As this book will show, *dakou* culture is more diverse and more ambiguous. It is important to note that the label emerged at a time when youth culture – and Chinese culture in general – was critiqued for having lost its political zeal. Yan Jun's claim to subversion can be read as an attempt to recuperate the marginal in a time when many observers flattened Chinese realities out under a singular blanket of alleged commercialisation that was assumed to co-opt and silence any potential for critique. As Wang argues rather belittlingly, 'The 1990s was actually an era that threw people into illusions, blindness, and horror, but this new thought appeals to shallowness and arrogance, exerting itself to cover a chaotic, bitter reality and at least to temporarily relieve anxieties.' (2003: 602) Probably even more nihilistic, if not cynical, is Geremie Barmé's *In The Red* – one of the most comprehensive overviews of the cultural field in the 1990s. Unfortunately, his overview comes with a wide array of unqualified and undertheorised adjectives to pigeonhole Chinese artists and dissidents. For example, in his view, 'The quality of [Cui Jian's] later work and the corpus of his music probably would have condemned him to a short-lived career in a normal cultural market, but the unsteady politics of mainland repression lent him a long-term validity and the appeal reserved for a veteran campaigner.' (1999: 131)[4]

This book will show how developments in music culture over the 1990s up to today challenge cynical accounts and easy generalisations. By now, *dakou* has also become a label of the past, of a time when, according to rock musician Feng Jiangzhou, people still had the ability to focus, to concentrate on and indulge fully in music. Now, with the emergence of the Internet, people live, in Feng's nostalgic view, in an utterly fragmented attention economy, and music is at most one of the many activities in which young people indulge:

> I used to buy a lot of *dakou* cassettes. I studied the music carefully with all my heart. I conducted very detailed work. Part of the reason was that my source of information was simply limited and detailed work was my only solution. I benefited a lot from this work style. Now there is a vast sea of information on the Internet, people listen to music casually. You just have so much information to receive that you don't know what one to choose. It has become my habit that I'm very selective in information, unlike the young people today, they know everything, but only a little.[5]

Balinghou

With the digitisation of music, the abundance of impulses has amplified. The current availability of sounds all over the world, where the most exotic or obscure sounds are just one click away on the Internet, has rendered the *dakou* market nearly obsolete. By the same token, beginning bands can easily upload their work. MySpace offers ample opportunities for Chinese bands for promotion and distribution – circumventing the music industry as well as the censors. In a country that seems particularly keen to periodise, these developments have given birth to yet another term for a generation conveniently classified by a decade: the 1980s (*balinghou*). This new generation of 'little emperors,' as they are often cynically referred to, all come from one-child families, born after the Cultural Revolution. For them, China has always been a country which is opening up, a place of rapid economic progress and modernisation, a place of prosperity and increased abundance, in particular in the urban areas. For this generation, 'June 4th' – the term commonly used to refer to the Tiananmen student demonstrations of 1989 – is an event of a long forgotten past, if they remember it at all. The Chinese Communist Party is a tool for networking; becoming a member facilitates one's career. Different labels are used, besides *balinghou*, for this generation, like *'linglei'* (alternative), 'the birds' nest generation,' and the *'zhongnanhai* generation,' named after a cigarette brand name. *Zhongnanhai* – also the central headquarters of the Chinese Communist Party, close to the Forbidden City – is the song title of one track by Carsick Cars, the band with vocalist Shou Wang, part of the 80s generation. He told me:

> Our generation has a different culture, the new generation feels more relaxed about music, about their life. The last generation took music very seriously, which I always respect, but this new generation plays music more for fun. Our culture is very mixed, you can get a lot of information from the Internet, so different bands think in different ways.[6]

In an essay posted on his blog on the *zhongnanhai* generation, rock critic Er Dong explains that this is a generation

> that is globally connected, modernised and diversified. Cui Jian is no longer their idol, they no longer consider rock'n'roll the weapon for revolution, none of them talks about idealism, romanticism, or any other 'ism.' They have been raised in the atmosphere of globalisation. (...) They have no set pattern of thinking, they don't have to worry about whether their lifestyle is "Chinese," which could explain why most of the new bands sing in English.[7]

This is a mobile generation that changes jobs, and combines that with making music. It consists of reflexive youngsters who skilfully navigate through late modernity. Or are they? New regimes of living provoke 'new ethical problems and dilemmas. As subjects learn to make their own choices and plan their own lives, this remains the fundamental bewildering question at the heart of what it means to be Chinese today.' (Ong & Zhang 2008: 16) Even more than the *dakou* generation, the 80s generation is part of the project driven by the state-global capitalism complex, propelling the creation of neoliberal subjectivities. Cosmopolitan worldliness plays a central role in this creation, producing a model of human nature that has, in Rofel's view, the desiring subject as its core: 'the individual who operates through sexual, material, and affective self-interest.' (2007: 3) Music is an important affective machine for the display and construction of this desiring self. In particular, youth functions as the prime agent of late modernity, for the newly developed regimes of living *demand* flexibility and openness (Ong 1999).

'Everyday I am somebody else,' sings Shen Lihui in one of his songs from 1997, an apt prediction of the spirit of the 80s generation, a spirit which became increasingly important in order to keep in tune with a post-socialist China of the 21st century. The celebration of agency as evoked by the references to individualism tends to ignore the more structural conditions that contain, steer and produce subjectivities like 'the 80s generation.' On a par with the assumed relation between modernisation and individualisation, this generation is often accused in public discourse of being selfish and overtly materialistic, a generation driven by pleasure rather than politics, for whom 'being alternative' – *linglei* (other species) – has become merely a lifestyle choice (J. Wang 2008: 228). A generation for which life has to be *niubi* – literally, a cow's vagina, metaphorically standing for cool and exciting.

It is also a generation often perceived to be overtly nationalistic and patriotic (Gries 2004; Hughes 2006; J. Wang 2008). Examples abound for this alleged rise of nationalistic zeal, such as the protests that followed the NATO bombing of the Chinese embassy in Belgrade in 1999, which NATO claimed to be an accident – to the disbelief of most Chinese. The protests and boycotts along the trail of the Olympic Torch Relay in London and Paris in April 2008, for which 'Western media' were critiqued for giving a biased coverage, serves as an example of the nationalistic zeal among Chinese youth. Blogger, writer, race car driver, school drop-out and proclaimed spokesperson of the 80s generation Han Han wrote with wit on his blog:

> Sometimes, it's really complicated. This is a country where you don't have the right to watch CNN, but do have the right to boycott it. Patriots, you go ahead, I will see.[8]

The sonic articulations of Chineseness I will analyse throughout this book may at times resonate with the discourse of nationalism, but are, just like that discourse, ridden with ambivalences and ambiguities. Just as the youngsters who protest against the US by throwing stones at the embassy may apply for a visa the next day, so too are ostentatious celebrations of Chineseness fraught with contradictions.

Dakou culture is characterised by an increased variety of musical styles, genres slowly bifurcated from the hard sound of rock further into a range of hyphenated styles. This increased diversity has paved the way for a more kaleidoscopic sonic cultural field, on which the *balinghou* generation have been able to build their subjectivities. Generalisations about the assumed egocentrism, patriotism or apolitical attitudes of these generations will prove, as my book will show, too sweeping and biased. As Han Han argues in defence of the 80s generation:

> As the previous generation was always working for the revolution, people keep on arguing that our generation does not have

any ideals. Sometimes you want to win a game, or buy a pair of sneakers, these are all ideals. There is no difference between these ideals. Sometimes I fall in love with a girl, so I want to get her, this is also an ideal. An ideal is actually a thought that motivates you to do whatever it takes (in Y. Zhang 2008: 105).

What does link the three generations as described in this section is their playing with difference; the attempts to distinguish themselves from earlier generations as well as – more importantly – their parents. Both making and listening to music plays an important role in the display and construction of these politics of identity.

The Geography of Chinese Rock

When I show MTV clips of Chinese rock to students, friends or journalists, they frequently come up with the same set of questions. First, the inevitable question related to place: What is Chinese about this? And second, related to temporality: 'This music reminds me of ten years ago.' Apparently, Chinese rock ought to be authenticated by exoticising it, and even then, they may perpetually be lagging behind. Place needs to be valorised while time ought to be conquered. This predicament, the denial of coevalness (Fabian 1983) in conjunction with the orientalist biased demand to insert sonic difference (Said 1978) betrays the hegemonic gaze (and arrogance) of 'the West.'

The response to the MTV clips points to one important axis guiding the Sinification of rock: the West versus East dichotomy. This binary relationship is as persistent as it is problematic. It is closely linked to the importance attached to authenticity in rock culture. However, there is a second axis running through the politics of rock in China: the North versus the South, conflated with the profoundly globalised distinction between rock and pop (see Figure 0.2).

Figure 0.2 *Geography of Chinese Rock*

The Cultural North (Beijing)

⇑

The Real West   ⇐   Chinese Rock   ⇒   The Fake East

⇓

The Commercial South (Hong Kong and Taiwan)

The rock mythology is important if we are to understand both this geography as well as the production of rock as a separate category (see also Stokes 2006). This mythology consists of a set of narratives which produce rock as a distinct music world that is, first and foremost, authentic, but also subcultural, masculine, rebellious and (counter) political. Not surprisingly, the perceived authoritarian character of the Chinese regime excites the perfect imagination to relive the rock mythology and its associated pop-rock dichotomy in this part of the world. By using the term 'mythology', I do not wish to suggest the existence of a 'reality' that lurks behind the mythology. Myth is a type of speech that 'makes us understand something and it imposes it on us.' (Barthes 1957: 117)

It is the rock mythology, as this book will show, supplying the glue that binds producers, musicians, and audiences together; it is the basis of the *production* of the rock culture. Authenticity is of crucial importance to the mythology, In the words of Herman and Sloop (1998: 2), 'The ideology of authenticity has provided the ground for a practice of judgment through which musicians, fans and critics were able to distinguish between "authentic rock," which was transgressive and meaningful, and inauthentic rock (or "pop"), which was co-opted and superficial.'[9] But before exploring the pop-rock distinction, let me first elaborate further on the theoretically more evocative West versus East axis.

The 'Real' West versus the 'Fake' East

When rock travels outside its perceived origin – the West – its makers face the problem of being labelled a mere copycat. The following is a telling account written by the Chinese female vocalist Long Hun, entitled 'Go West!', in which she elaborates on her frustrations when introducing the Beijing rock she 'is so proud of' to friends in London:

> But their reaction is always: 'Well, it's OK'. To them, these punk bands are just another group of punk bands, Tang Dynasty is just another heavy metal band, and they just don't have a clue to what's so good about Zhang Chu and Cui Jian. It really annoys me. I can only say: 'You don't understand.' Only some songs of Supermarket [an electronic band] still interest them, saying: 'This is interesting, strange music.' Also the tape of Chinese *guqin* [a 'traditional' Chinese string instrument], they play it over and over again. Strange, if it shows that there are indeed boundaries in music, why does foreign music manage to excite us and feel close to us? (in Long 1999: 24)

Her last outcry points to the crux of the globalisation of popular music: Why are the Chinese rock and pop fans so eager to listen to Western sounds, and not vice versa? And why have they developed an aesthetic sensibility toward popular 'Western' sounds and not the other way round? The cultural sharing which occurs when the sound of rock globalises is indeed conspicuously on Western terms (Kraus 1989: ix-x). The words of journalist Caroline Cooper are indicative:

> What the West thinks of as Chinese rock – slapdash Spears rip-offs and the bleating of Hong Kong pop stars – is all wrong. Consider instead the work of Thin Men. Jumping between classical Chinese Mandarin and the Mongolian dialect of lead singer's Dai Qin's home region, and often featuring traditional Mongolian sounds alongside classic electric guitar and keyboard... (Cooper 2000: online)

To her, sounds lacking identifiable Chinese characteristics are 'slapdash Spears rip-offs,' whereas rock, once it is Sinified – classical Chinese Mandarin, Mongolian dialect, traditional Mongolian sounds – is praiseworthy. Academics may reify this orientalising gaze; for example, Andrew Field valorises the 'real Chinese' while downplaying the alleged 'Western' elements:

> And these bands are creating their own music, albeit music that is sometimes heavily influenced by certain genres and subgenres in the West. Yet there is also an unmistakable influence of more traditional Chinese folk music on some of the bands, suggesting that the music is being glocalised, to use a popular term in academia. (Field 2007: online)

His remark serves as an apt illustration of why I think it makes little sense to think of rock in China in terms of being glocalised – as such terminology reifies and hierarchises cultural differences, as alleged 'copies from the West' are valued less when compared to assumed 'indigenous folk.'[10]

The mimicry of the Other – here Chinese rock musicians – meets with resistance and disapproval from the West. I consider this, in line with Bhabha, a hegemonic (colonial) attitude: 'Colonial mimicry is the desire for a reformed, recognizable Other, *as a subject of a difference that is almost the same, but not quite*' (1994: 86, italics his). Chinese rock often sounds and looks the same, *but not quite*. On this difference, this slippage of meaning from 'real rock' to 'old-fashioned rock', rests the hegemonic, defining power of the Western gaze. The moment rock music moves outside the arena of North America or the UK, to paraphrase

Chow, 'the term is almost always invoked with a national or ethnic qua-
lifier.' (2006: 78) Apparently, only the West has the hegemonic power
to claim universalism, while all others are delegated to ethnic and national ghettos. Rock from China carries the added burden of representing 'China' or 'Chineseness,' (Shohat & Stam 1995: 183) much more so
than Dutch rock music does, for example.

This hegemonic gaze from the West – in which musicians, journalists
and academics are complicit – is internalised in popular Chinese discourse. A look at two rock magazines in China – *Music Heaven* and *Modern Sky Magazine* – reveals not only the Chinese gaze upon the West
(extensive coverage of Western rock), but also the Chinese gaze upon
an assumed Western gaze (in reports that question whether or not rock
in China is 'just' a copy).[11] Figure 0.3 presents the cover of both magazines, one of which carries the headline 'Go West,' whereas the other
depicts the band The Cranberries. Given its status as the birthplace of
rock, the West not only sets the criteria for what rock ought to be, but it
is also imagined to be the omnipresent judge of Chinese rock. A special
in *Modern Sky Magazine* on hip-hop in China is indicative of the general angst: 'Compared to Western music, we will always be in a state of
copying. When we have something new, we will throw away the old
one. We have all sorts of music, but none is properly digested by us' (Y.
Zhang 2000: 19). In its elaborate references to generic labels from Western popular music and to Western bands, the Chinese gaze reveals a
desire to incorporate such sounds and classifications and a fear of incor-
porating too little or too much; it assumes a Western gaze, disciplining
and liberating itself, as I will show in this book, by developing authenticating tactics that involve articulations of place.[12]

Hard cultures

Following Appadurai, we can conceptualise rock music as a 'hard' cultural form. Commenting on cricket's embeddedness in 19th-century
Victorian values, in conjunction with the processes of indigenisation
cricket underwent in the 20th-century India, Appadurai advances the notion of the hard cultural form as a theoretical tool to understand the cultural flow of cricket. 'Hard cultural forms are those that come with a set
of links between value, meaning, and embodied practice that are difficult to break and hard to transform.' (Appadurai 1996: 90) Rock can be
considered a hard cultural form, with the rock mythology as its set of
links between value, meaning, and embodied practice. It imposes a relatively rigid repertoire of styles – all with their perceived origins in the
West – upon those active in the rock culture; as such, rock 'changes
those who are socialised into it more readily than it is itself changed.'
(Appadurai 1996: 90)

Figure 0.3   *Covers of Music Heaven and Modern Sky Magazine*

Hence the striking similarities in both sound and image, for example, of hard-rockers from Beijing and their colleagues in Jakarta or Seattle, with their leather jackets, long hair and unruly on- and off-stage antics. However, precisely because of the globalising force of the rock mythology, there is always the urge to make a difference and, in the case of Chinese rock, by localisation. The hard force of rock – a force that comes with a strong imagination of a clear origin: the West – *demands* localisation when the sound travels to places outside the West in order to become and remain authentic.

One example of this tactic of localisation comes from an old concert flyer of Cui Jian (see Figure 0.4).[13] For this flyer, Cui Jian borrowed from the imagery of the Communist Party. Whereas the Party 'liberated' the country on 1 October 1949 from a feudal regime, the flyer suggests that the rock of Cui Jian will liberate China from its current authorities. We see red arrows pointing to areas already liberated by the force of rock, whereas the shaded parts are yet to be liberated by our hero with his electric guitar. Just as the punks transformed the meaning of a safety pin (Hebdige 1979), so Cui Jian transforms the meaning of the glorified Communist past as embodied in a map of communist warfare.

Figure 0.4   *Flyer Cui Jian Tour 1992*

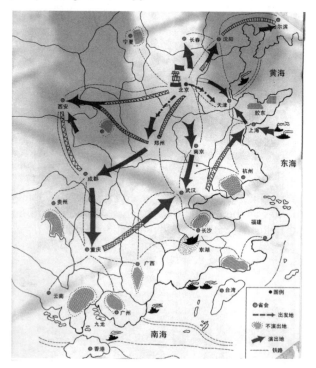

In constructing the rebellious image, he frames himself according to the hard cultural parameters set by the rock mythology, parameters that require such a localising move.

Appadurai's theorisation of 'hard cultural forms' helps to unpack rock's articulations of place, but it is important not to get caught in a global versus local opposition here, or to read rock in China as hybrid (or, indeed, glocal). Neither narratives of localisation or hybridisation suffice to grasp the 'the unfolding of the cultural movement over time.' (Condry 2006:17; see also Kooijman 2008) As Baulch argues in her study of punk and metal in Java, 'the "homogenous-hybrid" dialectic can blind observers to more complex interplays of power and nuances of meaning at the local level.' (2008: 7) As my book will show, both the scenic struggles within rock culture, as well as the exclusion of what I label the 'subaltern' sounds of female voices and non-Beijing bands, plus the Southern sound of pop: all these music worlds are involved in a struggle over and for recognition. Such struggles do not represent the waning of the nation-state, as Appadurai suggests in his model of globalisation revolving around the notion of *scapes*.

Rock in China presents a cultural field, like punk and metal in Java, where state power mediates the global, and where centre-periphery dynamics are also played out on a local and regional level (cf. Baulch 2008: 7). Furthermore, cultural struggles involve articulations of place (e.g. 'China,' 'Beijing,' 'Hong Kong'), rendering the sounds they employ *necessarily* incomplete and unfinished. Given the imagery already discussed of rock being a Western sound, all claims to locality are fraught with a cosmopolitan aesthetics. Baulch refers to this mode as the continuous 'gesturing elsewhere,' whereas I use the term 'cosmopatriotism' in an earlier publication (de Kloet & Jurriëns 2007), resonating with Regev's (2007a, 2007b) notion of 'aesthetic cosmopolitanism.' This latter concept refers to 'the condition in which the representation and performance of ethno-national cultural uniqueness becomes largely based on contemporary art forms like pop-rock music or film, and whose expressive forms include stylistic elements knowingly drawn from sources exterior to indigenous traditions.' (Regev 2007b: 319) Aesthetic cosmopolitanism emerges as the outcome of the intersection of and interplay between global fields of arts and fields of national culture (Regev 2007a). What is important here is not the implicit reification of an inside-outside or national versus international opposition, but the acknowledgement that processes of localisation, or better – articulations of place, through cultural forms like pop or rock, are necessarily incomplete and unfinished, that they are always deferred, and perpetually haunted by a global discourse of pop and rock.[14]

'Authentic' rock versus 'Commercial' pop

When one walks into one of the rather small number of record stores left in Beijing, (due to the Internet, many have closed their doors), one will find the rock tapes grouped together, set apart from what is categorised in popular discourse as pop music – the latter is perceived to be the inauthentic Other of rock. While the generic demarcation is global enough, the merchandise display in the Beijing store underlines another, more locally specific, demarcation: a geographical one. Whereas most rock comes from the north, Beijing, the pop music that hits the mainland charts generally comes from the south, Taiwan or Hong Kong (hereinafter grouped under the label *Gangtai* pop).[15] Mainland pop is conceived as a meagre copy of *Gangtai* pop.[16] Consequently, the global rock-pop divide has a geographical dimension that resembles and hence reifies popular stereotypes about the 'cultural north' and the 'commercial south.'

The pop-rock dichotomy has dominated academic and journalistic, Chinese and non-Chinese discourses on Chinese rock, and proves to be a crucial marker of distinction for musicians, producers, and audiences. Indicative are the words of Cui Jian: 'Pop music as a strictly commercial product, that is for money only, I am not interested in and am indeed opposed to' (in Barmé 1999: 361). Another example is provided by Sar, drummer in the Beijing rock band Thin Men:

> Rock music is totally different from pop... Rock comes from our souls, it is original music, composed and played from the same heart. Pop is the ultimate assembly-line product. (...) There is nothing genuine about it. It is not about expressing your truths but about manipulating consumers. (in Kovskya 1999: online)

According to Michael Dutton, 'apart from the marginal and marginalised niche market of heavy metal and rock, it is the sickly sweet songs of Canto-pop that fill the airwaves' (1998: 239). Such crude judgments and classifications as expressed by rock musicians as well as Western academics represent a general and typical opinion on Chinese pop: overtly commercialised and lacking any creativity. Which may explain why so far, despite its smaller audience and its limited appeal among the Chinese diaspora, it is mainly rock that attracts the attention of Western-based observers, be they journalists or academics. Several books, articles and documentaries have tried to grasp the significance of rock in China, and fewer academics embark on an analysis of *Gangtai* pop, although over the past years this is gradually improving.[17]

This Book

This book is driven by a double aspiration. First, to present an ethno-graphic account of China's music cultures over the past two decades, with a specific focus on the end of the 1990s, when reforms, commer-cialisation and globalisation were in full swing. Rather than presenting a static picture of a mirror, it is important, as DeNora writes, to 'try to specify how the social comes to be inscribed in the musical, if one is to spell out an account of how structural affinities or homologies between music and social formations might arise and change over time.' (2000: 3) Second, I wish to interrogate the terms and concepts with which we de-scribe and analyse such ethnographies. This deconstructive, theoretical turn is crucial if we wish to unsettle the old binaries that inform our thinking on 'Asia' and 'China.' (Wang 2003) This simultaneous task of description and deconstruction, of exploration and contamination in-forms my writing.[18]

Following Condry, I contend that to understand popular music in China, it is important to include the different actors and their interac-tions in the analysis – musicians, media industries, fans, writers, etc. (2006: 2). This book starts by studying the music scenes, continues with the audiences and producers, and pays due attention to the mutual interactions and dependencies between these actors. Chapter one ex-plores the sounds that, as 'hard' cultural forms, come closest to the rock mythology. These hard sounds are the underground bands, heavy metal, punk and hip-hop. The chapter does begin with a brief discussion, in-spired by the work of, among others, Dick Hebdige, David Hesmond-halgh and Will Straw, on why I have opted to describe rock culture in terms of scenes, and why I link this scenic approach to the construction of authenticity and the production of place in the analysis. Throughout the book, I will combine analysis with theoretical reflections and asides. In chapter two, I move on to discuss what I term the 'hyphenated' scenes, the scenes that are, indeed, less 'hard,' or softer, and hence less conspicuously drenched in the rock mythology. The music scenes dis-cussed here are folk-rock, pop-rock, pop-punk and the fashionable bands. In chapter three, I move on to the sounds that are generally mar-ginalised in rock discourse: those coming from bands outside the per-ceived centre of rock, Beijing, those from the female bands and, most notably, the opaque sound of pop. In this chapter, I will elaborate further on Arjun Appadurai's hard-soft distinction, proposing a recast-ing of that binary relationship into a clear-opaque distinction, a recast-ing inspired by the work of Mikhail Bakhtin.

These chapters are informed by a wide array of empirical data. I will make extensive use of the over 300 MCs and CDs I collected between 1992 and 2008, and include the jacket design, lyrics and compositions in my analysis.[19] Articles that appeared in the mainland press shed light on Chinese discourses on popular music.[20] I have also used books, published on the mainland, on Chinese rock and on Western rock. I carried out the fieldwork for this study during different periods: the winter of 1996/1997 (five weeks in Beijing); June to December 1997 (two weeks in Hong Kong and six months in Beijing); August 1999 (three weeks in Shanghai and Beijing); and April 2000 (five weeks in Beijing). I returned for different research projects in 2004 (three months), 2007 (two months) and 2008 (seven months), during which I carried out additional interviews for this book and continued to collect materials. During all these periods, I attended as many live performances as possible (an incurable habit that will continue also after publication of this book). The most important information for this study came from more than 100 interviews with record companies in Hong Kong, Shanghai, and Beijing, with rock and pop musicians from Hong Kong, Shanghai, Beijing, and Guangzhou, and with Beijing youth (see Appendix I for an overview of the interviews).[21]

Interviews with musicians usually took place over dinner, as this created an open, informal atmosphere which considerably improved both the quantity and the quality of the information provided. Some musicians were interviewed several times so as to trace their development over time (Qiu Ye from Zi Yue, Feng Jiangzhou from The Fly, and Zu Zhou and Cui Jian). With a few exceptions, the interviewed bands and singers are under contract to record companies. This study thus focuses on the more established part of the Beijing rock culture.[22] Over the past decade, due to new technologies, material has become much more readily available. Through YouTube, MySpace, numerous blogs, wikis and websites, the world of popular music in China has become just a mouse-click away. In my view, this abundance of data not only necessitates more refined methods of data collection and, particularly, selection, but it also points to the increased importance of interpretation and theory. The Web 2.0 era requires more rather than less theory. The crux here is not to take theory as a magic black box, but to insist on the continuous, self-reflexive process of theorising, in the words of Stuart Hall (in Grossberg 1996: 150): 'I am not interested in Theory, I am interested in going on theorising.'

In chapter four, I examine an often-overlooked domain in the study of popular music: the audiences. Drawing on Michel Foucault's notion of technologies of the self, in combination with Anthony Giddens' study on the reflexive self in late modernity, and Tia DeNora's work on music audiences, I scrutinise how (Chinese) music is used as a technology of the self, as a way to control life in a society that is in a perpetual flux. This chapter is based on different materials. To gain some basic information on Chinese youth and media and music preferences, I carried out a survey among 650 respondents. In addition, in-depth interviews were carried out with 32 youths introduced to me by Chinese friends. However, the most valuable source of information for this chapter proved to be the fan mail written by 80 rock fans to their favourite bands. This material was given to me by the record companies, and provides a unique view on the everyday importance of music; unique not only as such materials are not public, but also because they are not produced by or mediated through the research process.

In chapter five, I address the production of music in China, inspired by theorisations on the relationship between global capitalism and media policies of the nation-state, and between neoliberalism and communism, as put forward by – among others – Anthony Fung, Aihwa Ong, Jing Wang and Yuezhi Zhao. First I position the Chinese music market in a regional and global context, highlighting its small size. Second, I trace the peculiarities of the music industry in China, showing how specific cultural belongings inform the business, after which I probe the cat and mouse game of censorship that haunts cultural production in China. In the conclusion of this book, I theorise further on the intricate links between popular culture and politics, reading the rock mythology as a deparadoxicalising force. This is productive, as it propels the emergence of a wide array of music scenes. Yet the resulting hierarchies, coupled with the implied univocal readings, are in my view highly problematic. The key question becomes how to liberate the paradoxes from the power of the mythology, and as such, resist the working of what Alexei Yurchak (2005) terms a 'binary socialism' that pervades academic and popular discourse. Such a move would help us understand the workings of popular culture and its intricate links with politics without retreating to the safe grounds of cultural essentialism or reductionist accounts of 'reality.'

Throughout the book, I deliberately give ample space to the voices of the bands, the audiences and the producers, not as if these constitute an absolute truth – after all, interviews are profoundly performative occasions in which a preferred self is enacted. I invoke these voices, some loud and jarring, others more doubtful and slightly puzzled, but also those with irony and humour, to account for the profound multivocality – or, to use Bakhtin's word, *heteroglossia*, of music cultures in China and beyond. Take, for example, the role the 80s generations played in the aftermath of the Sichuan earthquake of May 2008. After the quake, many young Chinese volunteered to help, stirring up discussions in the media, as it was taken as a sign that a generation perceived to be selfish and materialistic turned out to be quite different. Rather than being hedonistic, they are, in the words of a Chinese journalist, 'a group of young people with strong patriotism, enthusiasm and responsibility.' (Y. Li 2008) To which I would hasten to add that there is still much more to the *dakou* generation, as well as to the 80s generation – a surplus or semiotic and sonic overflow that this book hopes to unfold.

1 Hard Scenes

Red Army crossed Chishui river relying on my bridge
Chairman Mao ate McDonald's in Shaanxi Province
A sleepless night
A wasted soft berth
Coca-Cola, right here right now
Zuoxiao Zuzhou, Such a Talker, 2008

A Scenic Move

The term subculture was coined in the 1940s and has since been used to describe and analyze all kinds of social groups (punks, football hooligans, homosexuals). The Birmingham Centre of Cultural Studies set the agenda in the 1970s with two major publications: *Resistance Through Rituals* (Hall & Jefferson 1976) and Hebdige's *Subculture, The Meaning of Style* (1979). Whereas the former predominantly uses class as the key to discovering subcultural meanings, the latter uses style and race as their organising principles. Hebdige unravels different youth styles, which according to him are 'pregnant with significance. (...) As such, they are gestures, movements towards a speech which offends the "silent majority", which challenges the principle of unity and cohesion, which contradicts the myth of consensus.' (1979: 18) Oppositional styles, which deliberately transform the meaning of symbols of the dominant discourse, emerge to counter dominant culture. Through accommodation or neglect, mainstream society is in the end able to pacify the potential threat of subcultures. Subcultures thus do not allow much potential for real change; they are, as Kahn-Harris (2004: 96) puts it, 'heroic failures.'

In later publications, Hebdige (1988) develops a more subtle approach, by adopting Foucault's ideas of power and surveillance. According to Foucault, 'Maybe the target nowadays is not to discover what we are but to refuse what we are. (...) We have to promote new forms of subjectivity through the refusal of this kind of individuality which has been imposed on us for several centuries.' (Foucault 1983: 216) Hebdige shows how different forms of surveillance emerged around the category 'youth' during the 20th century. He traced two dominant images of youth: youth as fun, and youth as trouble. For Hebdige, the subcultural response is a new form of subjectivity. 'Subculture forms up in the space between surveillance and the evasion of surveillance, it translates the fact of being under scrutiny into the pleasure of being watched. It is a hiding in the light.' (1988: 35)

In the last hundred years, discourses in China around the idea of 'youth' have increasingly come to resemble those in the West. In late imperial China, the term youth (*qingnian*) was 'restricted to males aged sixteen to thirty; it excluded girls, who were expected to marry as soon as they reached sexual maturity.' (Dikötter 1995: 146) In republican China (1911-1949), the term was universalised to include both young men and women. 'Youth' was turned 'into a powerful symbol of regeneration, vitality and commitment to modernity.' (Dikötter 1995: 147) According to Dikötter, 'The problematisation of "youth" into a social issue spurred the growth of a body of specialised knowledge, particularly in the new fields of social science, psychology and human biology.' (149) As in the West, this has resulted in a wide array of disciplinary practices and related normative pressures. Bodily inscribed differences between girls and boys produced gendered role models (Evans 2008). The normative pressure is especially evident in the medical debates on (or, better, against) masturbation (Dikötter 1995: 165).[1] 'In the adolescent, dress, diet, gestures, manners, emotions, speech, and thought were all to be disciplined for the building of character.' (176) Dikötter shows that apart from Western influences, these discursive repertoires were also rooted in a rich and diverse past in China itself. Traditional Chinese medicine, for example, argues strongly against masturbation, which is said to cause a severe loss of male energy (*yang*).

The Chinese Communist Party further institutionalised the category of youth by creating the Communist Youth League. Especially during the period 1949-1978, youth was a highly politicised unit (Gold 1991). In communist China, youth was regarded as the vanguard of social change (Geist 1996: 262). At the same time, 'young people are described as unfinished persons not yet belonging to society and not yet having established correct world-views and knowledge about life.' (Bakken 1994: 263) Thus, youth on the one hand was linked to hope, growth, and order (rather than to fun, as we have seen in the West), and on the other hand to something potentially deviant and dangerous.

The last youth rebellion in China – the 1989 student protests – was followed by two decades of economic reforms and prosperity, resulting in a widening of the gap between the rich and the poor (Wang 2003). With the growing importance of leisure time and consumption culture, during the 1990s, the term 'youth' was increasingly linked to ideas of fun and pleasure (Z. Zhang 2000). Consequently, as in the West, different modes of surveillance have been imposed on Chinese youths. The expectations of parents (whose authority is anchored in Confucianist ideology), the very demanding educational system, Chinese social scientists who develop theories about youth, and the role models produced by the Party, are all involved in the construction of dominant images of what Chinese youth should be – the good son, the hard-working student, the model citizen, the obedient student. The one-child policy has only increased the burden imposed upon Chinese youth.

Thus, not only the Party but also, and mainly, other groups are involved in the construction of the category 'youth'. By applying theories about subcultures, the response of rock musicians can be interpreted as a denial of these prescribed forms of identity, rather than as the *conscious* construction of an oppositional identity. What remains problematic in interpreting rock as a denial of prescribed forms of identity is that the pleasure of the music itself tends to be ignored in favour of a neat sociological analysis. The argument is also based too much on a rigid hegemony model. Culture is conveniently categorised; the emphasis is solely on difference, on deviance. Apart from a bias toward the countercultural, there is a strong masculine bias in subcultural studies (Bennett & Kahn-Harris 2000; McRobbie 1991; Muggleton & Weinzierl 2003; Thornton 1995: 5). Women are at best described as static objects. Finally, though my overview of critiques on the notion of subculture is by no means exhaustive, the term subculture invokes associations of youth, and privileges music consumption to the young. Despite a decades-long history, this link between rock music and youth is not that obvious anymore in the West or in China (Hesmondhalgh 2005). It consequently makes more sense to write of rock culture in China, and avoid labelling it a subculture. How does one present a comprehensive picture of this multivocal culture?

Chinese rock culture has often been described chronologically (Jones 1992; Steen 1996; Huang 1997). The idea of a New Sound Movement that emerged after 1997, as put forward by Yan Jun and Ou Ning (1999), imposes a temporality upon Chinese rock suggesting a neat and tidy development over time. In historicising rock culture, one easily falls into a narrative of progress or regress, rather than of coexistence and contestation. Such a historicising narrative is likely to reify and essentialise rock, and runs the danger of silencing the older, still active, bands and musicians, such as Tang Dynasty and Zhang Chu. I consider it more fruitful not to distinguish fixed periods, but to explore various fluid music scenes. These will provide me with a better anchor point from which to understand the boundaries within rock culture, and between rock and related cultural domains.

Musicians share my observation that the rock culture has become increasingly fragmented. One such example is Dai Qin, from the band Thin Men.

> The *yaogun quanzi* [circle of underground rock musicians] used to be a really supportive community based on the shared desire for unfettered self-expression through original music. Now the politics of trendiness and competition are disintegrating the circle. Now the circle is breaking up into small cliques organised around style rather than substance. Now people worry too much about what the market wants, and what's hip, and not enough about how to make the music that they themselves love. (quoted in Kovskaya 1999: online)

The scenic 'split' is interpreted by Dai Qin as a threat to the binding force of the rock mythology. His romantic reading of the past covers up all the fights and conflicts that have been part and parcel of the rock culture in China since its emergence. Style is considered to be shallow and empty, while the true rock spirit is about substance, about the expression of the self – in short, the rock mythology is once again reified. Dai's elegy justifies my decision to analyze different music scenes, since such an analysis might guide us to the different workings and/or boundaries of the rock mythology.

The advantage of speaking of scenes is that it does not overdetermine and homogenise the context, but classifies without separating a dominant culture from the music culture. It is, to put it bluntly, a concept with weaker political associations than the concept of subculture; instead, it directs the attention more towards the perceived specificities and aesthetics of the music (see also Bennett 2004; Bennett & Kahn-Harris 2004; Hesmondhalgh 2005; Kahn-Harris 1999; Pilkington and Johnson 2003; Stahl 2004; Straw 1997). The concept of scene also strikes me as less fixed; it is easier to imagine scenic movements (that is, music crossovers and audiences being attracted to different scenes at the same time) than subcultural movements. Boundaries of scenes are only momentarily fixed, and they frequently overlap. The act of writing makes it difficult, if not impossible, to capture this fluidity. Also, bands are increasingly eager to deny any possible classification, and through this performative speech act they claim uniqueness and thereby safeguard their authenticity. For example, vocalist Kang Mao from the punk band SUBS explains they are not punk: 'We don't believe in any doctrine. We don't believe in any medium and authority. We have never belonged to any community nor defined ourselves as a particular style.' (Wen 2004: 13)

What interests me is not a neat classification of the rock culture and the creation of yet another typology, but rather the generic processes, closely intertwined with the rock mythology, that produce different scenes. Crucial to this approach is the acknowledgement that genre distinctions and bifurcations play a decisive and productive role in musical practices and experiences and to the social organisation of musical life (Holt 2007).

Hesmondhalgh argues against the use of the term of both (neo-)tribe and scene. To describe music cultures as neo-tribes, as Bennett does in his 1999 study of youth, style and musical taste remains too theoretical, with little empirical grounding, he claims. Pilkington and Johnson make a similar point when they observe that theorisations on neo-tribes tend to ignore youth's own definitions, and lack much empirical research (2005: 266). To Hesmondhalgh, the term scene lacks clarity; scene 'suggests a bounded place but has also been used to suggest more complex spatial flows of musical affiliation; the two major ways in which the term is used are incompatible with each other.' (2005: 23) The first use, in which a scene is read as a cosmopolitan, inclusive sonic force, has been predominantly popularised by two important works; first, Straw's comparison between alternative rock and alternative dance music; and second, Kahn-Harris' study of the global metal scene (2007). The second, place-bound use of the concept of scene is apparent in Shank's book on the rock'n'roll scene in Austin, Texas (Shank 1994). This muddled use of the notion of scene, a global reading versus a local reading, is not productive, according to Hesmondhalgh, and he proposes thinking of music in terms of genre and articulation. In my view, the local and global implications of the concept are helpful in the context of 'Chinese' rock scenes, precisely because the global is so deeply implicated in the local, as I have argued in the previous chapter. I see the two readings as not mutually exclusive but instead feeding into each other. The idea of a scene can be smoothly combined with the notions of genre and articulation. Scenes proliferate around specific genres, these musical collectivities involve the participation of musicians, audiences, and producers, all of whom articulate specific social identities in and through music. Music both reflects and constructs (new) social identities. In the words of Hesmondhalgh, 'combined with genre, with its ability to connect up audiences, texts and producers, this notion of multiple articulations – including 'homogenous' ones – provides a much more promising theoretical basis for theorising empirical research than the recent alternatives.' (2005: 35)

The question is how to present the scenes, and which articulations to privilege. I will start off my description of a scene by pointing out its *position* within the rock culture. I will address its popularity and show how this scene is being discussed in China. This will illuminate how the processes of distinction within rock culture are being played out through generic preferences. Having positioned the scenes, I will move on to analyse their generic aesthetics – that is, the style perceived as distinguishing one scene from another – and show how these aesthetics, or the perceptions of such, authenticate the scene. This part is grouped under the label *authenticating styles.*

In the previous chapter, I showed how authenticity is of crucial importance in the rock mythology, and how it is inscribed into two dominant spatial dichotomies: northern rock versus southern pop, and the real West versus the fake East. Rock, as a hard cultural form from the West, demands localisation so as to authenticate itself. Place thus intersects with authenticity, yet for the sake of clarity, I have disentangled the two and discuss in the third section of my scenic analysis how bands negotiate *place.* Here, my concern is how place is an important signifier, and to unpack three prevalent images: ancient China, communist China and cosmopolitan China. I will also analyse how such articulations of place (or, indeed, deliberate placelessness) resonate with important political and commercial divisions within the imagined Greater China. This chapter explores the more 'hard' scenes of Chinese rock, the heavy metal, underground, punk and hip-hop scenes. The next chapter moves to the more hyphenated scenes: the pop-rock, folk-rock, pop-punk and fashionable bands. The organising logic (positions, authenticity and place) is similar in both chapters.

In restricting myself to these themes (i.e. positions, authenticating styles, and place) coupled with my desire to grasp the fragmented nature of Chinese rock, my analysis will, instead of presenting an in-depth analysis of a few bands, be more of a long and winding journey through China's rock culture. Since this book is not meant to be an encyclopaedia of Chinese rock,[2] bands will be included insofar as they shed a different light on the main themes of my argument. Then why do I devote most space to what I label the underground scene? Taste plays an important explanatory role, a role that is too often downplayed or ignored. As Frith argues convincingly, much of the pleasure of popular music lies in the endless discussions over it with friends (1996). Value judgements, and related processes of distinction, lie at the heart of music cultures. The music I keep on playing, also when I am 'home' in Amsterdam, comes mainly from the underground scene, the folk scene and Cantopop (see chapter three). This involvement explains why my analysis tends to become more elaborate for these respective scenes.

Underground

Positions – In the summer of 1996, three bands – NO, The Fly, and Zi Yue – gave a joint performance in Beijing. With hindsight, the performance might well be considered the public birth of underground music, as the scene is called in Beijing (*dixia yinyue*), and as 'noise' (*zaoyin yaogun*). Since then the bands have taken quite a different track, in particular Zi Yue, whose music is less discordant in comparison with the other bands under study. What links these three bands with other bands like Wooden Horse (MUMA), Tongue, Carsick Cars, P.K. 14, Queen Sea Big Shark, Hedgehog, Re-Establishing the Rights of Statues (Re-TROS) and the Second Hand Roses is their critical stance toward Chinese society, in most cases combined with an experimental sound. The sounds explored in the underground scene range from the new wave (*xin lang-chao*) – which in China is also called the depression style (*diliao yinyue*) – of Wooden Horse to the industrial noise of The Fly. Sale figures do not often exceed the 30,000 mark, a figure considered low by Chinese standards, and a figure that has most likely dropped over the past years given the use of download and sharing sites like MySpace.

Apart from being a musician, NO singer Zu Zhou (Figure 1.1), who was born in 1970, is a writer, poet, and painter, and has participated in several performance art activities. It is especially in the underground scene that links with other 'art worlds' are obvious. The Fly's Feng

Figure 1.1   *Zuoxiao Zuzhou (photo by the author)*

Jiangzhou is also an avant-garde painter as well as video-artist.[3] His first CD was released in 1997 by a small Taiwanese label and only appeared on the mainland market in 1999 on the Modern Sky label. A mainland critic concluded after listening to the CD:

> Chinese avant-garde art is usually impotent art. Chinese rock is usually hollow. What kind of chemical reaction will happen if we put these two things together? (...) The Fly has set new standards for Chinese rock and made us realise how hypocritical and senseless the so-called avant-garde rock music was. (...) Grunge, punk and noise are really the best ways to express avant-garde art because they are extreme. The lyrics of this album are controversial, they tried hard to use filthy words to improve their dirty, noisy and bad aesthetics. (Ai 1997: 42)

Being the avant-garde of the rock culture, the underground bands have close ties with the cultural avant-garde in China.[4] The above review was published before the CD was allowed on the mainland market. Despite government control, CDs find their way to music critics, who publish their reviews nationwide, thus indirectly promoting CDs that are supposed to have been banned by the government. Party hegemony, it seems, is far from absolute and uncontested. The underground bands were among the first to break with the perceived crisis of rock in China (see introduction). Their discontent with the rock culture is summed up by the words of Feng Jiangzhou:

> In China, from 1986 to 1996, for 10 years, Chinese rock remained pretty much the same, basically hard rock. So I believe that from 1997 there should be something new. But I can't jump too far otherwise there would be a displacement. What I am trying to do is to create something that is just beyond the existing rock'n'roll, to create the avant-garde in China.

The Fly has had two albums released, one in 1999 by Badhead (a sublabel of Modern Sky) and one in 2000 by Jingwen. Zu Zhou, under the name Zuoxiao Zuzhou, released its third album, *Zu Zhou at Di An Men*, on the Badhead label in 2003, a soundtrack for a movie called *In The USA* in 2006, the CD *I Can't Sit Sadly By Your Side*, also in 2006, and a double CD titled *You Know Where the East Is* released in 2008. He sells the latter through his website for a quite astonishing 500RMB; it is not for sale in the shops.[5] In April of 2000 Zu Zhou published his first full-length novel, *Barking at the Tomb*. Hao Fang writes in the foreword:

> *Barking at the Tomb* is a novel about the despair of a generation. Historical scars, political despair, economic banter and lost spirit all wrapped together and crying out; helpless, dejected, dependent, indignant and crazed, it is a casting out, a breaking out all of the symptoms of a generation of China's youth at the century's end.[6]

Zi Yue has released two albums by Jingwen. Both Feng Jiangzhou and Zu Zhou have over the years become involved in the music business as producers.[7] After the release of their second album, The Fly disbanded. Since then, Feng Jiangzhou has, among other career tracks,[8] moved to electronic music. Together with the Taiwanese band 3rd Nova, he has made an album the music style of which is known as digital hardcore. It presents an aggressive, upbeat, and angry soundscape, dominated by repetitive beats. The album marks a radical departure from the idea of a rock band; the listener is drawn into a noisy, computerised, aggressive musical world.

Authenticating styles – For Zu Zhou and Feng Jiangzhou, music functions as a site to negotiate feelings of anger and frustration, feelings young people are hardly allowed to express in Chinese culture. Both Confucian and Party ideologies stress the importance of conformity, and of obedience to parents, educators, and bosses. As Feng Jiangzhou said:

> I am actually very angry about a lot of things in China, like disrespect among people, the whole political system, but I do not have the courage to confront people directly, so when I write I can be very angry and aggressive.

Over the years this anger has slowly faded. The years since 1996 have given Feng Jiangzhou the opportunity to get involved in video art, music production, and the organisation of entertainment events, at times for the government. As he explained to me in 2008:

> In China, there are still many blanks, it's easy to cover these blanks. (...) Here in China, because there is no rule, you can do whatever you want. (...) I can be really angry, blaming them really hard in my daily life when watching TV, because things are just not right. At the same time it's not easy for me, for if I choose to love my country, I have to love the Communist Party, which is not an easy task. However, if I don't, it would be uncomfortable to live in this country. Also I'm working on some projects with the government. It's a dilemma. I'm watching what the govern-

ment is doing. Actually they are changing, but not enough. I believe things will get better in twenty years.

He explains how it is possible in China to enter new creative domains, to be the first in a specific field, and how in his view China is changing and becoming more open. Nevertheless, although sometimes less strongly than during the years of *dakou* culture, even today, underground musicians remain vocal in their criticism of contemporary Chinese society. Chinese academic He Li quotes from rock critic Kong, whose description of NO's music remains accurate, also for Zu Zhou's recent work:

> Zu Zhou's uniquely penetrating tenor, like a knife stained with blood and sperm, tears off everything ... His purely despondent bass divulges the loneliness towards the future and the destruction of the will to live. Their simple and weird minor-scale progression embeds anxiety and emptiness. It is not only a musical language, but also a spiritual wandering guided by some old instinctive language. Their irregular and airy sound texture constructs some kind of imaginary space. (He 1997: 88)

He Li states that 'NO is like a group of sadists from hell' (He 1997: 88).[9] Zu Zhou's critique of contemporary Chinese society is more a radical denial of meaning: 'I'm disgusted by Marxism; in my opinion, it has cheated me. (...) This is a senseless age, maybe the true age hasn't come yet.'

His discontent is translated into an ironic and absurdist, rather than angry, soundscape. The sounds range from ballads, to electronic beats and guitar noise. His voice is at times a high-pitched falsetto, and at others a Tom Waits-like grumble. In his 2008 album *You Know Where the East Is*, one song, titled 'Methodology,' is clearly a parody of the Party. The lyrics of the song come from the report delivered by Jiang Zemin at the 15th National Congress of the Communist Party. The song starts with the sounds of a suona, an oboe-like instrument with a distinct high-pitched sound, and we hear a Chinese drum in the background. Then the piercing, falsetto voice of Zu Zhou breaks open the 'Chinese' soundscape:

> Deng Xiaoping Theory, a continuation and development of Mao Zedong Thought, is a correct theory guiding the Chinese people in successfully accomplishing their socialist modernisation in the process of reform and opening to the outside world. In China today, it is Deng Xiaoping Theory, which integrates Marxism with the practice of present-day China and the features of the

times, and this theory alone, that can settle the issues concerning the future and destiny of socialism.

The sound is a distorted voice, bordering on falsehood; gone is the tranquillity an ancient instrument like the *suona* is reputed to exude, a tranquillity that to me signifies the myth of the peaceful, deep, traditional Chinese culture. What remains is an absurdist soundscape, in which the words by the lyric writer Jiang Zemin are parodied and inverted. Dadaistic elements characterise Zu Zhou's music and lyrics.

The Dadaist aesthetics of Zu Zhou's music shows similarities with the vulgar aesthetics of The Fly. In a Taiwanese review, the music of The Fly was compared to the guerrilla tactics of Chairman Mao. Instead of launching a frontal attack, the critic pointed out that The Fly was employing lateral movements to oppose dominant culture. Rather than writing about politics, as Zu Zhou often does, The Fly's singer Feng Jiangzhou prefers to write about sex. Sex – another topic difficult to discuss in China – signifies the political. But his critique covers more than solely the political:

> What is considered beautiful by a lot of people is simply a very popular notion of beauty. I don't think my lyrics are dirty at all; I want people to think again about what is beautiful and what is dirty. (...) The other reason I choose sex as the subject matter is as a reaction to the pop music of China. The government seems to at least condone if not encourage pop music, whereas it presents rock'n'roll with so many problems. I find pop music so superficial but it represents its own vulgar aesthetics. It would be very difficult for me to write very sophisticated lyrics as its critique. The only way to do so is to find another subject matter which could be as vulgar for the general audience and sex seems to be very appropriate to counter Chinese pop music. (...) Everything [in China] is just so covered up. In the past there have been extremely erotic books, pornographic material, but people hid them and presented themselves as gentlemen. We have a song entitled 'Gentleman'. In China, everyone wants to be that gentleman, and I'd like them to tear off that mask. Because if you're always wearing a mask, you don't exist; people should be real.

Feng Jiangzhou aims to subvert the ideology of pop by using provocative, vulgar lyrics. The implicit accusation that pop is both superficial and in line with the dominant ideology remains important for his positioning as a rock musician. Also, the idea of tearing away the masks people wear, in order to reveal their true, authentic identity, is closely linked to the belief that his music – in being open about sex – is an ex-

ample of authenticity. The jacket of The Fly's first CD features an art-
work by Song Yonghong, provocative scenes of a couple having sex
painted on the walls of a temple (see Figure 1.2).[10] The promotion
materials of The Fly point out that the recording is done in low fidelity.
The underlying assumption is that technology is falsifying. Thus, not
only the aesthetics of the lyrics and the music, but also the recording
techniques, negotiate notions of authenticity.[11]

Figure 1.2   *Detail of CD Jacket The Fly – The Fly I (copyright Modern Sky)*

The mirror The Fly offers the audience is as disturbing as that offered
by Zu Zhou. The sound merges grunge, characterised by its strong fluc-
tuations in tempo, with noise. Feng Jiangzhou's tormented and tor-
menting voice combines anger with a large dose of irony. The lyrics are

characterised by directness and absurdity, as shown by the following fragment from the song 'Nirvana':

> Since there is no light bulb in this village toilet
> Since there is no full moon tonight
> Since I can't fall asleep
> Since I want to play with myself (...)
> Under my ass shine rays of dawn
> I will bring with me the shit fragrance that fills the hut
> My nirvana, my nirvana

The Dadaist aesthetics of Zu Zhou and the vulgar aesthetics of The Fly are tactics of *symbolic inversion*, which can be defined as an aesthetic 'negation of the negative' (Babcock 1978: 19). This aesthetic negation confronts the audience with the lineaments of Chinese culture. It questions the normal in its focus on what is considered abnormal. It destabilises the illusory symbolic order. 'Such "creative negations" remind us of the need to reinvest the clean with the filthy. (...) The *modus inversus* does more than simply mock our desire to live according to our usual orders and norms; it reinvests life with a vigor and a *Spielraum* attainable (it would seem) in no other way' (Babcock 1978: 19). Symbolic inversion involves a societal, if not political critique, albeit an implicit, absurdist and ironic one.

Tongue's music and sound are also illustrative of the politics of the underground scene. Tongue's members are from Urumqi.[12] Their first album, *Chicken Coming out of the Egg*, was released by Modern Sky in 1999; a subsequent live album was published under Yan Jun's label Subjam. The band disbanded in the summer of 2004. Tongue's music is, like Zu Zhou's and The Fly's, full of noise. The tormented voice of leading vocalist Wu Tun – one of the vocalists on the song 'Methodology' by Zu Zhou analysed above – strengthens the dark atmosphere the music evokes.[13] Yan Jun writes on the difficulties Tongue's releases face when passing the censorship authorities (Yan 2002: 183). He refers in particular to the song 'They are coming,' of which the full lyrics are:

> The primitive men are coming
> The slave masters are coming
> The feudal lords are coming
> The democrats are coming
> Imperialism is coming
> Capitalism is coming
> Socialism is coming
> Communism is coming
> They are coming

The upbeat sound turns the song into an underground version of a pro-test march; the sound almost overrules the gloomy, whiny voice of Wu Tun, in the end of the song – when the last sentence *tamen lai le* is repeated all the time – a high-pitched screaming voice joins in, after which the song suddenly changes into the tune of the lullaby 'Frere Jacques.' The turn from a march towards a lullaby signifies, in my view, a moment of parody; it pokes fun at all the ism-s included in the lyrics. As such it can be read as a sonic manifestation of Lyotard's claim that the end of the Grand Narratives, such as socialism and communism, characterises contemporary postmodern culture (Lyotard 1984).

The underground bands signify the reappearance of the political in Chinese rock. These politics – the insistence on articulating a critique often silenced in the Chinese public sphere – are illustrative of the sub-versive potential of the rock mythology. They also authenticate the mu-sic. Their politics are noisier, more sarcastic and more absurdist when compared to their predecessors, among whom are the poetic, metapho-rical lyrics and melodic sound of Cui Jian. They do testify that the dis-placement of the political by the commercial throughout the 1990s, to adopt the terms used by Dai Jinhua (2002), has not been absolute. Furthermore, both domains do not necessarily exclude one another. On the contrary; as will be explained in chapter five, it has been due to the relaxation of government control that small, local record companies have been able to emerge, who contracted bands like Tongue and Zu Zhou. The reappearance of the political in Chinese rock is consequently embedded in a state-supported marketing of Chinese culture.

The sound of Zi Yue is more melodic when compared to the other underground bands. Its lyrics, however, share an articulate critique of contemporary Chinese society. Zi Yue's first album – the name means It Says or The Master Speaks, a reference to the Chinese philosopher Confucius – was produced by Cui Jian. Their CD jacket mixes specific Chinese symbols, such as a temple and a classic Chinese painting, with cosmopolitan images, such as high apartment blocks and oil barrels. A piece of jute connects these images with one another. The frayed ends of jute symbolise, according to vocalist Qiu Ye, the chaos of everyday life. To him, totalising narratives such as religion and communism try to cut away these frayed ends and turn life into a neat and tidy event, something he considers unnatural.

Qiu Ye claims to be very much inspired by Buddhist culture, and that he is striving for the perfection of Buddhism in his daily life. A closer look at Qiu Ye, his music, and his lyrics reveals that he is not losing himself in an uncritical celebration of the past. Qiu Ye is quoted on one of the band's promotional flyers:

Too many shadows of our ancestors are enshrouding our culture and our life. So-called morality serves only one class. It has only one aim: to enslave, to overthrow and to enslave again ... Looking at the so-called process of human history, whether it's religion, politics, law or economy, they are all closed cans suppressing and constraining human instincts, like putting you into a vacuum and suffocating you. They call it unity.

Like Feng Jiangzhou, Qiu Ye is already in his late thirties, and has been active in the rock culture for more than fifteen years. However, he released his first CD only in 1997, and it was praised as the best Chinese album of 1997 by 'China Broadway' (*Zhongguo Bailaohu*). The praise from rock critic Shang Guan (1998), who also refers to the crisis in Chinese rock of the mid-1990s, is indicative of the reaction to Zi Yue:

Just when we are lamenting the decline of Chinese rock and roll, Zi Yue brings us this delightful album. It is not only a pleasant surprise, but also a comfort – a comfort to all the hearts which have cooled down for such a long time. (...) This album, which is a bit psychedelic and full of punk spirit, enshrines the band members' (mainly its vocalist Qiu Ye's) sharp insights into the world as well as deep and painful metaphors of reality.

Metaphors are crucial if one is to understand the music of Zi Yue, and the lyrics dominate because of Qiu Ye's declaiming, rap-like singing style, resembling the style of the Red Hot Chili Peppers. In his song 'My Dear Good Child', Qiu Ye sings about the conflicts between a son and his father:

I have a lot of words in my heart
Actually I should have told my dad earlier
But every time before I open my mouth
Dad will give me a piece of candy
That's why I tell you: my child, I am contented, so should you be happy
Don't knit your eyebrows and pretend to be deep in thoughts
The nice things you eat, you drink, you wear are what your old man, me, has spent his whole life to get
Understand?
I try to bear it but it's unbearable
I have to tell you right away (...)
I say: the piece of candy you give me, Dad,
Is not sweet at all.

Qiu Ye impersonates both characters in the song. The music is full of twists and short interludes, and we hear Qiu Ye coughing and murmuring, through which he manages to create a sphere of intimacy with the listener, a sphere that authenticates the music. A classic generational conflict unfolds in this song between the son and his father. But at the same time, the personal intersects clearly with the political (or, to quote the still valid feminist slogan, the personal is political). The song reflects on the relationship between the Party (the father) and today's youth (the son). Tired of all the stories about the sufferings of the past, before the liberation of China, and severely disappointed by that candy called communism (or economic reforms, or anything else handed down to youth), the youths want to scream at the Party, talk about their disappointments, their dissatisfactions, their dreams. Yet they will be silenced by the stories of the past or, eventually, as in 1989, by violence. To read the father solely as the Party is too limited, according to Qiu Ye. In his view, the song can have different readings; the father also stands for patriarchy, just as it signifies the powerful working unit (*danwei*). Not only the music, but also the metaphoric aesthetics resemble those of Cui Jian, which explains why both are often compared with each other.

Place – Zi Yue's music is labelled 'opera rock', a reference to the specific vocals of Qiu Ye, which strongly resemble those in Beijing opera. The music presents a mixture of 'Western' rock with instruments considered traditionally Chinese. Vocalist Qiu Ye criticises those who, in his eyes, copy Western music, and does his best to stress the Chinese character of his music. He does so, however, with a lot of irony and humour, using Beijing slang and talking extensively in-between the songs during performances. Humour, irony and parody are important elements in the underground scene, producing a carnavalesque critique that challenges the hegemonic political and nationalistic discourse and pokes fun at established conventions (Bakhtin 1981).[14]

A review appearing in 2008 of the music of Zi Yue and its importance for China's rock culture illustrates of the fear of copying, as mentioned in the previous chapter, and the subsequent demand to Sinify the sound. Zi Yue is heralded as the first successful sonic translator:

> Rock music is an imported product from overseas and the most commonly mentioned weakness of Chinese rock is that Chinese people with no rock culture foundation cannot really truly fulfil this Western music style with authentic local content. In other words, the Sinification of rock music hasn't stopped ever since the first day it entered China. So, some people added *guzheng* and some people added *pipa*, some people added some Asian-

style lyrics, but no matter what they do, it all feels awkward and unnatural. Until 1996 when the first volume of Zi Yue was released. The instruments were all the same, guitar, bass and drums. But if you listen carefully you will find it is a mixture of traditional vocal techniques from old Chinese drama and Western rock and rap, plus he has carefully chosen traditional style music and Chinese lyrics with a little black humour and a lot of Beijing dialect. The whole album smells really Chinese. (Xie 2008: 106)

This review attests to the importance of the issue of globalisation and copying for Chinese bands, and points to the sheer impossibility of 'truly' Sinifying rock music. It is significant that it is a more alternative band, employing a sound approaching to the hard force of the rock mythology, which is being praised for its successful translation. Feng Jiangzhou from The Fly is also fascinated by 'characteristic' Chinese sounds, which he aims to combine with computer samples and sounds from electric drills: 'I am most interested in using Chinese instruments and revolutionary songs. (...) But I'd definitely refuse to make them sound beautiful; I'd try to make them sound uncomfortable. I like uncomfortable things.'

This conscious distortion of what are considered to be traditional Chinese musical expressions forms one important marker of difference used by underground bands such as NO and The Fly. The transformation of what are considered to be stereotypical Chinese sounds challenges the connotations attached to them. These connotations are, in the case of the *guzheng*, mainly quietness and deepness, signifying China's long history, and in the case of the communist songs, the heroic revolutionary past. Zi Yue is even more focused than The Fly or NO on making *Chinese* rock. For Wang Yue, lead vocalist for the punk band Hang on the Box, it is this inclusion of Chinese elements that she does not like: 'I don't like Zi Yue and NO! They have too many Chinese elements. I like more modern bands.'

To her, the Chinese elements stand for backwardness, for a pre-modernity, whereas the sound of rock, which she considers Western, signifies modernity. It shows how the negotiation of place is contested within the rock culture and functions as an important marker of difference between bands and, often, scenes.

Zu Zhou's refusal to use traditional musical instruments in a classical way sets him apart from Zi Yue, where the traditional sound is used to construct an '*authentic*' Chineseness. However, in both cases, the use – or abuse – of traditional instruments also underlines that this is indeed *Chinese* rock. The negotiation cum negation of the past, either by a conventional or a 'distorted' way of using traditional instruments, can be interpreted as an act of self-orientalising. Although the dissonant sounds of Zu Zhou's *guzheng* might not create the tranquil, peaceful, mysterious China evoked by rock musician Wang Yong, they are still intended to mark a difference from 'the West'. In the words of Feng Jiangzhou: 'Localisation of Chinese rock implies that the music should express contemporary Chinese society, so in the music such local flavour is a kind of spontaneous flow of your ideas and emotions towards the conditions you are living in. You are Chinese, living in Chinese social situations.'

He points to the importance of locality, of place, and the straightforwardness of his statement is in my view highly relevant: the Chineseness of Chinese rock is not to be found in its sound, nor in its lyrics, but merely by the banal fact that those making it are born in, living in and working in China. Those who demand more – the foreign journalists so eagerly looking for signs of Chineseness – fall into a hegemonic and orientalistic trap, one that, as I explained in the previous chapter, puts the West at the epicentre of rock music. Yet tactics used by bands to Sinicise themselves, such as Zi Yue's insistence on making a Beijing sound, do run the danger of constructing an essentialised Chinese identity.[15] Qiu Ye's wish to create a pure *Chinese* rock accommodates rather than challenges the dominant notion, namely the uniqueness of China – a notion currently very much in vogue in the Chinese political arena.

Heavy Metal

Positions – Heavy metal (*zhong jinshu*) seems to travel very well in China. Ding Wu used to play with the rock band Hei Bao. Unable to express his love for heavy metal, he left the band and, in late 1988, formed the band Tang Dynasty together with Zhang Ju and two American-Chinese students, one of whom is Kaiser Kuo. Their debut album in 1992 was an instant success. The importance of Tang Dynasty for Chinese rock culture can hardly be overestimated. They introduced China to heavy metal; during the winter of 1993, the piercing, high-pitched voice of Ding Wu could be heard in streets all over the country. They have toured throughout China and performed in big venues and stadiums. It was only in 1999 that Tang Dynasty released their second album *Epic*, the style of which very much resembles their first one. The response of both the media and the audience to the album was lukewarm (Tao 2000a: 3), and the band failed to regain the status it had gradually lost over the years. It remains to be seen if their third album, rather oddly titled *Knight of Romantic*, released in the summer of 2008, can change that predicament; critics label it as a rather unsuccessful attempt to return to the good old days, when the lead vocalist still had the

ability to use a high-pitched voice (S. Wang 2008: 146). Other bands –
such as Cold Blooded Animals, Twisted Machine, Thin Man, Face, and
Iron Kite – have fared better and attract a considerable audience. Like
elsewhere in the world, more extreme subgenres have proliferated, with
bands like Voodoo Kungfu, 641, SAW, Saving Molly and Last Chance of
Youth. The following is a critic's reflection on the popularity of heavy
metal in China.

> The bombardment of heavy metal prevailing in foreign countries
> was enlarged by our ignorance and blindness. That resulted in a
> rebellious image both in terms of appearance and mentality and
> caused a general impression nation-wide that rock 'n' roll means
> being mad. Fortunately, the age is progressing on the whole. (Hu
> 1999: 21)

Rather than disappearing, it seems that heavy metal has become more
and more fragmented and diversified in China since the mid-1990s, towards subgenres such as death metal, NU metal, and black metal. For
example, the number of death metal (*siwang jinshu*) bands, with Toma-
hawk being one example, is growing, according to Shen Lihui from
Modern Sky.[16] Following the global success of bands like Korn and
Limp Bizkit, NU metal (also termed rap metal), with bands such as T9,
Miserable Faith and Twisted Machine, all released on Scream Records,
has gained momentum in Beijing. The popular live band Thin Man borders in style on NU metal – its sound resembles Rage Against the Machine. This generic bifurcation is seemingly endless; for example, the
band Pungent Liquid classifies itself as Gore Grind. In an interview
they do their best, like the previously mentioned SUBS, to defy any classification and hence secure their authenticity: 'We don't need to define
ourselves because we are what we are. (...) We are more concerned
whether we present reality.' (Bei 2004: 22)

Authenticating styles – At first sight, the aesthetics of heavy metal comes
close to what the rock mythology is all about. The leather jackets, long
hair, motorcycles, long, loud guitar solos, and screaming voices signify
both rebellion and masculinity. Tang Dynasty's celebration of the past
and its related criticisms of the present prevail in the lyrics, the image
and the sound of the band. In their songs, they express their solitude in
modern times, their despair, and their search for a better world. A music critic commented on the band: 'In their music, they express their
true feelings towards life and their understanding of the world. (...)
They express in their own way a longing for a strong and influential
China: a return to the Tang Dynasty.' (Dao 1997: 27)

In line with the rock mythology, their criticisms of modern times are considered authentic, just as their historical claims authenticate the sound.

In the real world, the search for a different life has been far from un-problematic. The band has gone through hard times. After signing up with Magic Stone, they became successful overnight. Their CD is said to have sold over a million copies, and within a few months of its re-lease, more than ten pirated versions were on the market. Unable to cope with their instant success, problematic years followed. Addiction to drugs lasted for years, and in May 1995 guitarist Zhang Ju died in a motorcycle accident. They split with Magic Stone, which, according to the band, had not supported them during their hard times. It was only in 1997 that the band started playing again, for a short while managed by Dickson Dee from Hong Kong. Such stories of hardship authenticate their music; they tie in well with the rock mythology, and the perceived perseverance of the band underscores the fact that these are real, dedi-cated musicians. The stories keep on proliferating. Zhao Nian com-plains how they have always failed to make money: 'Rock in the West is a profitable, healthy business, but here it is twisted, we lost our money in the business, and we didn't complain, because we love music. But these horrible music critics on the Internet, they kept on talking bull-shit.' (Huo 2008: 8)

Their perseverance – against the industry, against the critics' judg-ment – serves as proof of their quest to make music, and hence authen-ticates the band. The archaic language of their lyrics further strengthens the chivalric pose, a pose that corresponds to the tradition of Chinese swordsman novels (*wuxia xiaoshuo*). Added to the masculine poses and archaic lyrics are the powerful compositions, some almost military-like, with strong melodies and unexpected twists. Through these chivalric aesthetics, authenticity is negotiated, an authenticity constructed around notions of being a *real, tough man* who dares to express loudly his dis-content with modern society. One element that further authenticates the music is the self-reflexivity of heavy metal. Following Giddens, late modernity is characterised by a self-identity that 'becomes a reflexively organised endeavour.' (1991: 5) This reflexivity is not just apparent at an individual level, but also a communal (and indeed scenic) one. As Wal-ser points out in his work, the strong performativity of heavy metal ac-tually points to the constructedness of, among other concepts, gender.[17] The spectacular poses of heavy metal (and, for the same token, hardcore punk) help constitute a reflexive community that is 'continually active, self-searching and contingent.' (Kahn-Harris 2004: 99; see also Lash 1994). Yet, Kahn-Harris pushes this idea even further by discussing the reflexive anti-reflexivity of black metal, claiming that the bands from the European black metal scene are reflexive in that they demonstrate a considerable awareness of the structuration and politics of scenes and the wider society. Yet they are also anti-reflexive in that they wilfully seek to exclude that awareness from scenic practice. (...) It produces a politics of depoliticisation in which the structuration of the scene and the consequences of certain practices are wilfully ignored. (106)

The spectacular chivalric poses of Tang Dynasty can be read as reflexive poses that help authenticate the scene. Their celebration of China's past points to a reflexive anti-reflexivity, in that they refrain from contemplating the political implications of such a celebration.

Place – The band's name reveals the band's longing for China at the height of its glory. During the Tang Dynasty (618–907), Chinese art and culture reached, according to popular notions, its highest point. In a comparison with the West, the record company states in the promotional material, 'The most important thing is that here you will hear the self-confidence of the Chinese, because they have done what you thought only Westerners could do.'

The symbolism in the music, the lyrics, and the video clips which present a sort of orientalist dream sequence, full of references to the traditional past, express a pervasive sense of cultural loss. There is both irony and a reclamation of popular nationalism (cf. Lee 1996: 161-164). Or, in other words, their celebration of Chineseness is simultaneously reflexive and anti-reflexive. Jones quotes Lao Wu, who at the time was bass player for Tang Dynasty: 'Rock is based on the blues, and we can never play the blues as well as an American. It's just not in our blood. We can imitate it, but eventually we'll have to go back to the music we grew up with, to traditional music, to folk music.'[18] (in Jones 1994: 159)

The irony is that his dogmatic, essentialist approach resembles Western discourses, in which rock is frequently linked to folk music in order to differentiate it from commercial pop music. The band's CD jackets represent the band as warriors for an old China; the jacket of their first album depicts red flags waving with the band's name written in archaic characters, against a background of an old Chinese painting, all signifying the celebration of ancient China. Tang Dynasty's longing for the past is expressed in their song 'A Dream Return to the Tang Dynasty' (Jones 1994: 160):

Wind – cannot blow away our grievances
Flowers – cannot colour over our longing for home
Snow – cannot reflect the mountain stream
Moon – cannot fulfil the ancient dream
Following the patterns on my palm

Branded there by fate
Following fate I fall into a trance
In dreams I return to the Tang Dynasty

American-born Kaiser Kuo, who left the band in 1989, replaced Zhang
Ju on guitar. He stressed that they do not want to challenge the political
regime. According to him, 'China is such a huge country that it needs a
strong leadership.' Kaiser sees their music as a kind of safety valve, as a
way for youths to release their emotions and energy, as a way to redis-
cover Chinese culture, to be proud of being Chinese. In his celebration
of Chinese culture, he draws a comparison with Japan. '[Japanese his-
tory] is going to be dwarfed by China. (...) Chinese culture is a gold
mine, there is so much to do. There are people who go crazy for these
Japanese samurai stories, but there is so little in them, and there is
such a well in China.'

The philosophy of the band resembles the nationalist ideology as expressed by the Party.[19] Kaiser voices popular notions of the supremacy
of Chinese culture over Japanese culture, as does the record company
in its promotional material. It is telling that this celebration of China
comes from an American-Born Chinese (ABC), which not only indicates an involvement of the diasporic Chinese community in cultural
production in mainland China, but also suggests that his strong identification with 'China' may well be motivated by a desire to erase the A
in ABC. Ironically, Kaiser's return to Tang Dynasty was severely criticised by other rock musicians. While Zhang Ju played the guitar in a
Chinese way, Kaiser is said to play it in an American way, which is un-
suitable for Chinese rock. Besides, he is said to be a bad guitar player
anyway. This hostility toward foreign elements epitomises the attempt
to make rock with 'Chinese' characteristics. It is ironic that a band
which excels in a celebration of Chinese culture should be faced with
these criticisms.

In 1999, Kaiser Kuo left the band after having had personal conflicts
with vocalist Ding Wu. According to the press, they got into a fight over
NATO's bombing of the Chinese embassy in Belgrade. As an American-born Chinese, Kaiser Kuo was said to accept NATO's apologies to
China, whereas Ding Wu – and most Chinese – saw it as a deliberate
attack on their country. It is again ironic that, despite his patriotic opinions, Kaiser Kuo had to leave the band over such an issue.[20] Finally,
when I met him in 2004, Kaiser told me he had read my analysis in
which I pigeonholed him as a conservative and patriotic supporter of
the current authorities (de Kloet 2000). He expressed his discontent
with the way he was presented. This points to an ethical as well as
methodological concern: how far can we go in reading and interpreting
what is said in one single interview, often taken over food and beer, and

how ethical is it to interpret his words in terms of excessive patriotism and a desire to become Chinese, rather than American-born Chinese? His words serve as important reminders of, first, modesty when analyzing interview data, and the danger of taking statements at face value, as signifiers of the true beliefs of the person articulating them. Interviews are performative occasions, involving specific displays of the self coinciding with the desired image of a band or a genre. Here, I am in line with Caldwell, who observes in his study of the production industry in Hollywood that interviews 'can be conceptually rich, theoretically suggestive, and culturally revealing, yet, we should never lose sight of the fact that such statements are almost always offered from some perspective of self interest, promotion, and spin.' (2008: 14)

Second, Kaiser's response reminds me of the importance of discussing academic work whenever possible with the people who are being analysed, to let the respondents talk back, as it were. Thirdly, my reading of Tang Dynasty as being patriotic resonates uncomfortably with stereotypes often heard about heavy metal in general, claiming its conservative if not racist inclinations. Bands often seem to deliberately slip into a controversial performative mode – articulating the cosmopolitan aesthetics of heavy metal (cf. Regev 2007a, 2007b, see introduction). A review of the band Voodoo Kungfu – the name already is a cosmopatriotic articulation – describes the band as follows: 'Its outspoken profile of misery, extreme pagan worship inclinations and its deeply intriguing religious character, combined with the bloody and cold stage decoration that is full of nationalistic sentiments is very controversial, and they amplify the idea of rebellion.' (Ang 2008: 43) Global aesthetics are inscribed into a nationalistic narrative producing a controversial and *seemingly* conservative cosmopatriotic culture sphere. Yet, as the work of Kahn-Harris has shown, heavy metal presents a much more complicated cultural sphere. He points to the poignant differences between public performance (and an interview, even when it is at home, over food, can be seen as a public performance) and the private sphere. As he observes, 'The central paradox in the black metal scene is that almost anything is publicly sayable and potentially usable in discourse, yet almost any difference and conflict can be privately worked through. (...) The private sphere effectively ironises the public sphere.' (Kahn-Harris 2004: 103) The 'Chinese' stance of Kaiser can thus be read as a public performance, meant to provoke, to claim a difference from, for example, the critical position of the underground bands, and are as such tactics to secure authenticity, more than statements reflecting an ideological positioning.[21]

Furthermore, even if Tang Dynasty's music is an attempt to essentialise cultural differences, it must be acknowledged that this act of 'othering' is also a commercial strategy. 'The band is an avowedly commercial venture, and in this light, its nativism (...) is perhaps less an ideological stance than a marketing device' (Jones 1994: 161).[22] The critique of the present, the references to the past, the stories of the band's sufferings, and the chivalric aesthetics – strengthened by the heroic charisma of vocalist Ding Wu – authenticate their sound. Their music world forms a contradictory space: it both challenges and accommodates today's political realities.

Hardcore Punk

Positions – Punk emerged during the long hot summer of 1976 in the area around King's Road in south-west London (Hebdige 1979: 25). Its birth coincided with the end of that other, certainly more violent, Cultural Revolution, the one led by Mao in the ten years prior to that summer. While China was recovering and preparing itself to reopen its doors to the outside world, the Sex Pistols shocked the Western world in 1977 with their release *God Save the Queen*. The excessive look and extreme sound challenged all possible stylistic conventions. It was a white rebellion, borrowing eagerly from the youth cultures preceding it, such as glam rock and skinheads. Punk emerged at a specific juncture in British society; it was not just a (somehow celebratory) response to the increase in unemployment, but also a *'dramatising* of what had come to be called Britain's decline' (Hebdige 1979: 87, italics his). What happened when punk travelled all the way to China, some twenty years after that hot London summer?

Entering the punk zone in Beijing feels like entering a zone where hedonism competes with boredom. It is a reality where beer is smuggled into the bars, and the hair (if there is any left) is dyed purple. Mohawks are combined with thick chains that serve as necklaces. Black mascara is eagerly applied around the eyes and to the body. Performances are a colourful attempt to turn life into a visual and sonic spectacle. Performances in small bars are part and parcel of the punk culture; live shows are characterised by what Field and Groenewegen (2008: 9) refer to as the 'intense fire of primal energy,' as negotiated through performance style, music style and cultural codes. Punk (*pengke*) – sometimes journalists or bands add the label hardcore (*yinghe pengke*) to differentiate it from pop-punk – proves to be a good source of inspiration for Chinese musicians. Although punk is the current rage, its circle is very small and active in only a few small bars scattered around the city. Every evening, the same faces show up, and most punk musicians play for different bands; it thus takes only a few musicians to form a scene. This was the case in 1997, and, surprisingly so, remains fairly similar in 2008.

Figure 1.3   *Punkers at the MIDI Music Festival of 2008 (photo by the author)*

The hardcore punk circle is marginal, in terms of both size and popularity, but is very visible given its extravagant styles. Some of the older and partly defunct hardcore bands of the Chinese punk scene are Anarchy Jerks, Brain Failure, Reflector, and 69 – these four are collectively known as 'Senseless Contingent' (*wuliao jundui*), under which they released a compilation CD in 1999 – Joyside, SUBS, SMZB, and the (already disbanded) all-female Hang on the Box. Their names signify anarchy and rebellion. Not surprisingly, Western reporters frequently write about Chinese punk, or film the bands, as this scene ties in best with the desired countercultural pose (see for example Messmer & Lindt 2008; Jefford 2009). And the bands perform accordingly. According to Peter from the band 69, China needs punk:

> Many people don't understand punk. I think punk is necessary for Chinese society. Chinese people valued patience for about 5,000 years. Patience makes Chinese people like animals, like slaves. They need punk, they need punk to fight for what they want. If you don't want to be a slave, you should be punk.

It does not seem an exaggeration to say that hardcore punk, of all the scenes I have observed, comes closest to the ideal embodiment of the rock mythology, or is the hardest sound of all – propelling a style that is simultaneously profoundly cosmopolitan as well as Sinified.

Authenticating styles – In punk, the ideology of musical talent is subverted; in its do-it-yourself (DIY) philosophy, everyone can make music. Just as the pogo can be considered an anti-dance, a rejection of harmony and elegance, the related music can be considered anti-music, a refusal to accept any convention on popular music. Other authors have already eloquently analysed Western punk (Grossberg 1986; Hebdige 1979, 1988; Laing 1985).[23] It suffices here to add one footnote to the history of punk: the seemingly anti-authoritarian stance of the Sex Pistols was carefully planned and marketed by Malcolm MacLaren and Vivienne Westwood. The authenticity of punk, negotiated through its excessive style and the DIY philosophy, was in the case of the Sex Pistols cautiously constructed. The DIY philosophy poses a fundamental challenge to this notion of skills and talent. Nonetheless, this challenge is not taken to its extreme in China (and quite certainly not in the West either). As in other scenes, there is good and bad punk according to the musicians. Based on a random reading of blogs, Wang observes that for many, 'Chinese punk is a fashion accessory for hip kids. It is not the "real thing."' (2008: 229) Apparently, not everyone is allowed to do it him- or herself, and the discourse of authenticity also haunts the members *within* a scene. The opinion of Peter indicates that the women of Hang on the Box do it the wrong way: 'Their music sucks. It's not music, it's just screaming. Even their lyrics are dumb, really dumb ...'

Compared to the underground band The Fly, who also stressed the importance of DIY, punk compositions are more basic. Punk songs are usually short with an upbeat rhythm and an aggressive singing style. Apart from the DIY philosophy, the focus on rhythm rather than melody presumably also renders punk more authentic. Rhythm is linked to the constructed and racist history of rock that goes back to the drums of Africa (which, through the blues, made their way into rock). The 'primitive' sound of the African drum is real and sexy, just as Africa connotes sensuality and authenticity. Frith (1996: 127-141) points out that equating rhythm with the primitive, the bodily, and the sexual is merely a product of European high cultural ideology.[24] Via Europe, these notions travelled on to China. Consequently, the authenticity of punk can be captured in a one-liner: *Just do it*, and do it real, do it in the rhythm of the heart.

The flyer for a Halloween punk party depicts what looks like a white punker being terrified by a spider (Figure 1.4). The flyer's design connotes rebellion and chaos, so this must have been an underground party. The text says in clumsy English: Will Hold Power, Just Saying 'No' to Leader. Such a provocative statement is not repeated in Chinese,

Figure 1.4   *Flyer for a 1997 Halloween Party*

because that would be too risky; instead, the Chinese text simply announces a punk party. More than being a conscious political statement against the Party, both this text and the design of the flyer signify in my view anarchy and rebellion, two core elements of the punk idiom. Peter's band 69 also performed at the Halloween party. Their well-known songs electrified the audience. Their music is fun – fun to dance to, fun to sing along with. A fan dressed up like a Red Guard told me how he longs for a new rebellion, like the one in 1989. Peter's voice was filled with anger, which he had explained to me earlier: 'Every show I am angry. The music makes me think about many things, about all the bad things in society, the things that make me puke. (...) This society is controlled by the government.'

Field and Groenewegen discuss SUBS' performance of their song 'Brother,' reflecting the anguish lead vocalist Kang Mao felt after the crackdown of the 1989 student protests, during which her own brother was one of the victims (2008: 19). Their observations of the performance point to the political potential of punk (or, as they aptly describe it, the on-stage exorcising of a violent trauma):

> Following the song, Kang Mao breaks to deliver a short speech in Chinese about the importance of rock music (ironic since most of the crowd by now is foreign). 'If only we can increase the audience of this concert by a thousandfold, if only China can be more open, if only people can learn to think more, if only, if only...' (20)

Yet however tempting it is to give a politicised reading of Chinese punk, most bands resist such a reading. 'Punk bands such as Brain Failure and Joyside are more cynical about the political significance of rock music and celebrate hedonistic mosh parties, dissolving potential political energy into a kaleidoscopic whirlpool of clashing bodies.' (Field & Groenewegen 2008: 25) The 'underground' punk-zines, whose aesthetics are very much in line with the flyer in Figure 1.4, explain punk in terms of a cultural struggle. The following was written by Hang on the Box vocalist Wang Yue (May 1999; the italicised sentence was already in English):

> The birth and growth of Chinese punk germinates the explosion of a cultural revolution, a counterculture, an anti-popular consciousness, and a great movement breaking entirely away from decayed and dated thoughts. The pioneering punkers in China will encourage the new generation of Chinese youth to run bravely towards a new century. They are making valuable contributions to China's cultural development. Let us hope for the growth of China's punk bands! At the same time, let us all shout: long live world peace! *Long live anarchism! Long live the Chinese punk!*

The appropriation of communist terminology can be read both as a parody of the Party and as an attempt to Sinify punk. The last, English sentence reads like a political slogan. This is merely a symbolic play, not so much aimed at revolution and struggle, as at pleasure, the pleasure of

shocking and provoking. At the same time, this text is an articulation of
the rock mythology; it positions punk as truly countercultural. The pleasure of hardcore punk lies in its spectacular performance of difference,
a difference both shocking and provocative. These punkers are anything
but good sons and model students. Because such a negation of normality challenges dominant norms, we can speak of a *politics* of pleasure.
In its negation of what is considered normal in Chinese culture, in its
celebration of a difference taken to the extreme, the politics of pleasure
is more spectacular and therefore more visible in punk when compared
to other scenes.

Although the aesthetics of punk in China might resemble that of
punk in the West, the ideological horizon of the former seems to be
broader. The e-mail Peter sent me is typical:

> Jingwen helped us release but the compilation is really bad cuz
> [sic] we have been ripped off. (...) I have good news, Levi's will
> use 69 to promote their new products, we just signed the con-
> tract. (...) Pretty good, right? I think it's the first Chinese main-
> land local band to have a deal with a big company like Levi's.

In line with the prevailing idea that record companies are untrust-
worthy, Jingwen is considered to have ripped them off. He proudly announces their cooperation with the multinational jeans company, Levi's.
Also, Peter is earning a living by trading in stocks and shares, thus brid-
ging the unbridgeable gap between punk and capitalism. Both examples
show that, although punk might travel well to China, the musicians create a broad ideological space in which to manoeuvre.

Place – 'Fuck' is the English word most eagerly adopted by the bands.
For Qiu Ye, from the band Zi Yue, this is a sign that punk only copies
the West and lacks any link with Chinese culture:

> One extreme case of copying is punk. They only copy the hippie
> lifestyle, not the music spirit. In China there can't be punk. Only
> in a wealthy country can punk appear because of the spiritual
> emptiness. What the Chinese play is fake punk. They just imitate
> the manners, like screaming 'Fuck You Fuck Me' without making
> clear whether they have the potency to fuck others.

His remark not only reifies the West as the imagined centre of rock; it
also signifies tactics of exclusion, as the subtext reads 'I make *real* Chinese rock, they just imitate.'

Punk, though, fights back and creates its own authenticating discursive battles directed against the rock culture in general. The 69's song

'Comments on Rock and Roll' is a frontal attack on so-called posture rock:[25]

> What are you doing?
> Everything you say is so hypocritical
> Everything you do is so disgusting
> *Fuck! That is posture rock!* (...)
> Don't fucking strike a pose
> Don't fucking do that
> It's all fucking bullshit
> All you cheating stupid X
> You cheating stupid X!

Peter voices clear political opinions. For him, being counter-political is part of the punk package. Whenever we started talking about sensitive issues, his girlfriend urged us to speak English, so that the neighbours would not be able to understand us. The name of the band is a reference to the sexual position '69', which, Peter adds mockingly, supports the one-child policy of the CCP (previously, the band was called The Dildos). It is at the same time a reference to the Cultural Revolution, a period idealised by Peter:

> I think the Cultural Revolution is like an anarchy movement. I like anarchy, you know. Like anarchy in the UK, I don't know why. (...) I think I'd be a Red Guard.
> *And then accuse your parents?*
> No, no, the Red Guards just wanted to destroy everything and then rebuild it.

The anarchy of the Cultural Revolution, however violent it might have been, is considered to be in line with the punk spirit. The revolutionary past not only provides a source of identification and nostalgia, but also supplies the punk scene with the symbols with which to articulate the Chineseness of their music. Such articulations are stronger when the place is located in the past (be it ancient China or communist China). In Peter's words: '69's music is not new, it's 1970s music, the British punk combined with the Cultural Revolution, it's a mixture. I also use traditional Chinese music. (...) because I think punk is white music, just as reggae is black music.'

Since the Chinese are not white, some 'yellow' elements have to be mixed into white punk. 69 adopts revolutionary classics and transforms them into quick, short punk songs. The cover of an 'underground' punk-zine depicts a scene where a communist shows the revolutionary road; the cover text runs (in English): 'In our great motherland a new era is emerging in which the broad masses are grasping punk thought. Once punk thought is grasped by the broad masses it becomes an inexhaustible source of strength and a spiritual atom bomb of infinite power.'

Li Peng – who shares his name with the former Chinese leader – is guitar player for different bands and reporter for this punk-zine. He wrote about 69:

> The band, whether intentional or not, has integrated Chinese musical elements into punk music. (It's not like some bands that only use *erhu* or *guzheng* to display their Chineseness.) The elements they use are mostly from the 50s and 60s, which makes their style revolutionary and powerful!

Li's view typifies Chinese rock bands' double urge: to distinguish themselves from other bands (that use traditional musical elements), as well as from the West so as to avoid mimicry (thus the invocation of revolutionary China). The quote shows how the demand of localisation is consciously negotiated within Beijing rock culture and forms one of the dividing principles. Not only does the pop-rock dichotomy set Beijing apart from Hong Kong and Taiwan, but specific appropriations of the 'Chinese' musical heritage mark a distinction, in this case, between punk and, for example, the folk-rock music where sounds from ancient China are used. Punk can be considered a very 'hard' cultural form. This explains the power of the punk aesthetics, which travel so well globally, yet also corresponds to my argument that hard cultural forms are being localised especially eagerly. Because it is considered Western, punk – as a hard cultural form – *demands* localisation.

Paradoxically, punk, more so than other scenes, seems obsessively involved with the non-Chinese, in particular the West and Japan. In their magazines, reporters frequently stress how foreign TV crews have shot yet another documentary on punk, and that band T-shirts are being sold in Japan and the US. The eager incorporation of English words is equally revealing. On the 2004 release by Joyside (Modern Sky), all songs are in (broken) English, just like the songs of female punkers Hang on the Box. For example in Joyside's song titled 'I Want Beer,' part of the lyrics state:

> What a dirty goddamn world too much shit I cannot stand everybody's a nightmare my sweet home's just a hell so fuck it!!! I want beer, I want beer, I want beer, I want beer oh dear mankind dog damn you I do have a heart but it's not for you now shut up your stupid faces I never care about you bastards fuck you!!!

An indicator of the importance attached to global recognition is the way the SUBS present themselves on their MySpace site:

> Inspired by bands such as the Hives, the Sonics and Fugazi, Subs' brand of garage-punk rock makes a distinct musical mark. The band's live performances feature vocalist Kang Mao's jumps, wails, dives and screams supplemented by the rest of the band's equally abundant energy. Thanks to an invitation to play at Oslo, Norway's Øya Festival and the small tour that followed in 2005, the band has won over a new European audience and garnered interest from local and international print and broadcast media. [26]

Punk's localisation goes hand in hand with a reification of the importance of the perceived origin of punk. This continuous gesturing to the global idiom of punk feeds into the ambiguous poses. Baulch's analysis of death metal in Bali also applies to the punk scene: 'By orienting themselves to a global elsewhere, they conflated established dichotomies such as masquerade/essence, East/West, and retained carnivalesque modes of resistance.' (Baulch 2003: 196) Because it is considered Western, punk – as a hard cultural form – ought to be localized. These are two sides of the same coin called globalisation, which has pushed the dynamics of sameness and difference to the forefront of global cultural practices.

Hip-hop

Positions – The year 2004 witnessed a hip-hop revolution in terms of fashion, lifestyle and music. It comes somewhat as a surprise that it took so long before hip-hop became part of China's music world. Some bands may be considered part of rock culture, since they record on small Beijing rock labels, but the ties between hip-hop and rock are generally flimsy. Hong Kong has been an important departure point for Chinese hip-hop. In the late 1990s, the Hong Kong collective Lazy-MuthaFucka (LMF) hit the charts (Ma 2002). In its controversial political stance, coupled with a celebration of Chineseness (for example in a song about Bruce Lee) – both of which are translated into Cantonese rap with a lot of slang and obscene phrases – LMF serves as a timely reminder that to equate Hong Kong with apolitical music is fallacious. It comes as no surprise that LMF is banned on the mainland, but a flourishing black market has ensured a significant impact on the emergence of local hip-hop culture. In 2004, Scream Records released debut albums by Yin Ts'ang and Sketch Krime, and New Bees released the album by Kungfoo. In April of the same year, a third hip-hop battle was organised in Shanghai, the final of which staged MC Black Bubble from Shanghai against MC Webber from Beijing – one of Yin Ts'ang's members. Resembling the power imbalance between both cities when it comes to popular music, DJ Webber from Beijing won the battle.

Chinese hip-hop has gained rapidly in popularity since its debut in China in 2000. According to a report in Channel [V] magazine:

> If the youth of the 80s were obsessed with heavy metal, the youth of the 90s with punk, then from the end of the 1990s up to the present moment, it is hip-hop that dominates the aesthetics and even life attitudes of contemporary youth. They wear hip-hop clothes, they choose hip-hop records, and they spend every weekend at hip-hop parties. (DJ Danny & Hang 2004: 100)

More than rock, hip-hop also serves as a strong signifier of modernity, of urban consumer culture; hip-hop is, simply put, hip. As Fung observes, 'In Chinese hip-hop, the joviality of love and romance and the bliss of ethnic harmony and festivities of important Chinese occasions are celebrated along with the ecstasy of consumption.' (2008: 97) When I attended a hip-hop party in the spring of 2008 in Yugong Yishan – one of Beijing's music venues – the place was packed with people in the typical baggy hip-hop outfits with big necklaces and tattoos on their arms. Men dominated, and rappers were constantly joining forces on stage. Striking was the sheer absence of a rock audience; this scene felt very separate, one driven by an aesthetics of coolness, of exuberant masculinity and a 'black' aesthetics full of references to the imagery familiar from MTV clips and urban magazines. In addition to the new albums, the battles and the hip-hop parties, Urban Magazine presents the latest hip-hop fashion styles to Chinese youth. Editor Himm Wong explains how hip-hop has become trendy: 'Most Chinese youth are just seeking a superficial kind of culture, and real people, those who study the spirit of hip-hop, are very few.'

Hip-hop is blatantly used in commercials, marking a radical break from the rebellious pose preferred by rockers. This incorporation of hip-hop into mainstream culture smoothes over the underground connotations of *dakou* culture, ushering China into a post-*dakou* period of globalisation and marketisation trajectories.

Authenticating styles – The ideology of authenticity is inscribed into hip-hop in its slogan 'Keeping It Real'. The realness of hip-hop is closely linked to ethnicity, and it is often argued that it is a quintessentially 'black' sound that presents an alternative, rebellious voice (see for example Rose 1994), a voice rooted in the streets of the Bronx. Other origins are often conveniently ignored in such ethnicised readings that single out the rebellious in hip-hop culture (we can indeed speak of a hip-hop mythology). For example, both the Latin-American influences on early hip-hop culture, as well as the party rap of Sugar Hill Gang that coexisted with the more politically inspired sound of, for example, Public Enemy, remain relatively invisible. The ease with which rap travels around the globe and is appropriated by a wide range of ethnicities – including Caucasian – suggests that the link between hip-hop and ethnicity is weak. This is also Condry's observation in his book on hip-hop in Japan; as in China, 'Japanese hip-hop cannot be explained in terms of racial dynamics.' (Condry 2006: 49) The ease with which hip-hop blends with local music genres, resulting in hybrid forms such as Kwai-to in South-Africa, attests to its globalising power (Allen 2004). The mainstreaming of hip-hop in the late 1990s, with megastars such as Eminem, as well as its continuous offshoots (for example, gangsta rap, metal rap, r&b and party rap) has further weakened the link between hip-hop and both ethnicity and rebellion. Nevertheless, as Mitchell observes sharply in his introduction to the edited volume on global hip-hop, 'Most US academic commentaries on rap not only are restricted to United States and African-American contexts, but continue to insist on the socially marginal and politically oppositional aspects of US hip-hop.' (Mitchell 2001: 3) Repeatedly, hip-hop is presented in academic and popular discourse as an essentialised, endemically African-American cultural form (5). The story from China helps to undermine and to counter this US-centrism.

When I asked MC Webber from Yin Ts'ang how one 'keeps it real' in Beijing, he explained to me how to him, it boils down to a personal journey of trial and error, rather than to abstract standards of authenticity:

> ... It's related to technique and art. You have to combine the kind of techniques others can't master with the kind of art others don't understand. Then you will get something new and a sense of – how should I put it? – just keeping on doing it, like me, I would create 100 songs and then choose the very best one out of the 100. What is real? What is fake? Basically it's very individual ... if you want to keep it real, it's very difficult. Keep on trying, just keep on trying.

Remarkably enough, references to China or Beijing are absent in his narrative. Yet, when he battled in Shanghai, he clearly made use of Beijing slang against his opponent, who used Shanghai dialect. Such very localised politics are part and parcel of global hip-hop culture; each country not only has hip-hop groups in its own language, they generally further differentiate into different dialects. This rooted-ness grants the sound a sense of authenticity. When we take a closer look at the assumed roots of Chinese hip-hop, when we try to define its place, the picture becomes blurrier.

Place – In its marketing of Yin Ts'ang, record company Scream refers to the ideology of 'Keeping it Real'; as they write on their website:

> Fronted by Chinese hip-hop national champion MC Webber, the group are [sic] insistent on staying loyal to the roots of the genre in the face of what group member Josh Hefferman called, 'the McDonaldisation of hip-hop.' (...) Looking ahead, the group hopes to further the education of Chinese towards 'true' hip-hop.[27]

It is quite ironic, to use an understatement, that an American rapper claims to teach the Chinese an alleged American cultural form ('true' hip-hop) in order to 'resist McDonaldisation'. This irony is played out on several levels. First, the composition of bands like Yin Ts'ang, with the strong presence of 'foreigners,' makes any attempt to 'truly' localise hip-hop necessarily ambivalent. The US members may signify a 'pure' hip-hop culture, as they come from the imagined homeland of hip-hop; at the same time, they are sabotaging any attempt to make 'real' *Chinese* hip-hop. Articulations of what Forman (2000) terms, in the context of East Coast versus West Coast rap, *the extreme local,* such as references to everyday life in Beijing are rendered ambivalent by the inclusion of the non-local in the making and performance of Chinese hip-hop. In the case of Chinese hip-hop, the American group members may well be read as signifiers of *the extreme global.* The same ambivalence surfaces, yet is at the same time denied, on their MySpace site, where the band announces the release of a new CD, stating that this 'will once again bring real 100% home-grown Chinese hip-hop music to the mainstream listeners.'[28]

Second, like punk, hip-hop can be considered a deeply cosmopolitan cultural text; its cosmopolitanism is both stimulating *and* resisting the localising urge. This makes a pure localisation or Sinification simply impossible. Hip-hop is bound to be read as a modern, 'Western' lifestyle, no matter how eagerly its styles are being localised or indigenised – which resonates with my discussion in the previous chapter of Regev's notion of aesthetic cosmopolitanism.

Thirdly, global hip-hop ideology is challenged by the Beijing groups. The appropriation of hip-hop by China's affluent urban middle class is equally indicative of the twist Chinese give to hip-hop ideology – it challenges the assumed link between hip-hop culture and the lower classes, just as the link between ethnicity and hip-hop is disrupted in a Chinese context. Condry (2000: 169) observes the same situation in Japanese hip-hop, which has never been part of a street culture, but instead was appropriated by hip middle-class youngsters in search of yet another trend. The decoupling of hip-hop from class and ethnicity, the absence of the ghetto or the 'hood,' as well as the erasure of sexism and ostentatious performances of materialism (for a critique on these aspects of hip-hop, see Gilroy 2000), proves that hip-hop can be very different from what it is today according to the dominant imagination.

If I am risking stereotyping hip-hop along the US-centric lines so powerfully debunked by Mitchell (2001), apart from the proliferation of global scenes helping to undermine these essentialised notions of hip-hop, within the US scene, the dominant imagination is also complicated by manifold manifestations which are much more diverse and often go far beyond the stereotypical golden chains and semi-naked women. In a similar vein, Eminem, among others, has also contributed to the decoupling of hip-hop from ethnicity. In China, the discourse of authenticity remains in place; its defining parameters are located in everyday life and teenage anxiety. Poses of rebellion have faded away, as has the conspicuous presence of barely-dressed women, golden chains and expensive cars. In other words, the problematic sexist and materialist aspects of parts of US hip-hop culture are erased, to be replaced by more mundane performances of the musical self. For Fung, this eliminates the subversive potential of hip-hop: 'Occupied with consumptive hedonism, individualistic narcissism, and materialistic pursuits, apolitical hip-hop music actually functions to soothe social upheaval and maintain the status quo' (Fung 2008: 97) One could also read Chinese hip-hop as subverting hegemonic (US-driven) notions of hip-hop culture, just as the aesthetics of the everyday may resonate more closely with the lives of Chinese youth.

The scenes described so far return in their sonic aesthetics to a sense of Chineseness, to an imagined construct called China. It is perhaps on this point that hip-hop culture adds the prefix 'post' to *dakou* culture, when it openly and immediately incorporates the West into its cultural practices. Illustrative of the break is the distance between rock culture and hip-hop culture. Although the same record companies contract recording artists from both domains, there is relatively little interaction between rock and hip-hop. In hip-hop culture, the global is increasingly located *within* the local. Through the immediacy and openness, by and large enabled by new technologies, with which Chinese musicians link up with their most conspicuous counterparts (the West), cultural – and national – boundaries become blurred. Illustrative of such processes of cultural synchronisation, as already mentioned, is the conspicuous involvement of Westerners in hip-hop. In Yin Ts'ang, only one out of its four members is 'indigenous' Chinese. MC Webber is a Beijing resident, two members are white Americans, one is an overseas Chinese from Canada. Sketch Krime works with four MCs from France, Britain, Japan and the US. Signs of localisation are abound in, for example, song titles from Yin Ts'ang: 'Welcome to Beijing', 'Beijing Bad Boy', 'SARS' and 'Yellow Road.' In their song 'SARS', Yin Ts'ang reflects upon the days that the virus controlled Beijing:

> Frequently wash your hands. Wear a mask, stay away from me, wear gloves, stay physically fit, don't use your hands to touch your face, I have come to invade, call me SARS, I was born in Guangzhou, in that climate I developed a vicious demeanour, who would have guessed, that it would go this far, little old me could make everyone so scared.

The reflection upon SARS localises the sound of hip-hop, along with the language of the lyrics. Yet, the mixed nationalities of the musicians make this localisation ambivalent. The inlay of the jacket again articulates the cultural and national ambivalence of this hip-hop band: 'One Chinese, two Americans, one Chinese Canadian, a three-nation troop! Foreigners sing Chinese songs, the first release of its kind! A breakthrough of traditional ideas!'

In the releases by Sketch Krime, the global is even more strongly located within the local. Although the story of Sketch Krime – a Yunnan native who moved to Beijing – features prominently in the marketing of the CD, the invited international MCs sing in their own languages (English, French and Japanese).

In Chinese hip-hop, it is profoundly unclear which nationality lies behind a production, which cultural influences have been most decisive and what role the floating signifier 'Chineseness' has played – if any. This does not result in an erasure of the localising urge, as the themes touched upon in lyrics, as well as the use of language, localises and Sinifies the sound of hip-hop. Simultaneously and openly, the West is directly incorporated – as if the two are being scratched and mixed at the turntable of a hip-hop DJ. In its close ties to commercial lifestyle cultures, and its link to a rising middle class, hip-hop is part and parcel of the marketisation of Chinese culture, just as it embraces processes of globalisation. Yet, in locating the global within the local, Chinese hip-hop poses a challenge to essentialised notions of Chineseness.

Interim

The hip-hop scene already pushes at the hard boundaries outlined at the start of this chapter. Its playfulness, its rupture with the *dakou* movement and its strong ties to hipness, lifestyle issues and an upwardly mobile rising middle-class culture make it difficult to proclaim it is a 'hard' sound driven by the rock mythology. In its insistence on 'Keeping it Real', hip-hop remains close to the authenticating drive of the rock mythology. Is the urge to localise, to make rock with Chinese characteristics, equally strong? This chapter has presented a long and winding journey through the scenic landscape of Chinese rock culture. The voices presented in this chapter present a longing for authenticity at a time when commercialisation and globalisation are in full swing. At the same time, this longing goes hand in hand with tactics of distinction – these can be sonic tactics, but also verbal ones, in terms of gossip and the ridiculing and critiquing of others. The field of rock is in a sense not that different from other professional fields.

The hard scenes presented in this chapter have developed different aesthetics to articulate their authenticity. Underground bands employ Dadaist, vulgar, and metaphoric aesthetics coupled with lo-fi recording techniques; heavy metal has its chivalric aesthetics; and hardcore punk combines DIY with an authenticating rhythm. Hip-hop is 'keeping it real' in its insistence on using local dialects, borrowing from a global hip-hop ideology and the related articulations of place. Already in hip-hop we have observed the intrinsic impossibility of Sinification; its cultural codes as well as the actual practitioners make this an excellent case of the cosmopolitan aesthetics of pop-rock culture (Regev 2007a, 2007b), and have inspired me elsewhere to label this a 'cosmopatriot' sound (De Kloet 2007). But what happens to Chineseness when the sound becomes less hard, less drenched in the rock mythology? What about the scenes fusing genres, almost pop in their identifications, such as pop-rock and pop-punk? In the following chapter I will explore these hyphenated scenes.

2 Hyphenated Scenes

Western style minds feel so great
Everybody is living in a fashion magazine
Open the TV this is a foreign modern life show
Close your eyes only illusion
New Pants, Fashion 1983, 2008

Multiplicity

The problem with juxtaposing the hard with the soft, West and East,
North and South, authentic and fake, local and global, and Han Chinese
to the ethnic minority, is that one freezes multiple realities and modernities into a rigid binary framework (Lau 2003). The scenes described
in the previous chapter are all involved in tactics of localisation, at times
critiquing Chinese culture, at other moments celebrating it. The hard-
ness of the sounds seems to relate to the eagerness to localise. These
tactics are played out in a cultural field whose aesthetics are inherently
cosmopolitan (Regev 2007a, 2007b), which necessarily renders them
incomplete and impure. The eagerness to localise comes with a continuous 'gesturing elsewhere,' (Baulch 2008), a gesturing towards a global
discourse of rock music. In an attempt to complicate the picture of sonic globalisation even further, and before moving to the scenes that are
more rigorously excluded from Beijing rock culture, this chapter explores the scenes challenging a clear-cut scenic approach by merging
different genres and by being highly self-reflexive. Being less forcefully
implicated in the rock mythology, these hyphenated scenes push the
limits of a binary approach and cheerfully refute neat generic divisions.

Folk-rock

Positions – Folk music is often considered an important part of China's
cultural heritage, and as such is studied by ethnomusicologists (see
Schimmelpenninck 1997). The genre has made its way into rock

culture, but rather than being an expression of rural traditions, the sounds that carry the labels folk (*mingge* or *mingyao*), folk-rock (*mingge yaogun*), or urban folk (*chengshi mingge*) are first and foremost 'individual' expressions of urban sentiments. Whereas other scene names are either a direct or a homophonic translation from the English, folk is the only scene whose name has a long and complicated history in China as well. Minorities use it to articulate their local identity, the Han Chinese use it to reify their long tradition, the CCP uses it to propagate a national unity that builds on the multicultural idea of ethnic diversity, and now the rock culture has appropriated it. Zhang Chu and Zheng Jun were both born in Xi'an and only later moved to Beijing. In fact, the song that made Zhang Chu famous all over China ('Little Sister'), expresses his loneliness and his longing for both his sister and his hometown.[1] Zhang Chu was mainly popular until the mid-1990s, but when I attended a comeback concert by him in May 2008, a concert held to support the earthquake victims in Sichuan, I was touched and surprised to see how the audience – mostly in their 20s – was able to sing along with his lyrics word by word. The other singers in my analysis, all less popular when compared to Zhang Chu and Zheng Jun, are Hu Mage, who comes from Inner Mongolia, Xiao He, who moved in 1995 from Hebei to Beijing and Zhou Yunpeng, a blind singer who moved from Shenyang to Beijing. The migratory experience is particularly apparent in the folk scene; most singers position themselves as troubadours from the provinces.

Authenticating styles – According to Frith (1996: 39), in Western folk music, there is ideally no separation between art and life. Folk music is not so much a reflection or comment on everyday life, as part and parcel of everyday life, an inseparable element of it. The folk singer is the regular guy, and he rejects glamorous stardom. As I will show, these aesthetics also distinguish Chinese folk-rock singers from other scenes. Instead, what is valued (or better, constructed and displayed) is 'the natural, the spontaneous, and the immediate' (Frith 1996: 40). Folk singers are troubadours, lyrical poets with a guitar. They reflect on the loneliness of urban life, and sing about nostalgia for their hometown and their longing for true love. What sets them apart from pop music is not only their refusal to be glamorised, but also and mostly the importance attached to writing one's own songs and lyrics. Folk aesthetics produce a discourse of authenticity based on notions of closeness, simplicity, and intimacy. As I will show in my analysis, the paradox of folk is that while its troubadours are supposed to be ordinary boys, they are so extraordinary that you rarely find them in real life; you feel very close to them because the real boy next door is very far away.

Zhang Chu fits in very well with the regular guy aesthetics of folk-rock. Interviews with him usually stress his personal life. He is depicted as a poetic innocent (see Hu 1997). Poetry, being regarded as the highest form of the literary arts, gives Zhang Chu an intellectual aura. In the late 1980s, he lived at Beijing Teachers University, where he participated with Yi Sha in a poetry group (Hou 1996).[2] Hou Ma writes about this period and how Zhang Chu composed his songs:

> Important was their rebellious attitude, directed against the hypocritical artistic atmosphere that dominated everything. This was really a time of emancipation, a time full of creation. (..) When Zhang Chu wrote music, he looked like a hallucinating wizard, humming endlessly as though controlled by a ghost.

This statement voices an idealised nostalgia for the 1980s, the decade of the great cultural debate, or cultural fever (Wang 1996). It also reifies the idea of the gifted artist who goes into a trance when writing his music, an idea that resonates well within the rock mythology. In order to set Zhang Chu apart from other rock musicians, the author continues to describe Zhang Chu in terms that articulate the folk aesthetics:

> Zhang Chu stays home all day. (...) He is more like a little animal or child, he is simple, curious and kind-hearted. His eyes are bright and clear, his expressions are calm and he laughs without any restraint. (...) If you want to talk to him on an equal level, you must be as innocent as a child and wipe out all the impure things in your mind. (Hou 1996)

Such notions as simplicity, innocence, and purity position Zhang Chu as a true artist, and his rejection of stardom is crucial for folk-rock. But Zhang Chu is depicted here as an extraordinarily 'regular guy,' an extraordinariness that lies in his boyish attitude more than in anything else. In folk, the extraordinary is located in the ordinary. Folk is a celebration of innocence, of the immediate and sincere, and only those who act according to its 'pure' aesthetics can enter the folk-rock scene.

Zhang Chu is extreme in neither his looks – on the jacket of his first CD (*Ashamed to be Lonely*, 1994) he is lighting a cigarette in a shabby room; on the jacket of his 1997 CD (*The Airplane-making Factory*) he is dressed in jeans and T-shirt – nor his music. On the jacket of his first release, record company Magic Stone introduces Zhang Chu as follows: 'He decides to look for more sincere and simple feelings. (..) He hopes people will find in his music some truer feelings, not just simple romance. He wants to be a narrator and stand with others; he does not want to be too aloof, to be too high or distant.'

In line with the folk aesthetics stressing notions of simplicity and innocence, Zhang Chu is deliberately presented as the regular guy. In his
lyrics, Zhang Chu refuses to reiterate the rock mythology; it is hard to
find clear rebellious statements, his metaphors are complex and not easily translated into a cultural or political critique. In the ambiguity of
his lyrics, Zhang Chu leaves open much interpretative space for the listener. Another critic observes that Zhang Chu's voice is 'lonely, weak,
and unfashionable' (Vincent 1996: 20). The power of his music lies,
apart from the poetic lyrics, in this strange voice. His high-pitched,
nearly off-key voice is like a desolate cry from afar, as though he is asking for our help, but only after he has put himself out of reach.

Hu Mage is a singer who comes from Inner Mongolia, whereas Xiao
He moved in 1995 from Hebei to Beijing. Hu Mage's 1998 album
Everyone has a little wooden stool, won't take mine to the 21st century has a
white jacket that depicts a childish drawing (see Figure 2.1).

Figure 2.1   *CD Jacket Hu Mage (copyright Modern Sky)*

The childish drawing on the white cover gives the album, in my eyes,
an innocent aura, its whiteness signifying purity and simplicity. The lyrics are printed in the form of handwriting instead of being typeset,
which constructs the singer as someone close to us, someone who has
written down words for us. The inlay shows snapshots of Hu Mage,
sometimes along with his band. Some have captions like '1991, graduated from Yiling secondary school' or '(...) stayed in Huazhong Teachers
University, accompanying classmates in their studies.' Like the lyrics,
these pictures construct Hu Mage as one of us, a nice guy who has fun

with his classmates, who studies and tries to find his own way in life. Both the imagery and the music articulate a sense of intimacy which authenticates the music. A Beijing critic shares my observations in his album review: 'Just like all sincere confessors, he all of a sudden becomes a real catcher of the heart, catching all the lonely hearts on a weekend night... Even I am touched.' (Zhahuang 1999: 17)

In his song 'Some Potatoes Go to the City,' Hu Mage starts laughing when he sings:

> Next door lives a cultured person, strange, but not really with bad intentions
> He says I am hardworking, brave, sincere, simple and without any desire
> He shows me an exercise book, full of words
> He plays music to me, which I don't like, too noisy

He is like a modern troubadour; the music is plain and simple, only the sound of his guitar accompanies the raw and unpolished voice of Hu Mage. He stresses his simplicity by positioning himself vis-à-vis a 'cultured person.' His music can be read as a nostalgic longing to retreat from contemporary urban society, towards a place beyond conspicuous consumption, an imagined place full of serenity and honesty.[3]

Xiao He's CD carries an equally long and poetic title as Hu Mage's, *A high-flying bird won't land on the back of a slow-moving cow*. It was also released by Modern Sky in 2003. The CD resembles the aesthetics of Hu Mage; this time the jacket is in earth colours, signifying naturalness, just as the handwritten lyrics point to simplicity and purity. On the jacket's inlay, Yin Lichuan writes on Xiao He's live performance: 'I believe Xiao He can survive in any environment, waiting for every opportunity to have fun and share it with others. Now he is performing in a bar amidst all sorts of people, but he behaves as if he's herding sheep on a little hill slope when he was young, so relaxed, so involved, and so happy.'

The last remark again underlines the nostalgic purity of folk, a purity that is often located in the rural, rather than the urban, and in youth, rather than in aging. The temporal element in folk's nostalgia remains ambivalent. Drawing on Chow, Leung argues that 'nostalgia is not simply a yearning for the past as though it were a definite, knowable object. Rather, nostalgia involves a "sensitivity to the movements of temporality." Understood in these terms, a nostalgic subject is someone who sits on the fence of time.' (2001: 430) The folk singer sits on the fence, his back turned to a time of conspicuous consumption, longing for the innocence of youth and the imagined purity and simplicity of an idyllic life. This longing returns in the lyrics of Xiao He's song 'The river of wolves':

The snow that will never melt and remain clean
The river that will never freeze and remain transparent
Wind, please caress her body gently
Make her speak slowly
Through the surface of the river
Through the tree leaves
Through the valleys
As a gift to the forever past
As a gift to the forever future

Folk singers evoke – in terms of lyrics, sound and image – a nostalgic longing for a life beyond the marketisation and globalisation of urban Chinese society and can consequently be read as a critique of contemporary China. However, ambivalently enough, in their own lives, the singers moved from the geographical margins of China towards its political and cultural centre. This pull to the modern capital comes with a nostalgic longing for a margin located in an ambivalent idyllic past. Idyllic because the object of nostalgia is futile, in the words of Stewart (quoted in Shih 2007: 108): 'Nostalgia is a sadness without an object, a sadness which creates a longing that of necessity is inauthentic because it does not take part in lived experience. Nostalgia, like any form of narrative, is always ideological. The past it seeks has never existed except as narrative, and hence, always absent, that past continuously threatens to reproduce itself as a felt lack.' The lack, located in an imagined life beyond modernity, capitalism, urbanism and consumerism, generates a utopian dream that remains impossible, a dream located in a past-future. The nostalgia evoked by Hu Mage and other folk singers is engaging with this paradox, positioning both singer and audience on the fence of time, longing for a past that triggers a desire for a different future – a past and future that are both, if we are to believe Xiao He, forever.

Xiao He, who has already played a key role in the alternative folk scene of Beijing for several years, discovered the talent of blind folk singer Zhou Yunpeng. They regularly perform together in bars like D-22. In both his music style (boy with guitar) as well as his image (casual) Zhou Yunpeng typically fits the folk aesthetics. Generally his songs contain a critique of modern life and he expresses his humanitarian concerns. Yet, one of his songs betrays a part of my analysis so far in its overtly political contents. 'China's Children,' which made him famous, was released in 2007. It is worth quoting at length, given its biting critique of the murderous nepotism of government officials. The song refers to a fire where officials refused to let the children escape, to a water disaster caused by the negligence of officials, to HIV infections, to coal mine disasters, and to a drugs scandal (the footnotes explain these scandals in greater detail):

> Don't be a kid in Kela-mayi, where the fire burns your skin, breaking mother's heart[4]
> Don't be a kid in the town of Shalan, where it's too dark in the water, you can't go to sleep[5]
> Don't be a kid in Chengdu, where your drug addict mother leaves you at home for seven days[6]
> Don't be a kid in Henan, where HIV laughs in your blood[7]
> Don't be a kid in Shanxi, where father becomes a basket of coal, you never see him again
> Don't be a Chinese kid
> They will eat you if they starve, not even comparable to the old goats in the wild,
> Who become threatening to protect the baby lambs
> Don't be a Chinese kid, fathers and mothers are all cowards
> In order to prove their cold blood, they gave your chance of survival to the officials, at the last moment

In the song, children join in the chorus, singing 'yah, yah, yah, yah,' as if they can't agree more with his lyrics; it is as if their voices were only recorded after they passed away. The sad, dark voice of Zhou Yunpeng, accompanied by a simple, bare and slow guitar sound, strengthens the gloomy atmosphere the song evokes. The scandals, the children who lost their lives, all of which he brings so vividly to mind, make this one of the most chilling songs I know from Beijing's rock culture.

In its celebration of purity and innocence, folk seems to negate any longing for rebellion, but this single song contradicts such a reading immediately. Another aspect deserving of further study is the strong sense of humour folk singers like Hu Mage and Xiao He infuse in their work and during their performances (see Groenewegen 2008), which renders the scene more ambivalent than 'just nostalgic.' It points to its multivocality. Not only is it possible to read the 'innocent' sound of folk as a critique of the processes of marketisation and urbanisation, but in songs like 'China's Children', there is a straightforward political critique, also showing that it is still too early to lament the depoliticisation of Chinese rock culture.

Place – The migratory experience is crucial in the work of Zhang Chu, Zheng Jun, Hu Mage, Xiao He and Zhou Yunpeng. In their references to their migratory past, they voice experiences that many Chinese share, not only students who leave their hometown for years, but also the migrant workers who flock into the city. In their references to migration, to a floating lifestyle, folk singers do not so much fixate place as point to its fluidity and mobility. The sound is characterised by a deliberate placelessness, a sense of being uprooted, which authenticates the sound. Other folk-rock singers, however, (and here I will elaborate on Zheng Jun) deliberately include references to the ancient, exotic China, references that also help to authenticate their sound. Zheng Jun's music contains many references to ancient China. He explains this by pointing to a perceived incompatibility between East and West: 'I think Western culture just tries to be comfortable, and Eastern culture is different: it cares about the spirit, cares about your own soul, about real life and life before birth and after death. (...) Eastern culture is for a few wise people.'

Zheng Jun positions the East versus the West, and reifies the clichés attached to this duality. He explained to me that he has learned to appreciate Western music, and attaches a notion of freedom of individual expression to it. His freedom lies in a search for the spiritual, a search based not so much on Christianity (his mother's religion), as on a celebration of Eastern mysticism. In his music he eagerly incorporates mythic elements, such as Tibetan folk songs or local opera. Zheng Jun's hit song 'Back to Lhasa' combines the voices of Tibetan women with the sound of his electric guitar. Despite its rather blunt structuralist generalisation, I will pursue a brief semiotic reading here. If we follow predominantly Western stereotypes, ethnic and/or rural women, like Tibet, signify authenticity, naturalness, and purity. At the connotative level, both Tibet and women are considered closer to nature (than either the city or man) in Western culture and, I would like to argue, also in urban China. To combine the feminine with the exotic results in an even stronger articulation of authenticity, an articulation that ties in well with the rock mythology.[8] Tibetan women articulate fantasies of origin and of nature (instead of culture). They operate as the constitutive externality of Han people, and propel an internal orientalism in China. The work of Louisa Schein (1997) shows how the Miao women serve as the feminised keepers of tradition and the exotic others, through which Han Chinese can perform their assumed modernity.

As Komlosy observes (2008: 50), 'By using these [traditional ethnic] sounds, Zheng is invoking noble, if essentialist, notions of non-Han peoples. In 'Hui Dao Lasa', Buddhist chimes and high-pitched, rough yet lyrical female vocals are used to express ideas of purity and strength associated, in popular imagination, with Tibetan peoples.' These fantasies feed into the construction of a primitive other that belongs to an idealised past and contrasted with the modern self, an integrated component of an alleged modern China. 'These fantasies are played out through a *generic* realm of associations, typically having to do with the animal, the savage, the countryside, the indigenous, the people and so forth, which *stand in* for that 'original' something that has been lost' (Chow 1995: 22). Chow refers to this invention of an imagined past (which in the case of Zheng Jun is projected toward a distant place) as a primitive passion, 'a fabrication of a *pre* that occurs in the time of the *post*' (22).

Zheng Jun, who comes from a higher class family in Xi'an, in which both Christian and 'traditional' Chinese culture are core values, and was educated in a 'communist' system, and then started studying foreign business, ended up writing the following lyrics (from his hit song 'Return to Lhasa'):

> That snow-capped mountain, that green grass, that beautiful
> Lama temple
> That girl, forever
> Lha ... yaaayeee ... sa, feels like my home
> Lha ... yaaayeee ... sa, my beautiful snow lotus-flower
> In the pure sky flies a pure heart
> Don't worry for tomorrow, don't bother about today
> Come come, let's return to Lhasa
> Return to the home we haven't seen for a long, long time

As Baranovich (2003) also notes, in its nostalgia for the natural and idyllic, the lyrics implicitly critique state-supported processes of marketisation. At the same time, as with Sister Drum, the inclusion of ethnic elements can be considered a self-orientalising move, here employed by a Han Chinese.

To summarise, folk-rock is a scene where predominantly male troubadours muse on living in a rapidly modernising society. In their quest for authenticity, for purity, they fit the rock mythology. In their nostalgic longing, they are sitting on the fence of time, emphasising the temporalities of our lives, and longing for a past that has never existed and a future that will never exist. In their negation of rebelliousness, they simultaneously push the limits of the rock mythology. As the case of Zhou Yunpeng illustrates, such a reading is not quite complete. This renders the scene both profoundly multivocal and ambiguous, and this multivocality and ambiguity lies at the heart of the power of folk-rock, as it creates a relatively large interpretative space for audiences.

Pop-rock

Positions – When I gave a presentation at the University of Amsterdam
to a group of twenty high school students from Beijing in February
2009, I asked them which rock bands they could name. The group, all
part of the generation born in the 1990s, looked puzzled; rock was
clearly not part of their life-world. Slowly some names emerged: Point
Zero, Beyond, Black Panther, Cui Jian, and Zang Tianshuo. With the exception of Cui Jian, these bands are generally classified as pop-rock
bands. This is the scene that most successfully crosses over to a wider
audience. The prefix pop can arguably be taken literally, pointing not
only to the sound itself but also to the popularity of these bands. The
band Black Panther (*Hei Bao*) started off playing rather heavy sounds.
After vocalist Dou Wei left the band, the music gradually mellowed and
became pop-rock ballads (*liuxing yaogun*). Neither critics nor audiences
were pleased with this development; a band which transgresses the
boundaries set by the rock mythology is believed to have lost its soul.
For Zang Tianshuo, the move from playing in a band to becoming a
pop-rock singer has been more successful; he gained rather than lost
fans. Point Zero (*Ling Dian*) started off as a pop-rock band from Mongolia and as such was very popular on the mainland. According to
critics, Zheng Jun has also moved toward pop-rock, as becomes clear
from the following review:

> The difference between rock and pop is very obvious. However
> hard the drums are played, and even strengthened with a sup-
> porting band, pop music remains pop music. Why do Zheng Jun
> and Ling Dian have to squeeze into this small alley of Chinese
> rock? Maybe if they took off this rock jacket, more young girls
> would become their fans. I really like Zheng Jun – if only he'd
> stopped after his second album. (Tianpigu 1999: 17)

His words reify the dichotomy pop versus rock, and clearly value the latter more: pop is something for 'young girls'. A hard sound does not
guarantee the label rock; only sounds that are framed by the hard force
of the rock mythology will be granted that label, I expect. My analysis of
the pop-rock scene will focus primarily on how these bands perceive
their position within the rock culture. I will show how pop-rock musicians rely on the rock mythology when it comes to being authentic, yet
challenge other aspects of the mythology, in particular its focus on the
countercultural.

Authenticating styles – When I told Qiu Ye I was going to a Zang Tianshuo concert, a cynical smile appeared on his face and he said: 'That's

not rock, it's pure pop!' For Gao Wei, the vocalist for pop-punk band Underground Baby, Zang Tianshuo has betrayed rock: 'Zang Tianshuo was not successful because someone said his music was provocative. Then he changed his style, and that's not good for rock. It's not rock at all, if you have difficulties and you change it, that's not rock.'

Being used to the small rock venues that were hardly ever fully packed and usually attracted a lot of foreigners, the concert turned out to be quite an experience. A fully booked Workers' Stadium hosted a Chinese audience that at a certain point enthusiastically sang along with the classic 'Friend' by Zang Tianshuo. Young and old, men and women, all joined in singing his hit singles. In my interview with him, and in journalistic reports, Zang Tianshuo stresses his aim is to reach 'the common people' with his music. Reports in the media tell how he visits people who are dying of cancer to sing a song for them (Shang 1997: 14).[9] Such catering to the perceived needs of 'the common people' authenticates his music; in his closeness to the audience he becomes more real, more human, compared to a pop star.

Zang Tianzhuo explains his move from rock to pop as follows: 'My ideas about human beings are changing from rock to pop. The reason is mainly because I have grasped the nature of music: although pain prevails, hope drifts above it, this is what I want to solve.' (in Fang 1997: 94)

He accuses rock singers of being too egocentric and pretentious; they don't take the taste of the 'common people' into account. He changed his focus from rock, which he equates with pain, to pop, which stands for hope. This is an interesting reinterpretation of the dichotomy, as he refuses to speak in terms of fake and real. Above all he plays the nice guy; he tries to avoid blaming other bands and instead advises them to stop criticising one another. Nevertheless, to me he complained about punk rocker He Yong:

> If you look at his performance, his attitude is not good, the audience didn't like it. Because of his act I had to postpone my performance for a long time. He exaggerates his sufferings under the government in order to attract foreign attention. (...) As to politics, I'd rather show my hope and expectation rather than encourage people to fight, because we cannot change things in this generation.

Being openly rebellious is equated by Zang Tianzhuo to catering to the West; a one-sided interpretation maybe, but it does acknowledge the Western gaze on China and its impact on the rock culture.[10] His narrative, like his authenticating positioning toward the audience, is informed by the rock mythology in that he claims to be true to himself.

In his refusal to rebel and to confront political or social problems, he at the same time negates the mythology.

The members of Point Zero are also eager to point out that they write their own songs; like Zang Tianshuo, they differentiate themselves from other scenes by foregrounding the importance of meeting the demands of the audience. According to their bass player, Wang Xiaodong, they try hard to make easy listening, melodic songs, and he cannot understand why rock bands make 'strange music'. Point Zero operates on the margins of the rock culture, yet ranks among the top when it comes to sales figures. Their aesthetics – 'cool' poses, leather jackets – signifies a refusal to be packaged, and also authenticates the band. According to a Chinese review, the audience should not be fooled by the rock image, as their music is more melodic. According to the critic, the band moves from the melodic toward pop, which makes it increasingly insincere (Anonymous 1997a: 34). In this critic's reading, the sound remains framed – or rather, imprisoned – within the pop-rock dichotomy and enforces the related stereotypes. Like Zang Tianzhuo, Point Zero negates the rebellious:

> Our performances are all legal, we never meet any trouble. I don't think the bands in China have difficulties with the government, but with money. (...) We are very proud to be Chinese, many foreigners ask us the wrong questions. Every country has its own system; foreigners can't understand it and shouldn't interfere.

From the perspective of other scenes, the pop-rock bands are anything but rock. They have betrayed the spirit of rock and are looked down upon. Their popularity among the audience is envied, but also interpreted as more proof that they are 'only' pop. According to Point Zero, the album sold nearly 300,000 copies within two weeks, ten times as many as a typical underground album.

Place – In his focus on the needs of 'the common people,' coupled with a public positioning as being a devoted Buddhist, Zang Tianshuo combines tradition with a socialist spirit, both of which make him a Chinese singer (Steen 1998). The positioning of Point Zero is more conspicuously connected to place; in their marketing, it is stressed that this is a band from Inner Mongolia, so as to set them apart from the Beijing bands. In line with Baranovich's (2003) analysis of the ethnic pull of rock music, in which he reads rock as enabling other ethnicities to carve out a place in the alleged cultural centre of China, the move to Beijing can be interpreted as a liberating one for the Point Zero members. Another, commercially-inspired reading may be more plausible.

JVC Hong Kong has licensed the Mongolian pop-rock band Ling Dian from Jingwen for the market outside China. It states in the promotional material:

> Inner Mongolia, a part of PRC, is a harsh, sparsely populated land. The winters are harsh (-40°C) and for entertainment the Mongolians used to (and in the plains still do) sing together. People living in such a harsh environment do not express their emotions easily. (...) Ling Dian has chosen to express their emotions through their music. (...) There has never been a Mongolian rock group before that can compare with Ling Dian. As originators of a sound they continue to develop a pop/rock sound that has the capacity to appeal to a wide audience. The Mongols are truly on the march!

The militaristic metaphor strengthens the importance the record company attaches to the geographical origin of the band – it is on the verge of conquering the whole of Asia. Commercial motives result in an articulation of place; the metaphor of war suggests that this is not a peaceful process, but that place is to be interpreted as something to fight for. The myth is that music is without frontiers, that it unifies people around the globe. How, then, is it possible that so many Chinese know of Bach and Beethoven, while so few Europeans or Americans can mention a Chinese composer? Indeed, sounds do not travel freely; they are confined by geographic boundaries, and as such are intrinsic to power games (Kraus 1989). The desire to break through geographical boundaries with rock music, driven by commercial motives, can also be interpreted as a cultural-political struggle. Mongolia, as the political and cultural margin of China, strikes back, after being imperialised by Western and *Gangtai* sounds – and this, ironically, is according to JVC, a transnational Japanese company. Again, the global reproduces the local as a commercial strategy.

In their refusal to strike a provocative pose or make controversial music – in terms of either sound or lyrics – pop-rock bands negate the rock mythology. There is no attempt to be rebellious; at most, they try to look cool. The challenge they pose to rock – they accuse other scenes of being ignorant about the public's preferences – has a communist ring to it; they want to serve the people. By including the preferences of the listener, they move away from the idea of the rock artist who hovers above the crowds to enlighten them. Instead they acknowledge that the audience is part of the process of making music. The pop-rock scene shows how the mythology is anything but uncontested, yet the fierce criticisms they receive from other scenes simultaneously demonstrate the power of the mythology.

Pop-punk

Positions – The pop-punk (*liuxing pengke*) bands, a label also used in the
promotional materials and by the bands themselves, are far more popular than hardcore punk bands. The first album by Catcher in the Rye
and the albums of Underground Baby, New Pants, and The Flowers are
grouped under the label pop-punk. All record companies are trying to
cash in on the pop-punk rage of the late 1990s: Underground Baby was
released by Magic Stone (1998), New Pants by Modern Sky (1998,
2000, 2002, 2006 & 2008), Catcher in the Rye by Red Star and Dong
Music – since 2007 a subsidiary of Universal (1998, 2000 & 2007),
and The Flowers released their first album on New Bees (1999). After
they wound up in a court case with them, they put out five more albums on EMI. Until 2008, the bands kept on selling well, securing a
remarkably stable place in Beijing's rock culture. Probably because of
their popularity, the bands are often disdained, for example by Beijing
rock critic Steve Vai (1999: 31): 'While the empty screams of punk force
the acceptance of the crowds, it also gives itself a new label 'punk pop',
as if they are afraid that no one knows what is popular now.'

For the hardcore punk bands, these bands betray the spirit of punk;
they are not real. Peter from 69 criticises Underground Baby:

> I like DIY, do-it-yourself, you know Underground Baby ... why I
> say they are not punk, it's because they depend on his father, his
> parents you know. Underbaby's drummer and vocalist, they're
> brothers, and their parents opened a restaurant, because of that
> money they can buy a motorcycle, they rent an expensive house.
> It's fake!

He also blames the New Pants for being pop; they are simply not cool.
Peng Lei, vocalist for the New Pants, reversed the critique and told me
that he considers hardcore punk out of date, and he doesn't understand
why punk is so popular in China. In any case, when it comes to sales
figures and media attention, pop-punk is far more successful than hardcore punk. In particular, The New Pants have kept on changing their
style, moving towards an eclectic mix of pop-punk, electro pop, and romantic ballads. The band toured in Australia in 2007, together with a
popular local hard rock band, Regurgitator.[11] In the five albums they released between 1998 and 2008 on Modern Sky (indeed, The New Pants
are one of the most productive and stable bands of Beijing rock culture), they explored different modes of arty playfulness.

Authenticating styles – As in hardcore punk, rhythm is an important
authenticating style, as is the DIY philosophy, although the latter is less

central. The spectacular performance of difference is replaced by a youngish, joyful pose signifying spontaneity. In their performances, the youngish pop-punk musicians cheerfully jump about to the rhythm of their songs. These gestures of spontaneity render the scene authentic. Their music is less aggressive than hardcore punk. The lyrics are often mischievous (intertwined with spontaneity), rather than provocatively direct. The youngish, mischievous aesthetics of pop-punk sets this scene apart from the others.

Underground Baby is caught in an in-between position. In their lyrics, and in their opinions, they openly voice their criticism of Chinese society, in line with the rock mythology, whereas their mischievous poses signify a search for a more playful, less politically loaded style. When I talked with vocalist Gao Wei about the lack of performances in the period around the 15th Party Congress, he replied:

> Of course the government hopes we'll shut our mouths. They think that rock incites the people, so rock is prohibited. I don't want them to put such limitations on us. (...) For a long time the government has suppressed rock, but didn't kill it. It left a small space where it is tolerated. (...) In fact, culture itself should not be a kind of weapon, but now it is.

His last remark illustrates the predicament of Chinese rock. Government officials (along with journalists and academics) manoeuvre rock into a countercultural position, not necessarily with the approval of the musicians themselves.

Shortly after our interview, Gao Wei changed his name to Gao Xing, which means 'happy'. Yet, the lyrics of their 1999 album *Awake* are gloomier than the joyful poses of Underground Baby suggest. In 'I Only Have Music,' Gao Wei sings:

> I can't see the ocean, nor the sky
> I can't see the good and bad of this world
> I don't have imagination, nor happiness
> I don't experience real life at all
> I only have music

Music is detached here from 'real life', as well as from imagination and happiness; music is portrayed as a lonely island on which to hide from society. Given the contents of their lyrics, Underground Baby remains pretty much in the 'rebellious' spirit of the early Chinese rock by, for example, Cui Jian. The following review reflects that position:

It seems that Underground Baby is doing something different from the happy punk music by other bands such as New Pants. They haven't given up the mission and spirit shown by China's rockers during the past 10 years. The title track 'Awake' is the one that touches me most among the Chinese rock numbers I have listened to in the last year. Its melody is helplessly sad and the cries in the song are tragic. It makes my heart ache. (...) Loneliness and helplessness, emptiness and edginess dominate the album 'Awake'. Such a mental state, common in but not restricted to puberty, exists in every society. (A 1999: 54)

Its reference to another band in the scene – The New Pants – shows how scenes are produced by journalists. At the same time, the scene is positioned in the wider context, namely the rock culture (and this album is considered to fit well into the history of Chinese rock), and, secondly, into youth culture in general (and this album is believed to reflect adolescents' angst, but at the same time reflects a general concern that is not restricted to puberty). As such, this review not only sets punk apart from other scenes, but also produces rock as a distinct music world.

Figure 2.2   *CD Jacket New Pants – Dragon, Tiger, Panacea (copyright Modern Sky)*

For Peng Lei of The New Pants, the lyrics of Underground Baby are rather old-fashioned, since 'they always sing about the tastelessness and emptiness in life and about sex.' The New Pants often work with cartoon images in their video clips, generally depicting naughty cats like Garfield or other mischievous characters. Their CD jacket of the album titled *Dragon, Tiger, Panacea* (Figure 2.2) depicts the band in their typical retro-style, with clothes that refer back to the 1970s and 1980s. We see them in joyful breakdance poses that somehow resonate with both the disco period at the end of the 1970s, as well as the breakdancing hype that swept over urban China during the 1980s. The box is designed like a traditional Chinese medicine box; music serves as the panacea (*rendan*) for modern life, and the CD title refers to an existing brand of herbal medicine. The dragon, the framing of the picture as well as the logo of the band at the bottom of the jacket, and the keyboard at the edges, evoke an atmosphere of an old fashioned Kung Fu movie, a reference that returns in the video clip of the title song, where the band members are doing Kung Fu, Millionaire Peng in a yellow outfit we know from Tarantino's film *Kill Bill*, the clip full of references to Bruce Lee. The New Pants appear in their clips in funky vintage disco outfits, re-enacting a disco world of the 1970s that never existed in China. This is combined with references to products made in China – and this mix of the vintage and the Chinese results in an utterly trendy, ambiguous and above all humorous space. This ironic and humorous re-enactment comes with an upbeat sound and lyrics sometimes in English, sometimes in Chinese, and sometimes in a weird hybrid mix.

The New Pants create a semiotic space that may best be described as an utterly self-reflexive intertextual minefield. According to Giddens (1990: 28), 'the reflexivity of modern social life consists in the fact that social practices are constantly examined and reformed in the light of incoming information about those very practices, thus constitutively altering their character.' The New Pants can be perceived as being a constitutive force for the emergence of a reflexive community. According to Scott Lash, 'Communities are reflexive in that: first, one is not born or "thrown", but "throws oneself" into them; second, they may be widely stretched over "abstract" space, and also perhaps over time; third, they consciously pose themselves the problem of their own creation, and constant re-invention far more than do traditional communities; fourth, their "tools" and products tend to be not material ones but abstract and cultural.' (Lash 1994: 161, see also Kahn-Harris 2004) In pop-punk, the self-reflexivity comes with parody, irony and ambiguity, tactics that entail a deliberate negation of the rock mythology. Already in 1997 Peng Lei was quite articulate in his wish to move beyond rock aesthetics: 'After 1995 people began to hate hard rock (...) We want to become more commercial, we will play at parties and festivals. We want to change the dominant ideas about rock, so that people start asking, is this pop?'

He does not want to talk about politics, nor to be critical. His desire to be commercial contradicts, and thus challenges, the rock mythology, but in his move to pop he also differentiates himself from *Gangtai* pop: 'That is not real music; there are so-called rock bands because people are bored with pop. There must be something in the lyrics that touches the audience, there must be something authentic and sincere in it.'

We thus see a reification of the rock mythology in the insistence on being authentic, and once again – it indeed becomes a bit tedious – pop serves as the constitutive inauthentic outside.

Bands are eager to note their difference not only from both pop and other scenes, but also from the bands that can be grouped under their own scene. Peng Lei's opinion quoted earlier on Underground Baby is indicative, as is his view of The Flowers: 'I think members of The Flowers are too young; they can't decide for themselves, the company decides for them. We're older and independent.' The rock mythology proves once again an empowering tool with which to articulate one's authority.

In terms of sales figures, The Flowers is more successful than the New Pants, and has been received very well in Taiwan, something very few Beijing rock bands achieve. The band released its double CD in 1999, entitled *On the Other Side of Happiness*. On the cover there is a very small line saying: 'China's first underage band', a remarkable selling point. At that time, they were indeed young boys, around 16 years old. They are the only *balinghao* (80s) band included in this scenic overview. In the songs of the first album, they reflect upon their life at school, and sing 'just want to hear that bell as soon as possible, just tell us school is over.' Although the lyrics can also be gloomy, the joyful spontaneous poses make it a cheerful album. The pleasure of pop-punk does not so much reside in the spectacular assertion of difference, as we have seen with hardcore punk, as in its spontaneity and naughtiness. The lyrics of The Flowers' song 'Fruits' are gloomy, but the cheerful upbeat rhythm makes it tempting to sing along with them:

> Mom, don't nag me no more
> Don't worry for me, don't feel sad (...)
> Let my body move my arms
> To dig up the lost happiness
> Oh, I'm pissed, leave me alone,
> I have had enough of such a life
> I'm pissed, leave me alone
> I want to live happily.

Apart from the interesting juxtaposition between a seemingly gloomy text and a cheerful, catchy sound – which turns it into a playful gloominess – there is an interesting intertextual reference here. The line 'I'm pissed, leave me alone' is in Chinese (or, rather, in Beijing slang), *fanzhe ne, bie li wo*. It was one of the lines that appeared in the summer of 1991 on T-shirts in Beijing. These so-called cultural T-shirts (*wenhua shan*) – others with texts like 'Life is a bore' (*zhen lei*) – were the creation of the Beijing artist Kong Yongqian, who was detained for questioning by the police that summer, but released after a few days (Barmé 1999: 145). His shirts were then officially banned. The song by The Flowers shows that a statement once forbidden by the Party has popped up again years later and in a different cultural domain. It further emphasises the power of popular culture.[12]

Over the years, like The New Pants, the musical style of The Flowers has diversified rapidly, including, for example, elements of techno and hip-hop. This generic flexibility seems to be more paramount in hyphenated scenes, as the playful attitude makes it easier to switch music styles, a change motivated by a wish to cater to the needs of audiences, in the words of vocalist Da Zhang Wei: 'We have to earn our living through music ... Pleasing our fans is our reason for making music and we don't care about other things.'[13] They do succeed in this effort; their fourth album *Blooming Days* sold 200,000 copies in forty days after its release in 2005, while the band appeared in TV extravaganzas and received music awards.[14]

Place – When I met Peng Lei, he was wearing a leather jacket with a Ramones patch. A Beijing music critic recounted how the New Pants started making music:

> I don't even remember who bought this *dakou* cassette of the Ramones, the Jesus Christ of punk. But the moment they listened to it, they fell in love with it. (...) This is the most honest kind of rock, the core of rock spirit. It burns in these three new persons who want to have their humanity and freedom. (Wang 1999: 22)

Peng Lei – who mockingly changed his name on their second CD (*Disco Girl*) to Millionaire Peng – thus openly acknowledges his main source of inspiration, a source that happens to be located in the West, and which comes closest, according to this critic, to 'the core of rock spirit'. However, compared to their hardcore counterparts, pop-punk bands are less involved in an articulation of the local. The youngish, mischievous aesthetics of pop-punk is thoroughly *dakou'ed*; Peng Lei said that he couldn't care less about the Cultural Revolution, since it occurred before he was born. In pop-punk, there is not such a strong

appropriation of communist imagery, nor are there references to ancient China. The references to traditional Chinese medicine as discussed earlier are combined with Bruce Lee imagery, that at the same
time evoke a Tarantino-like world – this intertextual mix strikes me as a
tactic not to localise rock, but to produce a trendy, self-reflexive and ironic sonic and semiotic space.

Instead, there is a longing to be part of a global pop-punk community, a longing reflected not only by the patch, but also by the desire of
these bands to conquer Greater China with their *international* sound.
The album *Disco Girl* by The New Pants is a prime example. Three of
the fourteen songs are in English. In 'Modern Sky' (which is named
after their record company) one line goes: 'But we are future boys.' In
what may count as the best documentary on Chinese rock – *Beijing
Bubbles* (Messmer & Lindt 2008) – we see the New Pants roaming
through Beijing and its vocalist Peng Lei in his own toy shop. Keyboard
player Pang Kuan explains: 'On our first album there is a song called "I
Am Okay". It is about the helplessness in adolescence. It says "No girlfriend today, no girlfriend tomorrow, and no girlfriend forever." I think
things like that can happen to all young people in the world.'

The ubiquitous gesturing elsewhere (Baulch 2008) is characteristic
for pop-punk – they tap into a global rather than a local structure of
feeling. The longing for the global is coupled to a focus on either the
present or the future. The past is at most invoked as a stylistic figure, to
create a trendy vintage look, whereas the longing of the hardcore punk
bands to be local is paired with a focus on the past. On their third album, entitled *We Are Automatic*, the style of The New Pants has shifted
more towards electropop, bringing back memories of Kraftwerk. Again,
songs in English are mixed with Chinese language songs. For example,
take the song 'Fashion' quoted at the beginning of this chapter. The
playful and ironic celebration of a cosmopolitan lifestyle resonates with
a *Zeitgeist* operating at the border of *dakou* youth culture, paving the
way for a post-*dakou* trend ruled by the *balinghou* (80s) generation. This
is a generation for which humour, ambiguity, playfulness and reflexivity
are of paramount importance. Which leads us to the final scene to analyze, the fashionable bands, a scene that is as eager as pop-punk to explore new sonic trajectories, employing similar self-reflexive tactics.

Fashionable Bands

Positions – When discussing Sober and Supermarket and the upcoming
DJ scene with Yan Jun, together with Ou Ning, the chronicler of the
New Sound Movement, they grouped these acts under the label fashion-
able bands (*shimao yuedui*), a label I appropriate for use here. The label

has thus been invented by observers rather than being used by the bands themselves. Sober often refers to Britpop when positioning itself, while Supermarket speaks of electronic music (*dianzi yinyue*). Other examples from the Britpop style include Convenience Store, but a band like Hopscotch would also fit this scene with their English lyrics and melancholic songs. Others, like music critic Tao Ran, refer to such bands as Supermarket as the future sound of Beijing; these bands have three main features: melody, cross-over, and schizophrenia (Tao 2000b: 24). Here I will discuss two bands – Sober and Supermarket – which are under contract to the record company Modern Sky, the company which has played such a pivotal role in the proliferation of different scenes in Beijing rock culture.[15]

Both labels – fashionable bands and future sound – inscribe a temporal element into this scene, and indeed, like the pop-punk bands, many journalists and musicians consider this scene emblematic of the New Sound Movement. In an article on what makes this movement different from the earlier generations, the (anonymous) author refers to a move away from idealism and heroism toward urban populism and realism. This move is reflected in a changing clothing style as well: from leather jackets and pants to casual wear, jeans, and brand-name sport shoes, and from long hair to short, sometimes dyed hair. Also the lifestyle of the musicians is considered different. While older musicians are believed to be very devoted and to lead a penurious life, the new bands live an easy, leisurely life in which music is just one of their many interests (Anonymous 1999: 25). Although I consider such attempts to write a chronology of rock merely as a discursive way to distinguish among scenes, the descriptions above allow us a glimpse of the perceived characteristics of the bands belonging to both the pop-punk and the fashionable band scenes.

Sober is far more popular than Supermarket when it comes to sales figures. According to Shen Lihui, their album *Very Good!?* sold more than 150,000 copies on the mainland and was well-received in Hong Kong. Their second album, *Demain, La Gloire*, was released in 2007. The fashionable sound of Beijing signifies, even more than the underground and pop-punk bands, a break with the earlier period of Chinese rock. They are positioned at the threshold of the new century; in their wake, the generation born in the 80s were able to experiment with cosmopolitan lifestyle choices, experiment with new sounds, different fashions and establish new global sonic alliances. The introductory words of Modern Sky on the Sober CD are indicative; in their sweeping terms, this band 'is no longer concerned with boring complaints and irresponsible screams. They ask questions and try to change. Let's start loving life and living, let's begin a new era together!'

Their blunt critique of the early sound of Beijing rock, coupled with the framing of these bands by journalists as belonging to the New Sound Movement, sets this scene apart from others. If we follow this statement, they suggest that they have moved beyond the rock mythology by refusing to be rebellious, a refusal we have also seen in the pop-punk scene with the New Pants. Bands such as Sober and the New Pants represent a rebellion against rebelliousness, and Shen Lihui's record company Modern Sky plays a pivotal role in this positioning, as will be discussed further in chapter five (see also Steen 2000). The aesthetic routes taken by the fashionable bands are strikingly different from pop-punk.

Authenticating styles – The music of Sober is a (post-)modern re-appropriation of The Beatles' sound, in ways reminiscent of the music of so-called Britpop bands such as Oasis and Blur. Before we look at Sober's music to see whether and how it is influenced by Britpop, we should be aware that many tracks were written in the early 1990s. As such, Sober might be considered Britpop *avant la lettre*. Sober aims to replace nihilism with pragmatism, and has labelled its style 'anti-formalist' (Tao 2000b). Such positioning betrays the educational background of Shen Lihui, an art-school graduate. The aesthetics of Sober is eclectic, and includes elements of pastiche, irony, and cosmopolitanism. Eclectic, given the different music styles used; ironic, as they make it clear in their video clip that they pose (for example, when they put on make-up in the clip); and pastiche, given the references to The Beatles, which gives them a cosmopolitan aura. This also becomes clear from the jacket of their first CD, in which their pose resembles the Beatles (see Figure 2.3). The lyrics from the title song of their 1997 album are:

> Your TV set breaks down and your eyes will be cured?
> Your watch stops, does this mean that you are happy?
> Does this mean that you are happy?
> Very good!? Indeed very good!? Very good!?
> To whom do I give Monday and Tuesday?
> To whom do I give Wednesday and Thursday? (..)
> All right! All right! All right! All right!

The refrain 'All right! All right!' is sung in English, giving the song a cosmopolitan ring. The accompanying video clip depicts the band in Beatles-style suits; we see four young Chinese men in a British look with an ironic smile drawn on their faces. According to Shen Lihui, the song is influenced by The Beatles, but he considers it postmodern, both in melody and lyrics.

Figure 2.3   *CD Jacket Sober – Very Good!? (copyright Modern Sky)*

Shen Lihui explained to me that to him doing business is as creative as making music. No wonder he sings in this song how his identity changes day by day. Gone is the die-hard rebel, with an angry voice filled with discontent. What we hear now is a radically different attitude toward modern life. The songs on the album are quite different from one another. Apart from the light-hearted, humorous songs, there are sad songs with a slow tempo, such as the last track 'Walking into Sleep'. Whereas some critics applaud Sober's move toward a new style, others accuse the band of straying too far from the spirit of rock (Tao 2000). The cover of the 2007 album seems to poke fun at the label fashionable band itself: it depicts a urinal of which the coating is in the style of a Louis Vuitton bag. As if fashion – the continuous celebration of new styles so much propagated by Sober's lead vocalist Shen Lihui in his multiple business activities – remains in the end something to urinate on (see Figure 2.4).

This ironic, self-reflexive move shows how Sober interrogates the rock mythology, both in its negation of rebelliousness and in its ironic and eclectic re-appropriation of styles and images. Such eclectic use of styles, mixed with Sober's claim to represent modern life, a claim I will discuss under *place*, also authenticates the music.

Figure 2.4 *CD Jacket Sober – Demain, La Gloire (copyright Modern Sky)*

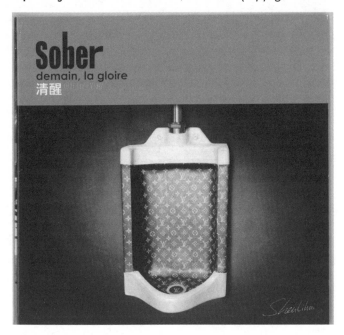

'Sometimes I feel that there is something amusing in the air,' is stated on the jacket of Supermarket's album *The Look*. Their CD is more coherent than Sober's, but it is not what I would call an amusing sound. This is synthesiser pop as we know it from Depeche Mode.[16] The album leads me to a virtual, computerised reality. In the shortest song of the album in terms of lyrics (*Explode*), Supermarket sings:

> Right now I'm afraid time may explode
> If I'm embarrassed, please don't care.

Clear-cut meanings dissolve in their electronic soundscape. What sets Supermarket apart from other bands is their electronic aesthetics. Neither the voice nor the lyrics are at the centre of their compositions, as is often the case with other bands; instead there is a kaleidoscopic sound, linking synth-pop with dance, drum'n'bass, and trip hop. This becomes especially clear from their second album (*Weapon 5x*), on which the electronic aesthetics is taken even further. The songs are titled *S1* to *S10*. The jacket, too, resonates with electronic aesthetics. It bears images of all the complicated sound equipment, images that authenticate the sound, for if the band has mastered technology to that

extent, it must *truly* be driven by the spirit of rock. In my interview with
band member Yu Shan, he did his best to negate any meaning:

> My music is music without style, I just do what I want to do and
> make music, it's very simple. (...) I don't have so many relation-
> ships with Chinese rock, I make music because I like it, I don't
> care so much about trends. (...) I'm not a good guitar player, so I
> ended up in electronic music.[17]

His latter remark suggests that he started to make electronic music because he cannot play the guitar, a statement that reflects a negation of
the rock mythology (where a gifted musician links his music choice to
his talents rather than the lack thereof). Like Sober, he does not take
this negation to the extreme, as is indicated by his answer to my question whether authenticity is important to him: 'It is the keyword of my
music; my music depends completely on the notion of authenticity.'

The electronic aesthetics of both the music and the band's image underlines the authenticity of Supermarket. In their wake, thanks to the
increased availability and accessibility of new technologies, many new
electronic bands have emerged in Beijing, such as Panda Twins and
FM3.

Place – The cosmopolitan aesthetics of Sober reifies the importance of
the global for the sound of rock. Shen Lihui has a desire to join the global world of music by adding a Chinese sound to it. 'Until now, the pro-
gramming has been dominated by the US, but the next century is likely
to bring a more multicultural mix where American youths will one day
watch Chinese rock bands.' (in Platt 1998: online)

Given the current pace of changes in Beijing, the cosmopolitan
choice strikes him as closest to reality: 'I don't think it's necessary to
add elements like an *erhu*, (...) Beijing has become very internationa-
lized. (...) I feel some foreigners are simply interested in something
strange, something exotic. Music should be true to modern life.'

His last statement shows how cosmopolitan aesthetics authenticate
the music. He constantly stresses the importance of accepting as many
musical styles as possible, and takes Japan as an example of an Asian
country which successfully incorporates the West without losing its national characteristics. Like pop-punk, Sober's focus on being modern articulates the global, which is located in the present or future rather than
the past. Also indicative of this global move are the words of music
critic Steve Vai (1999: 31): 'The emergence of electronic music has finally launched us onto the same track as the rest of the world. Different
kinds of hip hop, house, rave, techno, groove... When our styles and

characteristics are in line with the world, let's hope our techniques will be the same.'

It comes as no surprise that for other musicians, a band like Supermarket has gone too far, since it is perceived as lacking specific Chinese cultural characteristics. As folk-rock singer Hu Mage explains, 'You can't tell whether Supermarket's second album is Chinese or foreign music. I plan to make an electronic album, but you'll still know it's Chinese music.'

The fashionable bands opt for a sound perceived as being Western. In their desire to join the centre, they aim to place China on the global music map. Both pop-punk bands like The New Pants and the fashionable bands like Sober and Supermarket present a semiotic rupture: the overload of meaning has dissipated into a fragmented and dispersed field of possible interpretations. Whereas the earlier rock from China seemed to be drenched in the rock mythology, this new breed has a lighter, more playful and fluid attitude. The eclectic and cosmopolitan aesthetics of Sober is both ironic and playful; the band's image reflects a light-hearted play with musical styles, images and identities. In this, they have opened up a sonic field of possibilities on which a post-*dakou* rock culture is able to grow in the new, 21st century. A century in which English became the preferred language for some bands; a century also in which more and more bands made tours abroad, and a century when the Internet brought sounds from around the globe within reach.

Ending a Scenic Journey

The scenic move opens up a sonic field where different musical paths can be explored, where a plurality prevails above uniformity. But the plural world of rock in China remains enshrouded in the rock mythology. There is fortunately no need to proclaim the end, or the death, of rock in China. I have shown how scenes both challenge *and* reify the rock mythology. The power of the mythology remains unchallenged when it comes to authenticity. The importance of being authentic – a value rooted in the discourse of the high arts, where the unique artist gives expression to his or her pure personal emotions – links all the scenes.

The scenes have developed different aesthetics to articulate their authenticity. When looking at the scenes presented in this chapter, folk-rock has regular-guy aesthetics; pop-rock borrows from the rock idiom so as to show that they are real musicians making their own music, not for a small audience, but for 'the common people;' pop-punk adds a spontaneous, mischievous and self-reflexive style to the punk aesthetics; and, finally, the fashionable bands employ eclectic, cosmopolitan aesthetics and experiment with electronics, and thus authenticate their sound.

All scenes presented in this and the previous chapter eagerly claim to be real and are at pains to prove it in sound, lyrics, and image. This is a driving force – which at times is quite violent – behind tactics of inclusion and exclusion characterising the world of Chinese rock. Freud's concept of the narcissism of minor differences – a narcissism that drives many professional fields (such as academia) – is equally appropriate for rock music (Freud 1930: 61). The daily struggle to be real entails a desire to be different, and consequently leads to a politics of articulating difference.

Rock serves as a sign of difference and, depending on the scene, it can be quite a spectacular display of difference. The scenic authenticating styles often go hand in hand with a negotiation of place. Place is not only a politicised signifier, but above all it is turned into a style by rock musicians, a style that makes their music more or less Chinese. As I have shown in the previous chapter, especially the sounds that correspond so well with the rock mythology – heavy metal, hardcore punk, and the sounds of the underground bands – eagerly articulate their Chineseness, albeit with different implications. Being the hardest cultural forms of all the scenes, their urge to localise their sound, while at the same time including many references to the West, is stronger compared to the other scenes. The stronger a sound rocks, the harder it becomes and the more involved it gets in the negotiation of place.

The local is often located in the past, be it ancient China or the communist China of the Cultural Revolution. Two scenes eager to dissociate themselves from the rock mythology and its aesthetics – i.e., the fashionable bands and pop-punk – reverse the roles and gear their focus towards the West. In their desire to join the West, they focus on the present and the future rather than the past. Along with pop-rock, these scenes seem to be less involved in articulating the local. Interestingly, these are the most popular scenes now; pop-punk is popular among teenage youth, and pop-rock bands continue to attract a large audience and are the band names remembered by most Chinese youth. In general, over the last few years, more and more bands have started to sing in English, attesting to the cosmopolitan aesthetics permeating China's rock culture. The production of locality might sell well to the West, but does not guarantee local popularity. Being global sells locally, and being local sells globally.

3   Subaltern Sounds

The heaven is threatening with flames
The land is suffocated with words
The wind is flaring up clouds of violet
The people are embracing the dread
Who will arch his bow
And shoot the tongues of fire?
Who will steal the elixir
And fly to the moon to escape her desire?
Want to complain to the heaven?
But the heaven is not to be questioned
Want to curse destiny?
But destiny is not to be questioned.
Tatming Pair, 'Don't Question the Heaven', 1990[1]

Marginal Voices

Some voices are remarkably absent from the arguably fragmented world of rock in China. All the bands described in the previous chapters are located in Beijing; some of the singers moved from their hometown to the capital of rock to pursue their career in music. Releases from places outside Beijing are relatively rare; bands from, for instance, Shanghai are generally not taken seriously by the rock scenes in Beijing. Female voices are also rather scarce in Chinese rock, although their number has increased over time. Rock's aesthetics caters primarily to male identifications, so it seems, leaving little room for women to make rock. However central *Gangtai* pop might be when it comes to sales figures and media outreach, it is peripheral in the more 'serious' writings on music in Asia. As I have shown in the introduction, it is downplayed not only by China's rock musicians, but also by Chinese and Western journalists and academics. It is commonly assumed and asserted that a rock singer who has moved toward the world of pop has lost his or her soul.

Following Bakhtin, the rock mythology can be considered an authoritative discourse that generates uniform meanings and flattens out contradictions and ambiguities. In my scenic and genealogical approach in the previous two chapters, I have unpacked the productive power of the rock mythology, while I have simultaneously tried to address the underlying contradictions and ambiguities. In this chapter I will go one step further towards acknowledging the voices marginalised through the power of the rock mythology, and which can consequently be termed subaltern. The concept 'subaltern' is borrowed from a group of predominantly Indian scholars known as the Subaltern Studies Group, who tried to counter colonial discourse by giving room to heterogeneous and above all female indigenous voices (see Spivak 1988). As Spivak (1999: 281) asks herself: 'Can the subaltern speak? What might the elite do to watch out for the continuing construction of the subaltern?' Both the female voices in rock culture as well as bands that operate outside the perceived centre of Chinese rock, Beijing, pose a challenge to, respectively, the masculine and geographical hegemony of Beijing rock.

It is, however, the opaque voice of pop that poses a particular challenge to the authoritative discourse of the rock mythology. As will be argued, pop unfolds the *heteroglossia* of everyday life more so than rock does (Bakhtin 1981). In the final part of this chapter, I will discuss the transient, intertextual and multivocal opacity of pop and propose a recasting of Appadurai's hard-soft distinction into a clear-opaque dualism. This recasting is intended as a critical intervention in current debates on cultural globalisation that, as I will argue, ignore by and large opaque cultural forms such as 'commercial' pop music.

Gendering Music

Rock is a gendered domain. Its aesthetics – such as the leather jackets, motorcycles, screaming voices, and aggressive poses – predominantly signifies the masculine. The cliché runs: sex, drugs, and rock'n'roll, but such a one-liner has to be specified, as this is straight sex from a male point of view. Hard rock celebrates heterosexual masculinity; the term cock rock captures this male chauvinism rather well (Whiteley 1997: 67). With the increased dominance of hip-hop on the charts, the celebration of a (this time black) straight sexuality has reached new and problematic heights (see Gilroy 2000). This male bias (or, put differently, the spectacular performance of male power) can also be found in the Chinese rock culture, in which female voices are marginal.

Before exploring these female voices, it is important to briefly scrutinise the masculinity of rock music. Chinese men are subjected to struggles with Western hegemonic masculinity. Western masculinity emphasises a physical prowess described by Chow (2008: 339) as 'a "real man" having a body big, strong and muscular enough to consume alcohol, build houses and excel in sports.' In the context of this highly globalised discourse of masculinity, Chinese men face the problem of a convincing, embodied performance of masculinity (cf. Butler 1990). The delicate, feminine male heroes who helped define Chinese masculinity in the past are too much at odds with this discourse, resulting in a crisis of Chinese masculinity. Drawing on Wang Yuejin, Baranovitch indicates that rock can be read as an attempt to negate the crisis of masculinity in China. When Baranovitch writes that it is 'through rock that Chinese men and Chinese culture as a whole can regain their lost masculinity' (2003: 119), it is the Western hegemonic discourse of masculinity to which he is referring. Chow refers to a Chinese music critic, echoing the feminising discourse about Chinese men in the West, who hailed the music by a popular Chinese singer as '"the proof of a man's erection" against numerous effeminate singers of the current generation' (Chow 2008: 351).

Following Baranovitch, this may indeed help explain the popularity of rock in China. In addition, current female images in China also work against women's participation in rock culture. '[T]he predominant female image today in China is characterised by restraint.' (Baranovitch 2003: 156) The current search for a tough masculinity, in conjunction with the increased feminisation of Chinese women (Evans 2008), make the study of gendered performances in rock culture a timely one. Of course, Chinese rock is not naturally male, nor does it simply reflect the gender roles of society at large. Instead, it is actively produced as a male world by musicians, marketers (from a male-dominated music industry), and audiences, and is hardly ever questioned on this point by either journalists or academics, with Baranovitch (2003) and Wong (2005) as positive exceptions (see also: Cohen 1997). Following Baulch (2008: 9), the maleness of Chinese rock performers 'may be read as an attempt to root themselves in pre-existing and stable identity discourses, such as those of masculinity (which necessarily contain discourses of domination) while they experiment with others.'

Rather than further exploring the constructions of masculinity produced by rock (for that, see Baranovich), my concern here is with how female voices negotiate the masculine hegemony of rock. Indicative of this hegemony is a statement by radio journalist Xu Jie, who stated while discussing punk band Hang on the Box in a show in 2007: 'We might not expect female musicians to have the same superb techniques as their male counterparts. But Hang on the Box has proven that they do.'[2]

As I have argued, with Zheng Jun's use of Tibetan female voices, women, particularly when combined with ethnicity, have become key

orientalist signifiers for China's imagined primitive past. We can observe a wave of gendered products looking to appeal to a global audience, along with sexually explicit books from female authors like Mian
Mian (*Lalala* and *Candy*), Wei Hui *(Shanghai Baby)* and Chun Sue (*Beijing Doll*). The winner of the 2005 Idols-like competition *Supergirl*, Li
Yuchun, caused a national media craze. She is not only billed as the
outcome of the first democratic voting procedure in the Mainland; with
her androgynous look she also became the icon for gay and lesbian culture. Compared to the colourful exotic women as depicted by Zhang
Yimou at the turn of the 1990s, this current wave of Chinese feminine
mystique is located firmly in the contemporary, the urban and the sexually transgressive. Nonetheless, both Zhang Yimou's gendered por-
trayals and the popularity of young, hip and urban women underline
the observation that 'Chinese' femininity remains an important signifier, be it as commodity, as fetish, as symbol of either change or tradition, or as embodiment of the nation (de Kloet 2008a; Evans 1997,
2008; Hershatter 2007).[3]

In the case of Zheng Jun's use of a Tibetan female choir, women become the safeguards of an assumed tradition. Yet, in cases like Mian
Mian, Chinese women are signifiers of change for Western audiences.
Gender operates as the site where struggles over power take place.[4] The
books by Mian Mian, Wei Hui and Chun Sue depict a seemingly hip
and trendy urban lifestyle saturated with sex, rock and alienation. The
following fragment from Beijing Doll, where the author writes about
her affair with an up and coming rock star, is illustrative.

> Finally he phoned, and before he had a chance to say anything, I
> shouted, 'You motherfucker, get the fuck out of my life!' That
> was the last I ever heard of him. The magazine I Love Rock 'n'
> Roll had a line, I'm gonna skin rock 'n' roll,' and that's what I
> wanted to do to Zhao Ping, skin his rock 'n' roll exterior and
> show him for who he really was. (Chun 2004: 101-102)

What interests me most here is not so much the content of these books,
but more so the eagerness with which they are picked up in the West.
This eagerness underlines my point that in the Western gaze, Chinese
women operate as signifiers of change and possible resistance.

Rather than looking for resistance, my concern is more with the ways
in which female bands navigate in a male-dominated rock culture. I will
focus my discussion on four bands and two musicians, namely Cobra,
Queen Sea Fish Shark, Hang on the Box, Hopscotch, Luo Qi and Long
Kuan, all of whom have developed different tactics to position themselves in the rock culture: Cobra and Long Kuan by articulating their
musical expertise, Luo Qi by performing the bad girl, Hang on the Box

by inscribing gender into punk ideology, and Queen Sea Big Shark and Hopscotch by taking a cosmopolitan stance.[5] I thus distinguish four, partly overlapping tactics used by female rock stars to negotiate the phallic power of rock: the denial of gender, the dramatisation of gender (and of sexuality), the politicisation of gender, and the cosmopolitisation of gender.

Denial of gender

Cobra, one of the oldest rock bands in China, started in 1989 and performed regularly until they disbanded shortly after the release of their second album in 2000. The band members come from the Beijing Music Conservatory, went in search of more musical (and personal) freedom, and started experimenting with rock music. Their two CDs were released by the record company Red Star in 1996 and by New Bees in 2000. In 1999, the saxophone player, Lin Xue, left the band to go into business, following the trend of the 1990s during which 'doing business' – or 'plunging into the ocean' (xiahai) – were the magic words among Chinese youth (see introduction). Later, Yu Jin left China for Germany, representing the other trend of the 1990s, that of 'linking up with the tracks of the world' (Z. Zhang 2000: 93). In Europe, she formed the band Monokino, a band clearly pitched as a Dutch-Chinese cooperation, whose first CD was released by Modern Sky in 2008. Cobra is an established name in Beijing rock culture and is reasonably famous. The image of the band sold well internationally; their CD was first released in Germany rather than in China.

Cobra fits a reading of women as agents of change rather well. They are triple signifiers. First, the genre itself – rock music – signifies a movement towards change and freedom. So does their gender – female, in line with the examples stated above. Chinese women, more so than men, are signifiers of change. Finally, although to a far lesser extent as the ethnic and primitive element is absent, their gender renders the music authentic.

The triple signification under a Western gaze as outlined above explains why foreign journalists frequently report on the band, and why Cobra has toured in both Europe and the US. It also explains why the record company Red Star once planned to record English language songs. Their music is clearly influenced by new wave, the songs are moody, and the sound of a synthesiser accompanies the sad voice of vocalist Wang Xiaofang. However, Cobra remains in a domain where the performance of masculinity is crucial. In my interview with ex-guitar player Kaiser from Tang Dynasty, with which Cobra has toured a few times, he comments on their skills:

> I think that the girls ... I mean, they're great, I like them a lot,
> they're really good people. They don't have their heart in what
> they are doing, I know they don't. (...) If they weren't an all-girl
> band, they'd have split up already, nobody would be interested.
> What's novel about them is that they are all women. It's a sad
> truth.

There is an element of sexism in his statement that not only reproduces
hard rock as a masculine scene, but also excludes a female band from
the domain of rock by accusing them of being inauthentic: 'They don't
have their heart in what they are doing.' Cobra is aware of such stereotyping and the related hostility, and has developed tactics to secure a
place in the rock culture. Keyboard player Yu Jin explained to me how
they respond to the macho rock attitude:

> At the beginning when we formed the band we didn't know
> about this, we were part of the circle, we had a lot of friends.
> Everyone was nice to us. But later we found out they think we
> are funny and lovely. After some years, when we got better, we
> heard some male rock musicians who said we are just women ...
> In these eight years we feel we have never been part of this rock
> circle, you know, we were always outside because we are women.

Cobra is caught in the image of the 'funny and lovely' girls who happen
to play some music. It is a disempowering image, and excludes them
from the rock culture. The marketing of their record companies
strengthens this image: Cobra is promoted as the first all-female rock
band from China, thereby foregrounding their gender as the unique selling point – to their annoyance: 'Red Star is not so clever because they
don't have any ideas except that Cobra is the only female rock band, they
can only write this sentence. Sometimes we feel this is really bad.'

While singling out gender as a selling point might be explainable in
terms of marketing (although the rather disappointing sales figures for
their first album seemed to cast doubt on its effectiveness), it is interpreted by the band as a violent tactic, interpreted as a denial of their
music's stand-alone value.[6] The band's logo, which is used on the jacket of their second CD (released by New Bees), shows how gender is
used in the marketing of the band: The 'ob' in Cobra is transformed
into the symbol for the female sex (see Figure 3.1).

The power of the stereotypes as produced by both record company
('the all-female band') and their male counterparts ('funny and lovely
girls') is hard to resist. But they do have their tactics to resist and survive. First, Cobra derives its power as a real rock band from the rock
mythology itself. Vocalist Xiao Nan explained in an interview:

Figure 3.1 *Detail of CD Jacket Cobra – Cobra II*

> The key essence of rock is truth. You must be able to express the truth from within yourself. This is where rock differs from other types of music. Take for instance, popular music, where they can package what's already been packaged. They will try to do whatever they can to present the most perfect, most polished image, but rock isn't like that. (in Wong 1997: 4)

Pop, being the constitutive outside of rock, is once again victimised for being inauthentic, whereas rock tells the truth. This is not a gendered truth, but a universal one. In their song 'It's No Age For Playing,' they give expression to their search for truth, a search that seems noble and truthful in itself:

> There is no way to describe the emotion of today
> On every spot of the body the blood still flows
> It is impossible to express my feelings
> It resembles my childhood when I once tripped over
> You stretched out your hands towards me and helped me getting up
> It is like I have already forgotten that I have the strength
> I begged you, 'Let me go', but you said, 'It does not matter'
> Since long I ago had understood that it would be like this
> Why bear a grudge, the way is rough
> Living in confusion, remembering clearly
> I know it is no age anymore for playing

Gender does not play a role in the lyrics; instead, there is an articulation of the rock mythology. In their video, the focus is again on musical skills rather than their gender identity. As Wong remarks, after analyzing how the camera zooms in on the musical instruments time and again, 'Cobra's positioning of themselves as non-feminine bodies, both in [this] video and in live performance, is a strategy to deflect attention away from their gender difference and towards their abilities as musicians, *good* musicians' (Wong 1997: 9, italics hers; see also Wong 2005).

Long Kuan has played in an 'Asian' punk band in London, the Mika Bombs. Tired of being punk, she moved on a few years later, in 2001, to the Netherlands to join the electronic duo Arling and Cameron. A traffic accident in Spain cut their tour short, after which Long Kuan was forced to move back to Beijing in 2002. There she hooked up with Tian Peng from Supermarket (see chapter two), moving towards a sound that a journalist describes as 'a narcotic blend of moody, down-tempo beats and sultry vocals.' (Chan 2003: online) Shortly before the release of their album by Jingwen in 2004, entitled *'I love you most when I listen to music'*, she explained to me that gender does not play a role in her musical career. She did not consider it important and in general did not feel part of the rock culture, she explained. Her words very much resonated with Cobra's tactic of a denial of gender. Yet, whereas Cobra clearly opted for articulations of modernity, locating truth in rock, Long Kuan moves to a space outside Beijing, an ethnic and religious space. In the interview, she explained to me she was very much attracted to Buddhism and aspired to a life in nature. This long-ing appears in the video clip of her song 'Lotus Flower.'[7] We see her walking alone in a desolate landscape in Xinjiang, like a Chinese rendi-tion of an American road movie. She hitch-hikes her way into the mountains, gets a ride with a Muslim farmer and is accompanied only by her guitar player Tian Peng. Showing her dressed at times in ethnic clothes, the clip evokes a longing for an ethnic purity, located outside the hyper-modernity of urban China, at the margins of the nation-state. The music itself refers to modernity, yet this modernity is packaged in a nostalgic, ethnicised longing for nature. Femininity thus simulta-neously operates as a sign of the future and of tradition.

Neither Cobra nor Long Kuan is an example of girl power, nor do they reflect a negotiation of and play with femininity, as we know from Madonna. Instead, they pursue a strategy of denying the gender differ-ence, and they articulate their equality with other bands by stressing that – in line with the rock mythology – they are *real* and *good* musi-cians who dare to speak the truth in their music.

Dramatisation of gender

Luo Qi takes a different track altogether. She is much younger than the musicians of Cobra. Instead of being viewed as the innocent girl, Luo

Qi is the bad girl, similar to the previously mentioned new wave of Chinese women writers. Like these female authors, Luo Qi embodies the cliché sex, drugs, and rock'n'roll in a way only few musicians do. She is notorious for sleeping around, but as Yu Jin from Cobra remarks correctly, 'It is just not fair, I know she is sleeping around, but a lot of men are doing the same and nobody says anything.'

For a male rocker, sexual performance is just another indicator of being tough and cool, whereas for a girl it is a source of disapproval. In February 2008, this pattern quite dramatically appeared again during the Edison Chen scandal. After he took his laptop to a computer repair shop, hundreds of pictures of Edison having sex with more than ten famous female stars appeared online. The scandal occupied the tabloids of Hong Kong for weeks and became the leading news story both within and outside Hong Kong. Although Edison was heavily criticised and forced to retreat from show business, it was mainly the girls who were blamed for being indecent and immoral. Also, their nudity proved more shocking than Edison's and caused heated debates in the media.

The rock music of Luo Qi is authenticated by her own story. In 1992, aged 16, she arrived in Beijing, alone. After the divorce of her parents, she was raised by her grandparents. She quit school at 13 to join a song and dance group. In the press, the story was that her mother had more or less abandoned her in pursuing a business career abroad (Zhang 1997), implicitly reproducing hegemonic narratives of the importance of a stable family life. This past has assumedly distorted Luo Qi's life, as she stated in a magazine (Anonymous 1997b): 'Luo Qi said she became mature too early because her parents divorced when she was nine years old. She wants to be a good mother in the future.'

After arriving in Beijing in 1992 Wang Xiaojing, former manager of Cui Jian, discovered Luo Qi and introduced her to the Compass, a band he already managed (in line with the narrative that Luo Qi was abandoned by her mother, Wang Xiaojing told me in an interview: 'I know her much better than her mother knows her'). In her tight jeans and leather jacket, Luo Qi's image suited the rock idiom. Two years after her arrival in Beijing, Luo Qi lost an eye in a fight outside a bar. Since then, she often wears sunglasses or covers her eye with a piece of black cloth, like a pirate. She started using drugs and became a notorious drug addict in Beijing – until the evening of 14 July 1997, when she asked a Nanjing cab driver to take her to the nearest heroin dealer. In her own words: 'I was very fucked up at that moment. I said, "I am Luo Qi and I am looking for heroin, let me go home, I feel so happy, if you can I want to go to the hospital." '

Instead, the driver took her to the nearest police station, where she was taken into custody. She made it onto the front pages of the national newspapers. She was put into a 'hospital' for three months, during which time she 'recovered' from her addiction.

The use of drugs will never be tolerated by the Chinese press, but drug use by a girl is far more controversial.[8] Tang Dynasty's Ding Wu was also known for his addiction to drugs, and the rumour in the rock culture was that the death of their guitar player Zhang Ju was due to his drug use. These stories were not situated in a narrative stretching back as far as the childhood of either Ding Wu or Zhang Ju; they were simply rockers who used drugs. In Luo Qi's case, more explanation was required, as it concerned a girl. Using drugs does not fit the profile of a girl. It is treated as a dramatisation and negation of her gender identity, whereas for a male drug user, gender is not negated. The main reason given in the press clippings is also gendered, since it is her mother who is blamed. To rectify the mistakes committed by her mother, it was said that Luo Qi's ambition was to become a good mother. To serve as a good example for innocent youths, she agreed to act in a TV series based on her life (Z. Zhang 1997).

I interviewed Luo Qi just one week after she was released from hospital. Her sister joined her, clearly in order to keep an eye on her. During our talk, waiters came over to ask for her autograph, as the recent media display had made her even more famous. Luo Qi distanced herself from the pop stars in Hong Kong when she talked about a visit to the city:

> When they [the Hong Kong audience] saw me live, they thought I was a very good singer, that I was very different. I constantly rejected the clothes they wanted me to wear. They told me not to smoke in front of the journalists, but I just did that. I was very free, sat down on the street and so on.

She positioned herself as free and, in line with the rock mythology, she refused to be packaged. This refusal paid off; her CD sold around 600,000 copies. We came to the topic of her drug use, and her sister became very nervous whereas Luo Qi remained very easy-going. I asked her what happened exactly that night in Nanjing.

> Ah, so funny, so funny [laughing]. I have never seen so many policemen in my life. So many chances for me to get to know the Communist Party. I didn't know much about the Communist Party, but now I don't like them. They have no feelings, everything was very orderly. At 6.30 I had to get up, at 7.30 breakfast (...) It was like a jail.

It did help her stop using drugs, she said. So she was turned from a rock singer into a role model, into an example of how the Party helps those who use drugs:

> Before I went to the hospital most of the patients were forced into it, but after I went there many drug users went there of their own will, so I did promotion free of charge. (...) I think it's so funny. Before that I was a rock'n'roll singer and the government didn't support me. But now I have become a role model as an ex-heroin user and am on TV and so on. I have been interviewed by many government papers and they forget that I'm a rock singer.

Her life story renders Luo Qi's music authentic, as the story of the bad girl who sleeps around, drinks, uses drugs, and gets into dangerous fights. It is a narrative used in the marketing of her music. The text on the jacket of her album that was released the year she was taken into hospital runs: 'This is Luo Qi, who has experienced fame, pain, emptiness and illusions. We hope she can defeat the pain in her body and her heart and walk onto the stage to sing together with her fans the song "Come back".'

The panoptic power that cast her as a bad girl was suffocating. In her words, it was too much to live under such conditions in China, and she was unhappy. 'I just don't like Chinese politics, it's disgusting. And in China many people think I'm very strange, that I'm a bad girl because I drink too much, smoke too much and use drugs. Too many people think I'm a dangerous girl.'

The bad-girl image sells, but at the same time marginalises her in real life. Consequently she moved to Berlin in 1998 to record a new album. In an interview with German radio, she gave both political and personal reasons for her move. 'My life wasn't that bad, but the situation for rock musicians is difficult in China because of the government. But I also had personal problems since I'd started to use heroin. (..) Then I left for Germany to start a brand new life here.' (Bentoni 1999: online)

However, she later moved back to Beijing, where she still lives. Luo Qi negotiates the masculine bias of rock not so much by denying gender, as was the case with Cobra, as by dramatising it – by performing the bad girl. She did the things Chinese girls are not supposed to do, and thereby marginalised herself, from both the rock culture (only boys may be naughty) and mainstream society. Her life story is well known all over China, and that made her want to escape the country – only to return a few years later.

Politicisation of gender

Hang on the Box appeared on the cover of *Newsweek*. When we add women to punk (the scene closest to the embodiment of the rock mythology, as I showed in chapter two), the attention of the West is guaran-
teed. Attention is what they want. They explicitly voice their ambition to
become famous, and after releasing three CDs on Scream records and
touring in the United States and Japan in 2003, they gradually succeeded in this aim. Their singer and guitar player Wang Yue is quite a
sight in Beijing with her short purple hair (see Figure 3.2).

She is a *liumang* in the eyes of her parents, a label she very much re-
sents. She considers herself part of the *dakou* generation. To her, the

Figure 3.2   *Wang Yue (photo by the author)*

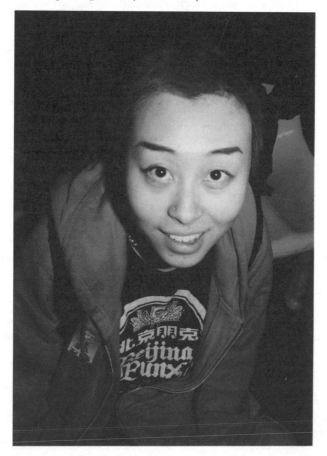

mission of the band is clear. 'Our band advocates women's rights; we think the position of women should become equal to that of men. In our opinion, 21st-century women should be able to do what they want to do.'

A punky form of shock therapy is used to get the message across. Both the sound and the words are as direct as possible. The lyrics of the song 'Asshole, I'm Not Your Baby,' which were published in the semi-official magazine *New Music New Life*, are written in English with deliberate grammatical mistakes, since they do not like lyrics in the first place (in: S&M 1999: 10):

> You dick in my hole
> You dick make me feel horny
> Suck my clit
> Seven hundred years

Hang on the Box politicises gender and inscribes it, often in its most explicit form (that is, sex) into punk ideology. This makes them different from the other hardcore punk bands, and is also a clever move in terms of marketing. In the punkzine mentioned earlier, Hang on the Box's bass player Mi Lina writes about how boyfriends treat her:

> When he asks me why I don't care about my life, why I have so many friends, why I don't behave like a real 'girl', I am just like a picture he fails to understand. He only wants to put me on display in a suitable place in his home. He's a stupid X! In the place where a mirror should be, he puts up a picture. From that moment on, we say goodbye!

Like other women rockers, they feel they are not taken seriously by their male counterparts. Wang Yue complains that she always names other punk bands as her favourites in interviews, whereas they never do the same to her. She expressed the familiar complaint: 'Because we are women, we have to make much more effort to prove that we're really good.'

Hang on the Box was the first Chinese rock band to release an album with only English lyrics. While opting for English lyrics is a clever move in terms of global marketing, it might also make it easier to escape censorship.[9] Wang Yue is clear in her rejection of articulations of Chineseness. 'I think that Chinese rock should work itself out of its regional confines. Rock does not originate in China, it is Western music. It is not appropriate to incorporate Chinese national culture into the music. Good music should be international.'

Although her argument reflects an essentialist interpretation of cultures, it is provocative in the sense that it counters the dominant trend in other rock scenes where priority is given to a Sinification of rock. By 2004, the band had not only added a male player but also declared a move away from 'Western' punk towards Korean and Japanese popular music. This may well be a move to cater to regional audiences; at the same time, it decentres the West, and it is a significant break away from the Chinese gaze towards the West when it comes to popular music. However, their CD released in 2007, after which the band disbanded, remains in a punk idiom, and is again in English. Its title is revealing: *No More Nice Girls*, attesting to their tactic to politicise (and capitalise on) gender. In an interview, Wang Yue reflects upon the CD title:

> In the last few years China has changed a lot, the status of women has increased, they get respect in every field. Now you are lucky to be a rock girl in a third world country, unlike Cobra and when we started, when Chinese culture was not developed or open enough. Now people's vision and ability to accept things has improved. Girls get more chances than boys in music, maybe someday we should speak for the boys. (Zong 2008: 8)

Her teleological narrative denies the pertaining male bias in Chinese rock culture, just as it rather naively claims a feminist turn that is hard to trace if we analyse today's China (Evans 2008).

Cosmopolitisation of gender

In the wake of Hang on the Box, more bands followed in using English lyrics, among them Joyside, Subs, Hopscotch, and Queen Sea Big Shark. Remarkably, among these bands, only Joyside is all-male; all the others have female vocalists. It seems as if female bands or singers are less involved in performing Chineseness, and can more easily adopt singing in English. Their use of English also signals a cosmopolitan belonging, which becomes clear when we look at Queen Sea Big Shark and Hopscotch. When I attended a performance in Mao Live house of the band Queen Sea Big Shark, it was just a few days after the big earthquake in Sichuan on 12 May 2008. The performance was to raise money for the victims, as all performances claimed to aspire to during that time. Nevertheless, when the band appeared the crowd cheered. The mischievous, cheerful smile on Fu Han's face resonates in the music as well as the lyrics. The lyrics may be deliberately written in clumsy English, but this increases the fun value ('Shit girl! What does the 21st century youth against? Hey girls! Hey boys!). The lyrics sometimes refer to gender, but refuse to differentiate, so it seems, like in the song titled 'Kiss! Kill! Bang!':

Men are losers and women are bitches
Don't you see the evil inside of me?
Men are bitches and women are losers.
Don't you see the jealousness inside of us?
Men are liars and women are speakers
Do you hear the evil inside of me?
Men are speakers and women are liars
Do you see the trick play between us?

Gender roles are swapped, creating the idea that it makes no difference to be a man or a woman. The electronic staccato sound accompanying the lyrics makes it a cheerful song, one to sing along with, to celebrate the coming of an egalitarian society. When interviewed for the magazine *In Music*, lead vocalist Fu Han explained that, with them, 'young people can now see a real rock act, rather than watching sissy boys on stage.' (Li 2008: 11) Here she withdraws into a posture of masculinity, affirming the gendered character of the rock mythology.

Queen Sea Big Shark won the prize for best rock act in the 2007 Annual music chart awards (Y.Y. Li 2008: 11). While joining in the pogo dancing during the concert, screaming childishly along with the others 'money fucker money fucker,' I realised things had changed over the past decades. Seriousness has been replaced by a joyful energy, long hair by trendy hairdos, to be constantly adjusted in front of the mirrors in the toilets, and people cheerfully sing along with the English lyrics. The feeling is more cosmopolitan, more decadent, more of a global urban youth culture. We are in China, but not quite. This may well express the zeitgeist of the generation born in the 1980s, who have not experienced any political turmoil and who grew up in a time of prosperity. Yet the illusion of equality assumed in the performance and the lyrics is undermined by the reification of the assumed masculinity of rock, and hence reaffirms rather than challenges the status quo.

The cosmopolitan aesthetics are clear in the video clip of Hopscotch's song 'A Wishful Way.' The clip is shot in the Stockholm subway, thus visually it is literally gesturing towards the global world of rock culture.[10] Both the subway line as well as a departing plane evoke a strong sense of mobility, of a world and a life in flux. The desolate, lonely voice of vocalist Tian Yuan creates a melancholic soundscape, as she sings dreamily in a style that moves beyond rock aesthetics, resembling the style of the fashionable bands as discussed in the previous chapter:

All I want is a good chance
For we can live underground
All I need is a sharp knife
To cut the tails you are afraid to show (...)
All I dream is a wonderful place
For I can build myself a world
Dream in a wishful way

Hopscotch was nominated for best rock band of 2002, along with Tongue and Zi Yue. Vocalist Tian Yuan also distances herself in interviews from an aesthetics of rebellion and revolt, and instead articulates the ordinariness and dreaminess of everyday life, as she explains:

> Sometimes (...) you will feel life is wonderful. Sometimes, however, you feel there is no meaning to life, you might think about committing suicide, and have many different attitudes to life. 'A Wishful Way' is an attitude. The reality of life is not what you imagine, but you can dream in reality. (in Qian 2007: 236-237)

In her choice of dreams rather than a critique, she positions herself as different from other scenes, she explains why she refrains from clearly articulating darkness in her song 'Soldier'. I do not purposely express that kind of darkness in this song. Many bands want to be different, their songs are very negative. You feel that their music is very dirty, dark, and hopeless.' (in Qian 2007: 238)

To summarise, Chinese female musicians face a difficult task; they have to find not only their own music style, as do all bands, but also ways to negotiate both the masculine bias of rock as well as current modes of Chinese femininity dominated by restraint. The examples I have given show that they have developed different tactics. Cobra and Long Kuan try to promote their musical capacities and deny their gender identity; the tactics developed by Luo Qi show a dramatisation of gender by performing the bad girl in 'real' life; and the punk band Hang on the Box has borrowed its power from the punk ideology, in which the band politicises gender by explicitly rebelling against patriarchy. The more cosmopolitan and decadent style of Queen Sea Big Shark and Hopscotch turn gender into a cosmopolitan, bohemian lifestyle. They are least of all concerned about the demand to make rock with Chinese characteristics. In particular, female singers use English lyrics, and the negotiation of gender may prove more urgent than the negotiation of place. This opens up a freer space, in which linguistic and cultural boundaries can be more easily neglected. Yet, when we read this analysis in terms of structure rather than agency, we see how Chinese female musicians operate as signifiers of an assumed gender equality (denial), of cultural transgression (dramatisation), of political change (politicisation) and of a global modernity (cosmopolitisation). Whatever tactic they choose to negotiate the male bias of rock, female musicians operate in a cultural field considered quintessentially masculine, as well as carry the burden of representing a China in transition; they all too often serve as a proxy for something else, and are hence deprived of their individuality.

Southern Vices

The marginal position of women within rock does not render them necessarily more tolerant toward other subaltern sounds. Wang Yue, for example, voices clear opinions on rock from Shanghai. 'Fuck, fuck, fuck Shanghai! Shanghai is very shit! Shanghai is a very fashionable city. Because most people focus on money and enjoyment, there are fewer people who're willing to make rock music.'

Almost a decade after that interview, her opinion has not changed a lot. On the 2007 release *No More Nice Girls*, in the song titled 'Shanghai,' Wang Yue sings:

> What is Shanghai?
> Rich white cock and hungry yellow chick
> What is Shanghai?
> Stupid white cock and sharp yellow chick (...)
> Shanghai is a beautiful city
> Shanghai is a stupid city

Money and enjoyment are conceived as being incompatible with the spirit of rock. Shanghai is perceived as a glamorous and fashionable city that is trying to regain the decadent flavour it had in the pre-World War II and pre-Revolution years. As a colonised place, Shanghai was once the entry point for Western sounds. Berlin had Marlene Dietrich; Shanghai had Bai Guang (Jones 2001; Steen 2000; Steen and de Kloet 2005). Why, after half a century, did the sound of rock enter China through Beijing, rather than Shanghai, and take root there? There is some truth in the stereotypical claim, so it seems, that the hypereconomy of Shanghai is hostile to sounds that do not sell that well, including rock. One also needs more money to lead a leisurely life in Shanghai, money a rock musician usually does not earn. These might be some of the reasons helping to explain why the rock scene in Shanghai is much smaller than that in Beijing, but they fail to explain why the same goes for other, comparatively less prosperous cities such as Xi'an, Chengdu, and Kunming. The words of Guangzhou rock singer

Wang Lei are indicative of the resentment among southern bands: 'As long as you're from Beijing, even your fart is good. But if you're from any other place, you're nothing. Especially in rock music. This is a big problem... I'm very angry.'

No wonder this perceived attitude of Beijing triggers the desire to challenge the centre. When writing about his stay in Lanzhou, Yan Jun – the chronicler of the New Sound Movement – writes that he was 'trying to help the local rock and roll force to subvert the feudalistic musical authority of the capital city.' (Yan & Ou 1999: 86)

I will not embark upon an analysis here of the reasons why rock's epicentre in China is located in the capital, but I would like to observe that over the past decade, rock music seems to have gained popularity in other cities. The bias in journalistic and academic writing towards Beijing may be complicit in producing the image of Beijing as rock's capital. Komlosy (2008), for example, gives an elaborate overview of the rock and disco scenes in Yunnan, and shows how generic distinctions between, for example, punk and nu-metal, play a crucial role in the identity politics there, in the same way as I showed earlier in Beijing. She shows how bands use music to negotiate a sense of Yunanneseness, and how 'Yunnan's lingering reputation in the Chinese popular imagination as a wild frontier attracts certain elements of the scene. Yet, the association of Yunnan with non-Han peoples also draws those looking for a lost, pure China, one free of commercialisation and corruption. Music provides a place where these contradictions can be explored, and where new identities can be forged and manipulated.' (Komlosy 2008: 66) Specific, ethnicised imaginations of Yunnan thus feed into the proliferation of a multifaceted music culture, proving that Beijing does not own exclusive rights to making alternative music.

Here, I wish to explore the cultural scene in Shanghai and the music of Wang Lei, the rock singer from Guangzhou, so as to give space to both their music and to their views on the centre. I will show how the rock mythology remains the most powerful binding force of rock cultures outside Beijing, and how, given the dominance of Beijing, these subaltern rock cultures are at pains to distinguish themselves from the centre. To do so, they employ two tactics located along the, by now, well-known axis of commercialism versus authenticity and the local versus the global. As I will show, they claim to be more authentic and more cosmopolitan than Beijing bands.

The authentic south

Beijing rockers downplay music from Hong Kong as being too commercial and too slick; many cultural analysts also hold such views. Musicians from Shenzhen, a special economic zone close to Hong Kong,

are haunted by a similar stereotyping. In a report on the rock scene of
Shenzhen, the author writes (*Punk fan* 2000: 12):

> I think we all have to accept the seemingly absurd fact that the
> more advanced the economy is, the more backward the rock and
> roll. The beautiful city of Shenzhen offers a good example. In-
> deed, the city is a migrant workers' and workaholics' heaven, but
> a rock musician's hell. Among the few rock bands, Heathen is
> just like its lead vocalist Liao Kai's pet dog. He loves it, but he
> has to pay a high price to raise it.

Such a reification of the rock mythology, here coming from a journalist
who is most likely located in Beijing, is often voiced by the musicians
themselves, for example by Li Weiyun from the Shanghai-based band
Seven: 'Shanghai has too much business, so money is a problem, you
have to make money, there is a lot of competition. Beijing is China's political city, the cultural life is very good in Beijing.'
    But then he gives a twist to the narrative:

> I think Beijing rock is somehow not good. There are too many
> bands, but all of the same kind, they are all punk. Like Flowers.
> Shanghai bands are different, if one band plays grunge, then I
> don't want to play grunge. (...) The bands in Beijing are very
> businesslike, Shanghai bands never think about money, they just
> enjoy themselves.

Other bands also accuse Beijing of being too commercial. The narrative
that considers commercialisation harmful to the authentic spirit of rock,
resonating with the rock mythology, is employed by those on the margins to discredit the centre of rock in China. Despite the fact that
Shanghai is seen as an overtly commercialised place, bands manage to
make rock, which renders their music more authentic than that of the
musicians from Beijing, who have dollar signs in their eyes. The best
rock grows in a barren place deprived of a cultural industry. Shanghai
rockers reify the clichés about Shanghai, that it is a commercial place
ruled by the twin brothers 'work' and 'consume,' where fashion prevails
above character, and where prostitute bars cater to foreigners (see: Sun
1999, 18-19; Farrer 2002, 2008). What they are trying to say in this reification is that if a rocker can survive in such a location, he must be
more than real. In a report on the Shanghai rock scene, Sun (1999)
writes:

Rock singers in Shanghai are not rich. Record companies are like hospitals: they're afraid of dirty things, they don't like rock and don't think it can make money.

The margin – like the centre – eagerly reifies the clichés, as they empower them when they are framed within the rock mythology. Guangzhou-based rock musician Wang Lei is a case in point. In a report on the rock scene in Guangzhou, his position is described as follows (Y. Zhang 2000: 16):

> Wang Lei's music is created amidst all the resistance, confusion, and interference surrounding [Guangzhou]. Not every city in China can produce a voice that is strong enough to resist the suppression of the entire city. Guangzhou, however, has succeeded in squeezing out this passionate and melancholic Sichuan guy. Wang Lei turns the dust, congestion, humidity, and solitude into one nightmare after another, one scream after another ... what is both disgusting and interesting about Guangzhou, is its chaos.

The music of Wang Lei accompanied me on my trip through China in 1995. I bought the tape in Wuhan, and all the songs on it are related to the theme of leaving home and heading toward an unknown future; as such, his music makes the ideal travelling companion. The opening (and title) track of his 1994 album *Journey Man* starts with the familiar sounds of a railway station. The high, lonely, and at times desperate voice of Wang Lei explains how he feels lost after leaving his father's home:

> I am the only one at the railway station
> Full of sadness, I am completely lost
> I want to cry, it is not easy
> I want to laugh, but I am afraid I lack the courage
> Where should I go now?
> Where should I go?

Since 1994, Wang Lei has released albums on a regular basis, something which is quite unusual in the rock culture of China, where most bands release one, or at most two albums. Some of Wang Lei's albums are more acoustic, while others deploy a stronger rock sound. In his music he integrates elements of Sichuan opera (he was born in Sichuan Province in 1971).

After a trip to France in 2001, Wang Lei changed to electronic music, and when he performed in Amsterdam in October 2005, he switched to reggae. All his generic changes are indicative for the great cultural mobility of Chinese artists, a mobility all the greater when compared with their Western counterparts, where bands and singers generally remain committed to a specific genre and where genre swapping would soon be considered a sign of inauthenticity. This provides musicians in China with a greater freedom to explore different genres and styles. This flexibility can also be observed in other domains, such as at an art show titled 'The street belongs to all of us' in May 2008 in Beijing, where one piece exhibited was by Li Zheng from Shenzhen. He was described as an 'intellectual, manager of real estate, blogger, initiator of the City on the Bicycle project.' This combination of identity labels is unlikely to appear at an art show in the West.

Despite being one of the few musicians with a rock oeuvre of his own, Wang Lei remains a marginal figure in the national rock scene, since he is based in Guangzhou. A report from a fan from Wang Lei shows how his image remains framed within the rock mythology:

> Only after he got onto the stage did Wang Lei return to himself. He shouted without constraint and sang with a voice full of grief. His songs and voice astonished me: How could such excellent music exist in Guangzhou! (...) His image is not polished; he just belongs to himself and his badly injured heart. He is a simple man. (Li 1995: 4)

His voice and the perceived pain and despair in his songs signify authenticity, and authenticity is something one does not expect in a city like Guangzhou. Which, again, makes the rock from the south a sort of hyper-rock.

The musicians are aware of the marketing potential their outsider position provides. When I asked Wang Lei, after he had complained to me that he resented the cultural atmosphere of Guangzhou, whether he would prefer to move to Beijing, he confessed he would rather stay in Guangzhou, since he was a unique figure there.

> Perhaps the biggest advantage to me is that I live in Guangzhou. In Guangzhou no one makes music. Whether I'm good or not, as long as I know I'm making music, no one will influence me.

The lack of an established rock culture gives him more space to manifest himself; in Beijing, he would have to fight more to get attention. He gives the Chinese media a more poetic reason for staying in Guangzhou: 'Because Guangzhou depresses me, makes me suffer and thus gives me the impulse to express various emotions and to create music.' (Zhang 1995: 8)

The journalist further strengthens his narrative by concluding that 'the depression of the south is sublimated in his independent and pure song. Wang Lei has always been a stranger to the entertainment circle of Guangzhou; he is solely devoted to his music, he disdains the popular sweet and slick style.'

Guangzhou, a city whose popular culture is to a large extent colonised by Hong Kong, is positioned as lacking any true culture, and pop is once again downplayed as sweet and slick, whereas the voice of Wang Lei is considered independent and pure.

The cosmopolitan south

When we move back to Shanghai, the gloominess of Wang Lei is replaced by a more playful attitude. Walking through the streets of Shanghai, it is tempting to sing cheerfully along with Madonna's 'Material Girl.' In the newly renovated Xintiandi area, which opened in 2001, the CCP First Congress Meeting Hall is situated in the heart of a glamorous shopping and bar area, including the inevitable Starbucks. Here one is bound to conclude that we are indeed living in a material world, one in which even communism is commodified into a bright and shiny tourist attraction. One venue in the Xintiandi area, the Japanese-owned Ark, regularly features local rock acts, but the high prices as well as the interior style (the whole place is occupied by tables and chairs) erase any possible 'underground' flavour. No wonder one of the regular bands performing in Ark, Cold Fairyland, was surprised at the enthusiasm of the public in Beijing when they participated in a rock weekend in May 2004.

The 'alternative' circle of Shanghai is relatively small and rather mixed. Writer Mian Mian is also involved in organising rock parties, together with her close friend Kasper, and jazz singer Coco often shows up at rock concerts. They at times meet at the gallery and performance space Room With a View. With his androgynous appearance and tongue piercing, Coco strikes me as a newly-born, decadent, could-be-star of a new century. He tries to mix Chinese traditional music with jazz, and experiments at the same time with techno. To him, politics makes Beijing the centre of rock. In his words:

> In China we have a saying that goes 'Wherever there is pressure, there will be fights'. So when politics imposes more control, things develop more quickly. In Shanghai they put more emphasis on business, and culture doesn't follow anymore. I think it's bad. (...) I think Shanghai is a bitch, feminine, like a wealthy girl from a wealthy family. She can be very happy one moment, and

upset the next without giving any reason. It's very hard to deal
with someone who is very changeable.

Coco points out that because the cultural climate is so harsh in Shanghai, it produces a smaller, yet more dedicated, alternative scene. The
metaphor of Shanghai being a bitch (and then, I imagine, of Beijing as
the husband trying to control her), is appealing. Given his gayish appearance, it come as no surprise that Coco feels an outsider in the rock
circle. 'They think "Hey, I'm a rock singer, you're a fucking jazz singer,
I'm very alternative". I mean, if you're really alternative, you can accept
many things and then you can be alternative.'

The Tribesman used to be the only venue in Shanghai for rock performances. It was located close to the Fudan University, which is rather
far from the centre. It was a hot summer night in August 1999 when I
went there to attend a rock party. It was a dark and sleazy place, with
bad sound equipment. Rock band Seven performed their depressive
new wave songs, after which Crystal Butterfly took over. Their music is
inspired by U2, according to their guitarist Pang Pang. In his view, the
fact that their band operates in Shanghai is very important:

> You know, Shanghai is not really Shanghai. It's not so much a
> national thing, but a matter of cities. Just like you don't have
> American rock, you have rock from Seattle and New York. In
> China it's the same: We don't have Chinese rock, but rock from
> Beijing and rock from Shanghai.
> *How are they different?*
> In Beijing, people are more focused on this Chinese theme,
> Shanghai people don't like Beijing songs so much, they think it
> has such an attitude.

His view is interesting as it counters the idea of China's uniqueness
and instead encourages one to look for local differences. Although he
didn't use these words, he claims here that Shanghai produces cosmopolitan rock, whereas Beijing makes Chinese rock. 'I just want to make
good rock music. I feel that many foreigners like Chinese rock, not
really because they like the music, but because they like Chinese rock. I
don't want to make that kind of music, I want to make good rock music.'

The refusal to Sinify rock, one that I also observed among the female
voices, sets him apart from Beijing rock; this can be considered a tactic
to resist the hegemony of Beijing. He is merely part of a world culture,
rather than positioning himself as Chinese. Such a negotiation of place,
which here produces a cosmopolitan locality, sets Shanghai bands apart
from the Sinified rock of, for example, Cui Jian. For Qing Dao, singer

for the band The Maniacs, the difference between Beijing and Shanghai is related to politics:

> In Beijing they include more political topics; in Shanghai we don't want to include politics. Many Shanghai bands don't like Beijing. I think one reason is that Shanghai music is less famous. Second, they just scream whahwhahwhah; it's not really strong, it's just macho.

During the rock concert at The Tribesman, one girl had passed out drunk on the floor. I was amused when she turned out to be Kasper, the organiser of the party. I met her a few days later for an interview. Born in 1977, she is part of China's *dakou* generation. She got into the alternative scene after listening to *dakou* CDs, watching Channel V, and exploring the Internet. She had just quit her 'boring job' for a Shanghai record company and was trying to make a living on her own by organising parties. Job-hopping is a rather popular practice among Chinese youth. Her music taste is eclectic: She likes Karen Mok, Aaron Kwok, and Anthony Wong (Cantopop stars), as well as Cui Jian, Portishead, and Underworld. She explained to me how she once tried to be punk: 'I used to be a singer in a female punk band, but they thought I was too commercial. I'm too much into fashion, and I don't want to take a bus, I want to take a taxi. They didn't like me because of that.'

She didn't behave in line with the rock mythology and didn't survive in the world of rock. Mian Mian – the female writer and organiser of local rock parties, ex-drug addict, and a woman notorious for sleeping around – also has quite a few musicians who are antagonistic towards her. She is celebrated in foreign media (for example, *Newsweek*) as China's most controversial female writer. Her little book *Lalala* contains her life story, and the following fragment offers us a glimpse of this alternative reality which, indeed, caters so well to what the West likes to see in China: women, youth, sex, and rebellion. It's the flip side of the mythic East, but remains part of the same coin – the part called 'the oriental other', in which femininity operates as the sign for transgression and change. Mian Mian writes:

> It seems that fighting stimulates his desire for me. Every time after we fight, he makes love with me in a brand-new way. In our carnal contacts, I remain passive. I enjoy being masochist, which gives me endless pleasure. Sometimes I'm ashamed of myself. I don't know if there are others who make love like us. My helpless body. I don't know whether my orgasm is physical or mental. Ever since Qi told me how she fainted during her orgasm, I'm no longer sure whether I ever have an orgasm. It's a

scary seduction. I want to possess a perfect body, a perfect me.
But when do I have the power to be sure? (1999: 47-48)

Just as Kunming gives birth to a rock culture that allows different articulations and identity performances when compared to Beijing, linked
to the popular imagination of Yunnan as a transgressive as well as a
pure place, so does Shanghai feed into a different scene, one that is
more cosmopolitan and less concerned with Chineseness. Mian Mian
gained global recognition with her book *Candy*, which has been translated into English, as did other writers like Wei Hui, Chun Sue and Mu
Zimei (who achieved fame by publishing her sex life with, among
others, rock star Wang Lei from Guangzhou, on her blog). According to
Lu, these writers showcase on the one hand 'the politics of liberation
and excess in the Chinese experience of modernity,' while, on the other
hand, 'by posing to be sexual, young, beautiful, amoral, rebellious, and
anti-intellectual, the female writer aspires to create a media reaction
and become a celebrity.' (Lu 2008: 169) Given Shanghai's (self-) image
as a cosmopolitan city of decadence, it comes as no surprise that it plays
such a prominent role in the rise of what is termed 'body writing' in
China.

Whereas Lu claims such writing can be found in any country, and
that it is neither politicised not orientalised (Lu 2008: 175-176), I would
like to repeat my earlier argument that claims the opposite, namely that
women are the ultimate markers of (political) change, and the eagerness with which the West picks up their voices betrays an orientalist
gaze that feminises 'the East'. Neither a celebration of such authors nor
the debunking of them as being pulp is of much help if we are to understand the cultural significance of these works. It seems more fruitful
to see them as articulations of a *dakou* youth culture ushering in the
21st century, as negotiations and representations of the 'ongoing
struggle by Chinese youth to reconcile individualistic and collectivist
orientations'(Weber 2002: 366), through an exploration of the themes
of individualism, personal aspirations, growing alienation, immediate
gratification, individual qualities, admiration of foreign things and political critique (ibid.). Rather than blaming the body writers for producing
pulp literature, or repeating the worn-out complaint that they cater to
the eyes of the West (a complaint common about Chinese artists who
make it in the West which is voiced frequently within China as well as
by foreign 'China specialists'), the more urgent question such work
poses is whether the focus on the body in the end proves beneficial for
(Chinese) women. Zhong doubts whether this will be the case, when she
writes that 'the gradual equating of women's issues with 'femininity'
and 'sexuality' within this cultural turn (...) overshadows the fact that
women's issues have always been also socio-economic issues.' (Zhong

2006:637) The danger in the celebration of new femininities lies indeed in its potential erasure of issues of class and inequality, a danger that can also be translated to rock culture in general, where the spectacular display of difference generally obscures issues of class and social inequality.

Cities outside Beijing offer a symbolic space to explore alternative (and also gendered) articulations of youth culture. The art-punk of the band Top Floor Circus draws on a quite different aesthetic reservoir: rather than sexuality, their work invokes humour, parody and irony as the building blocks of their performances. The Modern Sky music festival in October 2008 had a special timeslot for Shanghai bands, during which vocalist Lu Chen was not only the master of a ceremony that poked fun at both Chinese culture as well as communist culture (in its mocking use of a typical communist way of speaking); he also delivered a parody on the Olympic Games. In their version of the hit song 'Beijing Welcomes You', turned into 'Shanghai Welcomes You', he sings:

> Shanghai welcomes you, welcomes you to come shopping
> Don't forget to bring your RMB
> Shanghai welcomes you, What's so special about the Olympic Games?
> Shanghai Welcomes You (...)
> The pretty girls at Huaihai Road
> Are No.1 around the whole country (...)
> Shanghai welcomes you, What's so special about the Olympic Games?
> Let's get together at World Expo[11]

Lu Chen plays out the clichéd references to Shanghai in this song, exaggerates them, thus poking fun at the stereotypes people from Beijing generally employ when describing Shanghai. He did so at a time when Beijing was the epicentre of the world in hosting the Olympic Games, and in his ridiculing of the Games he mocks the nationalism propagated by the officials and decentres Beijing as the centre of Chinese culture.

Of course, not all bands are as keen to discredit Beijing. For example, the band Cold Fairyland, whose female vocalist Lin Di is also a gifted pipa player, clearly include numerous references to Chineseness in their dream-like soundscapes, which resemble the music of Dead Can Dance. As they write on their website:

> The Cool Zone is really a new species in eastern musical ecology.
> A modern Chinese sensibility, magical lyricism, and a trance-like synthesiser all make this album a strange flower. (...) Lin Di sud-

denly found a new, spontaneous musical language all on her own. It is a language taken from Chinese culture, but expressed in an innovative way.[12]

The band clearly expressed their preference for performing in Beijing, commenting positively on the enthusiastic response of the audiences.

This tour through places other than Beijing has led us from Wang Lei in Guangzhou to rock bands, jazz singers, and controversial female writers in Shanghai. The voices of the margin are often at pains to perform their exclusivity, their difference. They are above all certainly *not* like the centre, which renders them even more marginal. Interestingly, the rock mythology is not so much subverted as used as an empowering narrative. First, those who can make rock in such culturally desolate places as Guangzhou and Shanghai must be even more authentic, more sincere, than their Beijing counterparts. Consequently, cultural stereotypes often heard in Beijing are reified rather than challenged.[13] Second, most voice a critique about Beijing being arrogant, having an attitude, and being too political and too concerned with making rock with Chinese characteristics. Some prefer a more cosmopolitan rock style, and in doing so negate the importance of Sinifying rock. The Shanghai rock bands, gay jazz singers, and controversial female writers hope to be less local than Beijing, so as to revive the cosmopolitanism of the old Shanghai. The poses are somehow more decadent, more fashionable maybe, but remain drenched in the rock mythology. If we are to interrogate the rock mythology, we should go further south, to Hong Kong and the seductive sounds of Cantopop.

Seductive Sounds

In theorising the globalisation of (popular) culture, the distinction between hard and soft has proven valuable in understanding the dynamics of a hard culture like rock music when it traverses cultural boundaries. Earlier I have demonstrated that the hard force of rock – a force that comes with a strong imagination of a clear origin: the West – *demands* localisation when the sound travels to places outside the West, in order to become and remain authentic. Chapter two has shown that for the more hyphenated scenes, this urge becomes less conspicuous. Then what about the soft sound of pop? Does the hard-soft theorisation offer equally relevant insights in understanding the globalisation of the soft? In the final part of this chapter, I would like to revisit Appadurai's hard-soft distinction as discussed in the introductory chapter by focusing on Chinese pop. Appadurai does not offer any inquiry into the soft as he does on the hard. Nor does he name a concrete soft cultural form such as the hard cultural form cricket. Cryptically, he remarks that soft forms 'permit relatively easy separation of embodied performance from meaning and value, and relatively successful transformation at each level' (1996: 90). Given the juxtaposition of rock versus pop, it seems logical to label pop a soft cultural form, as it is difficult to come up with a coherent set of narratives which together constitute, for instance, the pop mythology. Pop's meanings and values seem indeed, relatively speaking, easily separated from its embodied performance.

However, if we were to follow this theoretical line, we not only run the danger of reifying the pop-rock dichotomy, but, more importantly, of ignoring one fundamental difference: while rock musicians are preoccupied with articulating their distinction from *Gangtai* pop (the South) and from the perceived origin (the West), pop artists usually do not display the same urgency. Pop stars in Hong Kong and Taiwan, for instance, are concerned about their direct competitors, also from Hong Kong and Taiwan, rather than their loud Northern colleagues. Instead of distinguishing themselves from the West by localising tactics, pop stars couldn't care less about recreating the latest fads in the global pop scene. The discourse of localisation I have traced for rock is absent in pop. Neither in imagery nor in sound (apart from the 'choice' of language) is there an articulated attempt to localise *Gangtai* pop.[14] Musicians are not involved in debates over their Chinese characteristics, as the Beijing rockers are. This, however, does not imply that pop is not a globalised sound; on the contrary, as I have noted earlier, it is precisely the sound of pop that is popular among the diasporic Chinese communities across the world. Pop may be rock's constitutive outside, but the opposite is simply not the case. While acknowledging the theoretical value of the hard, its 'obvious' opposition does not bring us very far in thinking through the globalisation of pop.

If the hard cultural form of rock is embedded in its meanings and values (authentic, rebellious, political), pop defies being straightjacketed into a cluster of negatives (inauthentic, non-rebellious, apolitical). If rock musicians in China continue to perceive their musical origin in the West, *Gangtai* pop collapses the West with the Rest. Cultural forms are perhaps like snow: crystal clear when hard(ened), opaque when soft. It is this opacity which explains why Appadurai remains silent when it comes to the soft, just as I consider it to be the reason why relatively few academics have embarked upon a serious analysis of *Gangtai* pop, whereas quite a few have done so for Beijing rock (see introductory chapter, endnote sixteen). Yet in these studies, the parameters imposed by the hard form of rock remain so powerful that either the 'authentic', 'political' voice of pop is privileged, or the focus is solely on the meaning of the lyrics, ignoring the inherent opacity of pop.

The transparency of the voice of rock, with its insistence on authenticity, may be productive in creating rock as a distinct music world; at the same time it confines the proliferation of meaning. The clarity of rock is countered by the opacity of pop. To appropriate De Certeau's thoughts on the power of popular culture in everyday life: the sound of pop 'ceaselessly recreat[es] opacities and ambiguities – spaces of darkness and trickery – in the universe of technocratic transparency, [it] disappears into them and reappears again, taking no responsibility for the administration of a totality.' (1984: 18) I therefore aim to recast the hard-soft distinction into a clear-opaque dualism. In the terms of Mikhael Bakhtin, the rock mythology can be considered an authoritative discourse (1981: 349). Its unitary language lacks ambiguity, and is a result of hegemonic forces. According to Bakhtin, transparency in language represents a hegemonic closure of meaning, signalling the power that social interests can bear on discourse (Garvey 2000: 377). To Bakhtin, 'a unitary language gives expression to forces working toward concrete verbal and ideological unification and centralisation.' (1981: 271)

Absolute transparency is, however, not possible, since unitary language still has to navigate through the multiple forces of *heteroglossia*: the contextual conditions insuring that words uttered at different times, under different conditions, by different people, will acquire different meanings. Utterances are therefore 'fundamentally "impure" or hybridised constructions, complex amalgams of different points of view, (...) they always evince a multiplicity of actual and potential meanings.' (Gardiner 2004: 37) By acknowledging the opacity of pop, I aim to explore the possibility of the appropriation and remoulding of words and sounds, which increases the multiplicity of meaning; it propels (or in Bakthin's language: seizes) the possibilities of new dialogues. Pop's opacity unfolds the *heteroglossia* of everyday life, as opposed to the unitary language of rock that represents 'the ideological control of signification' (Garvey 2000: 380). In the following and final part of this chapter, I will therefore make a rupture from the clear, hard world of rock and dive into the more fluid opaque waters of *Gangtai* pop.

Hong Kong-based pop singer, songwriter and producer Anthony Wong's works and career offer a particularly relevant case to analyze opaque cultural forms. In 1985, Anthony Wong started his career as one half of the electronic duo Tatming Pair, creating numerous hits in Hong Kong during the latter half of the 1980s. After the duo split up in 1990, Wong continued his musical career as solo artist and producer. Compared to his Tatming period, which has received some scholarly interest – again privileging the political and rebellious dimension of the duo's music (Chu 2000a, 2000b; Lok 1993) – Wong's solo performance remains surprisingly under-analysed, as if the hard and its embedded meaning and values persist as the major, if not only, legitimising force in studying *Gangtai* pop in academia. In 2008, Anthony Wong was listed as number 1 in the list of 20 best musicians of Hong Kong by *Time Out* Magazine.[15]

Tatming's synthesiser pop resembles the music of the Pet Shop Boys, but – as Wong quickly remarked in order to guarantee authenticity – both duos started out at the same time. This suggests that pop singers are as eager to claim the authenticity of their sound as their rock colleagues are. His desire to be more independent, which was realised later in the founding of the production company People Mountain People Sea, shows how pervasive the ideology of the rock mythology is.[16] It also functions as a marker of difference, as he claims to be more in control than the big stars. He says, 'We want more autonomy. Actually, I think I have a lot of autonomy already, compared with others, but I still want more.'

Wong attempted to distinguish himself from both Chinese rock and Cantopop by stating that:

> We don't just sing about love, nor are we simply anti-establishment. We have put more humour in our music and the context of our music is more complex. We talk about sexuality, about weird subjects you can't find in Chinese music. We wrote a song about voyeurism; you don't find this kind of thing in Chinese music, not even in Cantopop.

His words indicate that the world of pop may be as fragmented and scenic as the world of rock, just as it is too premature to claim that pop equals inauthenticity. The question of how to make sense of pop, however, remains more urgent. Below I will map out three planes which together constitute the opaque sound of pop: transient, intertextual and multivocal.

Transient opacity

Pop captures the feelings of urban life, in particularly its fluidity and mobility. Today's pop songs are known by everyone: their banal melodies are imposed upon audiences in taxis, shops, and bars, but are normally considered outdated within a few years. Indicative are the lyrics and sound of Anthony Wong's song 'Ave Maria':[17]

> I want to be high every day
> And change by night and day
> Like Maria, reincarnated,
> Pregnant by night and day
> Look at the glamorous goddess

Forever branded on my skin
You look so beautiful
(illness contracted in daylight always breaks out in the dark)
I exist till now

The song captures the feeling of living in a culture that is in a constant
state of flux, characteristic of urban clusters like Hong Kong. There is a
celebration here of the banal, the temporal, the fluid, and the superficial. It might well be the power to sensationalise the present that makes
pop such a pervasive sound. The sound that accompanies 'Ave Maria'
may be compared to the sound of Australian pop diva Kylie Minogue.
The catchy melodies of her global hits (*Lalala lalalalala – I just can't get
you out of my head, boy!*) are, like Anthony Wong's, as banal as they are
effective. Once they settle down in the sonic parts of the brain, they are
hard to drive out. If we hear the same song a few years later, the sound
will remind us of that year 2002, when the song hit the charts. The banal sound will have become old-fashioned, but manages to forcefully
bring back memories of a time past. Pop's temporality paradoxically at
the same time immortalises it. To invoke the classic Kantian categories
of time and space: whereas rock relates more strongly to space, pop relates more strongly to time.[18]

Anthony Wong claims to be inspired by the sounds of James Last,
which to him resemble the Muzak we hear in the shopping malls of
Hong Kong. As Rey Chow points out, 'If we are to look for a contemporary "expression" of the idealist infinity traditionally associated with
music, Muzak is exactly that – an infinity, but an infinity vulgarized.'
(1993: 205) James Last is only one source of inspiration; some songs
are a reinterpretation of existing songs, some from the late diva of
Gangtai pop, Teresa Teng, others from popular Kung Fu series turned
into an anthem for the street kids of Hong Kong, and still others draw
on the old decadent songs from Shanghai. Anthony Wong is not so
much defamiliarising the familiar sounds of Hong Kong from both the
past and the present as merely tweaking those sounds.

'I exist till now,' sings Wong in 'Ave Maria': the transient reinvention
of the self is accomplished by conspicuous consumption, the driving
force of Hong Kong culture. The familiarity of the song resembles a
culture in constant flux. It presents a smooth surface noise that accompanies the listener when shopping, when taking a cab, or when queue-
ing up for McDonald's in order to add the latest gadgets (that come
with a meal) to the collection. The song, which had 'Day and Night in
Causeway Bay' as its working title (Causeway Bay being the primary
shopping area of Hong Kong), is about a girl fantasising about becoming somebody else, an idol, by an incredible metamorphosis; just like
Mary, probably not by immaculate conception, but through some more

mundane shopping.[19] Given the song title, everyday banality and vulgarity are injected with a sense of religiosity, a religiosity that aspires not to eternity but to the here and the now.

Intertextual opacity

Due to the different roles Cantopop stars assume – they often appear in movies, TV series, and commercials, and show up constantly in the tabloids and in TV quizzes – they are more media personalities than musicians. Pop stars are intertextual chameleons; they provide multiple possibilities for identifications and as such create a universe of their own (Witzleben 1999). The world of pop star Leon Lai, one of the four 'heavenly kings' of *Gangtai* pop, is a complex one. It is at times sexy (when we see him dancing in a wet shirt in his video clip), can be violent (when we come across him in a movie), may motivate us to buy a new mobile phone (when he acts in an advertisement for the Orange network), or aspire to virtue (when he helps UNICEF to save the world in Brazil).

The intertextual dimension of pop intersects with a discourse of inauthenticity – pop is perceived as a plastic, commercial sound. If a pop singer can also be a movie star or an actor in commercials, he or she is not purely a musician; the pop musician is fake and commercial. The self-referential inauthentic aesthetics of pop challenge the notion of the authentic artist and the idea that true art is everlasting. Pop's artificial intertextuality is a force that counters the authenticating drive of other art worlds like rock. Pop not only refuses to disguise the importance of packaging, control, and artificiality – as rock does in order to produce the authentic artist – but even celebrates it. The author – a crucial actor in the construction of authenticity – of a pop song is present in its absence because it is hard, if not impossible, to define him or her, since the composer, lyricist, artist, record company, and producer are all intimately involved in the production of a song.

During a performance in Berlin in the summer of 1999, Anthony Wong disappeared into a corner of the stage, and continued singing while an actor mimicked him centre stage. This act was a deliberate play with the artificiality of pop. It signified a love of the unnatural, confused the real with the fake, and as such was a self-reflective act. Which leads us back to the notion of authenticity. Pop turns authenticity, in a creative, self-reflective move, into a style. In the pop world, style prevails over content, just as aesthetics triumphs over morality (Sontag 1964: 287).

Pop parodies the ideology of authenticity, but rather than reading it as a performance of inauthenticity, I prefer to read it as a Bakhtinian way to unfold the different possible authenticities within popular music.

Grossberg states that in pop, 'the only possible claim to authenticity is derived from the knowledge and admission of your inauthenticity' (1993: 206). 'The whole *notion* of authenticity ... is one that comes to us constructed by hegemonic voices.' (Spivak & Gunew 1993: 195) Pop's fiddling around with rock's unified language of authenticity is a parodic-ironic reaccentuation that, by making both listener and performer aware of the hegemony inscribed into the idea of authenticity, also opens up ways to rethink it. A rethinking located in ironic laughter, which is a liberating, transcending and uniting force (Bakhtin 1986: 134-135).

Multivocal opacity

Given the disappearance of the Author in pop, it becomes possible to speak of pop in different voices. Pop singers do not pretend to sing in one 'voice', but in many voices or roles. In one song, they may be entirely disillusioned about love, in the next entirely sanguine, then very strong, and then so fragile. The multivocality is further multiplied by the karaoke phenomenon, where each and every karaoke singer may appropriate the songs with his or her voice. Karaoke enables Mary walking in Causeway Bay in the shopping mall to slip for a few minutes into her desired star persona. A K-song (*k-ge*), a relatively new term in the *Gangtai* pop music scene, refers to a pop song that is particularly good for karaoke, in the sense of sentiment and vocal range. The high proportion of duets in *Gangtai* pop releases follows the popularity of karaoke, further stimulating the multivocality of pop.

A look at a section of the lyrics of Anthony Wong's song 'Next Stop, Heaven,' is illustrative of the multivocal potential of pop:[20]

> And then
> So much desire, so little time
> Should I go shopping, sight-seeing or have a little ride
> Sit next to me, and look into the eternity of this very fine day
> Till I am gay enough to say
> See you next time
> Take a deep breath
> And tell me you are fine
> Think of me for a while
> And see how life makes our love a crime
> Time after time.

There is a playfulness in these lyrics, along with the reference to a forbidden love. It remains unclear, however, what the nature of that love is. It is not difficult to interpret the song as referring to a homosexual affair doomed to failure under the current Chinese sexual regime, but other interpretations are equally possible. Wong's play with camp, gender and sexuality can also be traced on the cover of his CDs *In Broad Daylight* in Figure 3.3 and *Like Water* in Figure 3.4.

Figure 3.3   *CD Jacket Anthony Wong – In Broad Daylight (copyright Emperor Entertainment Group)*

Both the lyrics and the jackets reflect the multivocal aesthetics of pop. This multivocality provides space to play with gender and sexuality. The image on the jacket is, among other representations of pop, smooth, artificial and inauthentic, androgynous. The face covered with diamonds along with the smoke in the forefront render him ambivalent, mysterious and campy at the same time. Anthony Wong remains deliberately ambiguous – or better: opaque – about his sexual identity, but incorporates clearly homosexual themes. Such themes are never rendered fixed, but instead are always open to negotiation, redefinition and reinterpretation (Hawkins 1997: 125). Wong's play with the sexual self is indicative of the multivocal, ambiguous playing with identities. Anthony Wong plays with his image, eroticises it, adds a queer layer to it, while resisting coming out as gay. Also here the importance of karaoke needs

Figure 3.4 *CD Jacket Anthony Wong – Like Water (copyright Emperor Entertainment Group)*

to be acknowledged, since karaoke enables the listener to become implicated in that same play, to perform as sexual selves behind the doors of a karaoke bar different from those he or she is allowed to perform in public spaces.

Live performances are an important site for such identity games, which makes pop performances a spectacular display of multivocal pop aesthetics. Performances by pop stars are above all visual and musical spectacles; the audience has to be entertained. Gone is the importance of 'real' live music; there is no need to play endless riffs on a guitar until your clothes are soaked with sweat in order to authenticate yourself. What counts in the world of pop is pleasure; the better you entertain the audience, the better you are. Anthony Wong changes his extravagant clothes several times during a performance in order to slip into a different image, just as he constantly changes his hair colour. We see him in a shiny silver outfit, after which he changes into a white suit made of feathers and then into a suit resembling the Union Jack.

Femininity, Locality and Opacity

The subaltern sounds explored in this chapter provide us with a more ba-
lanced perspective on popular music in China. We are confronted with
the masculine bias of rock music; female voices have developed tactics
to overcome this bias through denial, dramatisation, politicisation, and
cosmopolitisation of gender. However, all these tactics rely heavily on
the rock mythology, and as such the female voices do not offer a radically new interpretation of rock – and why should they? The same goes
for the rock scenes in places outside Beijing. There, the rock mythology
is not so much negated as used as an empowering narrative. Those
who can make rock in such culturally desolate places as Guangzhou
and Shanghai must be even more authentic, more sincere than their
Beijing counterparts. Consequently, cultural stereotypes often heard in
Beijing are reified rather than challenged. All bands are at pains to
point out their difference from Beijing rock, rather than from *Gangtai*
pop, which shows how such organising dichotomies are anything but
fixed. If we are to truly explore the boundaries of the rock mythology, a
look at *Gangtai* pop proves most rewarding, as my analysis has shown.

When trying to explore the soft, Appadurai's conceptualisation proves
untenable. Under his hard-soft distinction, a large domain of popular
culture, among which the opaque sound of pop can be included, remains
undertheorized. I therefore propose a recasting of the hard-soft distinction into a clear-opaque dualism, precisely to subvert this privileging of
the hard, to offer a theoretical tool better geared to understand the globalisation of cultural forms, and in the end to reshuffle the (global) power
mechanism often inherent in the option for the clear and hard.

I do not wish to present a critique of rock as such, but of its constitutive discourses, and thereby the global distribution of discursive power
over cultural forms. It is my contention that when we place the opaque
sound of pop in the foreground, we will also open up mental pathways
to rethink the discursive clarity of rock and the power that insists on
such clarity. Pop unfolds what Bakhtin may call the generic *heteroglossia*
of popular music, and consequently renders the clarity of the rock
mythology more opaque. Pop does not use the direct shock tactics punk
uses, nor is there the anger present which characterises much rock music. The topics are more mundane; like the sounds, pop lyrics often
constitute a surface, transient noise that resonates deeply with everyday
life. Those lyrics and sounds are not only knots of a wider intertextual
web, they also speak in different voices, through different media. Being
an opaque cultural form, pop is characterised by a transient banality, an
intertextual artificiality and a multivocal ambiguity. Pop brings to mind
Oscar Wilde's claim: 'I adore simple pleasures, they are the last refuge
of the complex' (in Sontag 1964: 288).

4 Musical Taste and Technologies of the Self

I have a small question: please tell me what the value of life is. My teacher
told us, for those who have no dream, life is a shame, and I think that
maybe you can give me a dream. The teacher told us that we must have
correct values and ideas about life and the world. So, what is correct?
Din Qing in a letter to the band Heaven

My point is not that everything is bad, but that everything is dangerous,
which is not exactly the same as bad. If everything is dangerous, then we
always have something to do.
Michel Foucault (1997 [1983]: 256)

Music and Society

The words of Din Qing in a letter to the band Heaven attest to the
power of music; she turns to the band in search of alternative values
and ideas about life, different from the ones she receives at school and,
most likely, at home. It shows how music is integrated into the fabric of
everyday life, simultaneously pointing at the agency of the listener –
who, after all, uses music in her search for values – as well as the structural power of the sound – as she believes that music will provide her
with the answers she is looking for. Music audiences generally receive
less academic attention when compared to music scenes, probably even
more so when it comes to Chinese rock culture. An understandable
bias as the spectacular poses, provocative lyrics and subversive sounds
all literally scream for attention, both academic and journalistic,
whereas mundane and private listening practices are more difficult to
grasp. The meanings of music proliferate in the dialogue between the
work and the audience – and this is, I would argue, a two-way dialogue.
The works speak to the audience, just like the audience speaks to the
work (Bal 2002; Frith 1996).[1] It is tempting to treat a musical text as
though it were solely the expression of the artist, e.g. as though the anger in Zu Zhou's voice were just his anger, thereby ignoring the anger
experienced by the listener.[2] This chapter presents an attempt to explore

how audiences use music as a technology of the self, showing how music consumption provides 'a means for self-interpretation, for the articulation of self-image and for the adaptation of various emotional states associated with the self in social life.' (DeNora 1999: 32)

Foucault employed the notion of 'technologies of the self' in the later stages of his work. Having analyzed the structuring and productive power of discourse, the workings of governmentality, and the intricate ways in which citizens are disciplined, in the second and third part of his history of sexuality he turned towards possibilities of living life as it were a work of art. As he writes, 'Perhaps I've insisted too much on the technology of domination and power.' (Foucault 1997 [1982]: 225) According to Foucault, technologies of the self 'permit individuals to effect by their own means, or with the help of others, a certain number of operations on their own bodies and souls, thoughts, conduct, and way of being, so as to transform themselves in order to attain a certain state of happiness, purity, wisdom, perfection, or immortality.' (ibid.)[3] For Foucault, these technologies do not revolve so much around knowledge of the self, which to him is enmeshed into disciplinary practices which limit rather than open up possibilities for the self, but reside in care of the self. This care of the self involves practices of living built upon the idea that there is no fixed self, and 'from the idea that the self is not given to us. I think that there is only one practical consequence: we have to create ourselves as a work of art.' (Foucault 1997 [1983]: 262)

Music serves as an important ingredient in this constant production and reproduction of the self. It does so in myriad ways: it helps us to relate to other people, it serves to regulate our well-being, it makes us relate to our bodies, and it helps us position ourselves in society and hopefully navigate the cracks of the disciplinary discourses that impose prefabricated identities upon us – to name but a few examples of the power of music. Of course, genre plays an important role in such technologies of the self. The words of Yin Zheng, a high-school student, in a letter to Modern Sky record company are indicative: 'If you're a rocker who truly loves punk, then the underground is your paradise. If you're a mainstreamer who worships all the pop idols, then this is your hell.'

For a devoted rock fan, this may be an important distinction in taste through which the self is differentiated from other taste cultures. Yet, as I hope to show in this chapter, rather than an articulation of a taste hierarchy (Bourdieu 1979; Gans 1999), everyday listening involves a complex array of technologies of the self which cannot solely be reduced to the need for distinction.

These technologies have become increasingly reflexive under the conditions of high modernity and the related de-traditionalisation of society. As Giddens writes, 'In the post-traditional order of modernity, and against the backdrop of new forms of mediated experience, self-identity becomes a reflexively organised endeavour. The reflexive project of the self, which consists in the sustaining of coherent, yet continuously revised, biographical narratives, takes place in the context of multiple choice as filtered through abstract systems.' (Giddens 1991: 5) Given the inherent unreliability and unpredictability of knowledge and expert systems such as the media, the reflexive self needs continuous symbolic labour in order to maintain itself. Media, including music, are becoming increasingly important as symbolic toolboxes in this process of reflexivity; music provides the sonic and aesthetic means through which identities are articulated and group boundaries are formed. It is surprising that music has not been studied that much in relation to technologies of the self, whereas a 'focus on intimate musical practice, on the private or one-to-one forms of human-music interaction, offers an ideal vantage point for viewing music "in action," for observing music as it comes to be implicated in the construction of the self as an aesthetic agent.' (DeNora 2000: 46)

Rather than framing China in terms of late modernity, it may be more useful to think of China as passing through a rather short period of compressed modernity, a period that started in the late 1970s, accelerated throughout the 1980s, yet only entered full swing in the 1990s. Amidst this maelstrom of changes, ushering China into a state of permanent change and flux, driven by the rhetoric of the perpetually new, the urgency to reflect upon the self, to develop technologies of the self, seems to me at least as pivotal and urgent, if not more so, as it is in the UK, the society on which both Giddens and DeNora base their work. As Ong and Zhang write, in a privatising China, 'the reinvention of selfhood and personal privacy are embroiled with new kinds of knowledge and information that participate in shaping "the new social."' (2008: 16) The question to be answered, then, in this chapter, is what technologies of the self are actually enabled by popular music.[4]

To engage with this question, multiple methods have been used: given a general lack of ethnographic research on Chinese youth cultures (exceptions are Fong 2004; Rosen 2003; Weber 2002), I consider it important to let the audience literally speak in this chapter, hence the abundant inclusion of quotes. To gain some basic information on Beijing youth – i.e., about their values and aspirations – and their media use and music preferences, I decided to carry out a quantitative analysis. I approached the electronics concern, Philips, which agreed to cooperate in my 1997 survey among 650 youths in Beijing.[5] To acquire further information, I conducted 32 interviews with Beijing youths.[6] One method that goes beyond the approach of the 'academic that is probing for information through questions' comes from the fan mail I analysed. In total, 80 letters from fans to their favourite bands are included; these letters were provided by the three record companies:

Magic Stone (Taiwan), Red Star (Hong Kong), and Modern Sky (Beijing). These letters attest to the power of music; fans from all over China take the effort to share their deepest emotions and thoughts with band members they most likely have never met and whom they only know through music. They provide a unique tool to explore how music is used as a technology of the self. The data on which this chapter builds is from 1997, the heyday of *dakou* culture, and the moment of China's opening up, when marketisation really took off. The age mentioned refers to that year. These are voices marking a pivotal moment in Chinese youth culture: *dakou* culture has facilitated the opening and changing of Chinese society, benefitting the 80s generation I introduced earlier in particular. For that generation, the search for identity and authenticity has only gained more significance – with music as a vehicle to articulate technologies of the self – rendering the argument in this chapter probably more rather than less relevant for the current *balinghou* generation. Before exploring these technologies, it is important, however, to map out the context in which these technologies are developed. This mapping will already reveal one important aspect of music as technology of the self, as music helps to articulate generational differences.

Youth in Fin-de-siècle Beijing

In chapter one, I briefly pointed to the multiple forces controlling the everyday lives of Chinese youth: parental control and expectations, the educational system and the political environment. The renewed popularity of Confucianism (Bell 2008) has only increased the pressures. Rosen (2003: 101) distinguishes three changes in youth attitudes since the 1990s: first, Chinese youth is drawn to global culture to a greater extent than anticipated by the government; second, the state has been successful in promoting patriotism among Chinese youth; and, third, the diminished interest in politics has not solved the crisis in faith but has led to a greater concern with one's own self-interest. These trends, which became very visible in the development of the *dakou* generation, have become more pronounced after 2000 among the 80s generation. The picture that emerges in Rosen's account is of an increasingly cosmopolitan, patriotic and individualistic, if not egocentric, generation. Especially over the last decade, the patriotism of Chinese youth has received considerable journalistic attention (Fong 2004; Gries 2004). In these stories, Chinese youth is perceived as overtly patriotic and individualistic, as a generation that differs immensely from the students who occupied Tiananmen Square in 1989.

Discourse on Chinese youth is also often quite negative in China; the 80s generation is blamed for being too individualistic and lacking morality. In the words of Cen and Li, 'The past two decades have created a moral confusion for youth in China. Meanwhile, the education in moral and social values that is offered our youth in school, family and society has not been up to the required task.' (2006: 165) In these narratives, the voices of young people themselves are hardly included (see also the introductory chapter). In this section, before exploring the sonic technologies of the self, I want to recuperate their voices and explore how young people write and talk about their family, the education system and politics.

First, the Chinese family. What is quite remarkable is that only 28.9% of the survey's respondents agreed with the statement 'I usually have the same opinions as my parents' (among rockers, this figure was lower, i.e. 20%). Yet, nearly 90% agreed that they 'got along well with their parents' (among rockers, this was 86%, slightly lower than average). So, whereas many youths dare say that they disagree with their parents, they are less vocal when it comes to classifying this as living in disharmony with them. Harmony prevails, and with the sufferings from the Cultural Revolution still vivid in their minds, parents seem to firmly uphold the importance of learning – at least, that is what their children are given to understand. The story of Qin Ming reappeared in most interviews, because many Chinese families are caught in different narrations of the same suffocating past:

> My mother suffered a lot during the Cultural Revolution because her father was accused of being a counter-revolutionary, just because he wrote an article in which he said that sparrows are good for agriculture. At the time, Mao was telling everyone to kill sparrows, so her father was labelled anti-revolutionary and she couldn't go to university to study, even though she'd done very well at school. So she went to the countryside and worked with peasants for about ten years.

Many students pointed out that the pressure put upon them by their parents to study hard and succeed in life is strongly affected by this violent period in modern China. The impact is strengthened by the one-child policy in China. All frustrations, anxieties, hopes, and failed opportunities are projected onto a single child, a burden often hard to carry for Chinese youth. But the hardships suffered by the parents, combined with the value attached to harmony, make it hard to rebel. As Zhi Yong remarked:

> When I have friction with my parents, I tell myself that they are my parents, that they support me, love me. It's irresponsible of me to make them angry. Of course, it's not always my fault, but

I don't think I should make them angry. They work so hard and have experienced so many hardships, I don't want them to feel uneasy.

Memories of the Cultural Revolution, when youths rebelled against both parents and teachers in such a violent way, has made the word rebellion in a Chinese context more dubious compared to the situation in the West. In the West, the youth rebellion of the 1960s is frequently romanticised by its participants, as well as by younger generations, as its message of peace and love remains seductive, as do the fashions from that era.

Chen Shirong is a girl from a small town in Sichuan who now studies in Chengdu. In her letter to the band Heaven, she turns to a band to share her feelings. This attests to the power of music. She writes about her loneliness and the burden she experiences from the family. Her letter is worth quoting at length, as she expresses very well the burden Chinese youths feel they bear:

> Maybe you wouldn't understand how sadness and angst started to show on the innocent face of a 12- or 13-year-old girl. I have always been a girl who wants more from life. Since childhood, I always have my own ideas. But in our place, it's called being rebellious. So I've always suppressed my ideas, trying to be an understanding and obedient child. For my parents, for my brothers and sisters, I'm willing to sacrifice everything. I always believe that I am responsible for my family, my relatives, and my friends, for their happiness. Therefore, I study hard, hoping to become somebody and let those who know me be proud of me ... I wish I could have already taken over some of the burden from my parents. I wish I could have ventured into the world and not allowed them to support me through university. But still I accepted my father's arrangement, because that's his hope, his love ... Ideals, career, responsibility. They make me want to leave everything behind and escape into decadence. I've lost my confidence and courage. I've become weak and helpless. (...) I wish to be challenged by another soul so I won't be numb anymore. I really need comfort. Those beside me do not understand me. I'm very tired. I need someone to lean on, to take away all my burdens ... What I like most is listening to music quietly.

Her words merely represent the struggle to shape one's own life in a society where parents demand obedience and expect the child to go to university – which provides an environment where hard work and perseverance are required. These are feelings and experiences shared by

many Chinese – both old and young – as they discover how very difficult it is to survive in such an increasingly competitive society offering
so few certainties or traditions to cling to. She expresses the feeling that
music is what helps her to carve out her own space, to create her own
sense of home, a reflexive place where she feels comfortable. The generational conflict in China seems less vocal, more subdued, than that in
Western societies. Yet, the expectations of parents, along with an extremely competitive education system, put a heavy burden on the
shoulders of the young generation. Economic reforms have also increased the pressure, as the job market has become more competitive
since the 1990s.

Second, the Chinese educational system. I usually asked the respondents in my interviews what they consider to be most restrictive aspects
of Chinese society: politics, the educational system, or the family. Politics was usually regarded as being too detached from everyday life.[7] The
educational system was most commonly referred to as the biggest ob-
stacle in life. It is far too competitive, the system of teaching is considered outdated, and 'political education' is a bore for many students. The
following quotes provide representative examples:

> Schools will teach you nothing; only the text book will teach you.
> The teachers are bound to teach you the lessons and give no
> further information. You have to pass the entrance examination,
> so you have to study all the boring things. (Qin Ming)

> The education system restricts personalities, and only cares about
> examinations. I felt that my life in middle school was like life in
> hell, nothing funny, only those examinations. I think the educa-
> tion system is too cruel, it ruins personalities. (Lui Jiayue)

> The education system decides on a person's future only through
> some examinations, just like in ancient times. (...) In political
> education, we studied the five phases of human society; now we
> study so-called philosophy, which means we should develop cor-
> rect ideas and values about this world. (Liu Fangfang)

The irony in the words of Liu Fangfang, a middle-school student, is telling. Not everyone takes the propaganda seriously – she speaks of 'so-
called philosophy'. When the teacher fails to make clear what life's all
about, some, like Din Qin, whom I quoted at the opening of this chapter, turn to rock music.

Third, the political environment. Given the structure of the educational system, it is no wonder that Zhang Yongping started writing a letter to Modern Sky during his writing class. 'I believe you [Modern Sky]

will become even better. We are still young. The revolution is not yet completed, comrades, we must continue working hard!'

His last quote comes from Sun Yat-Sen, who was referring to the overthrow of the Qing Dynasty; it was later adopted by Mao Zedong and became one of his most famous one-liners during the communist revolution. The act of writing during class can be considered political, and even more so due to the parodic use of communist jargon. In fact, the educational system, like the ideology of the family, is closely intertwined with politics, as Liu Xin argues correctly: 'I think politics is in education all the time. My parents have to make a living in society; they live within a certain political environment, so nothing can be separated from politics.'

Nothing can be completely separated from politics, and however savvy audiences and students are in decoding messages, propaganda undoubtedly leaves its traces, as does government propaganda elsewhere. Most striking in my interviews was that especially the younger interviewees uncritically repeated the voice of the Party on the issues of Tiananmen, Tibet and Taiwan. When asked for their feelings about June 4, 1989 (when they would have been around nine years old), some said:

> During that period, some counter-revolutionaries incited our youths, who are weak in their thoughts and easily become excited. (Qu Nian)

> At the beginning, the students only wanted to make the government's bureaucracy better, but then they were used by some counter-revolutionaries. Sometimes young students will overdo something, but soon they will do something to construct socialism. (Wei Wei)

Although students in their twenties usually did not repeat the voice of the Party, they refused to get involved in the issue. It belongs to the past and signifies a time when politics was pervasively integrated into daily life. Hung Xin is glad about the depoliticisation of everyday life: 'I think that during 1989, the political zeal of the people was quite high; since then, people just want to take care of their own things and feelings, it is a kind of shift. I think this is good, it's more realistic. I don't think a high political zeal is a good thing.'

Given the impact of the Cultural Revolution, the period when Chinese youths shared tremendous political zeal, it is not so surprising that today's youths want to take a step back from the political. Some look back to that political period with a certain jealousy and wish they could have joined it. Their hope is to bring back the political in the minds of Chinese youth. Yu Jie (in 1997 a 24-year-old student of Chinese literature at Beijing University) is an example of this. He is very vocal about the current political regime, and his aim is to express his ideas to as many people as possible; he told me he wants to 'enlighten' the people. In his view, the impact of June 4th on Chinese society has been great:

> As for the intellectuals, their attitude and methods have changed a lot. June 4th is like a cliff dividing two ages. If the movement hadn't failed, I think the thoughts and changes brought about by the reforms of the 1980s would've had a good influence on China, but now it's all been lost. June 4th is also a watershed in my life; before it I had no thoughts of my own, but since then I've begun to think independently.

With such an attitude, it's no wonder he feels quite lonely:

> Of course I feel disappointed and sad that Chinese youth is so much focused on money. I feel very lonely. Today I have few friends to talk with. But I have to analyze the condition rationally. People indeed care more about material life, which is good as we are still so poor and developing. Democracy and freedom are still far away from the common people in China.

Unlike others, who can hardly imagine that such events could happen again, he believes it is quite possible that the Party will face a similar challenge in the future:

> I can see unemployment and the poor state of Chinese peasants and the difference between city and country life, we also have different people in China, the minorities ... the government cannot solve these problems, so I think the possibility of another June 4th still exists.

He concisely summarises some major issues in contemporary China. The rural-urban divide and related issues of poverty, the suppression of minorities, and rising unemployment remain highly topical political issues in 2009. Yu Jie managed to publish a collection of essays entitled *Fire and Ice* (1998), and has since then published extensively and become one of China's most outspoken social critics. He claims his opposition to the regime to be rooted in Christianity, and when he met US president Bush in 2006 he asked him, with no result, to plead in China for more religious rights (Hoagland 2006: 7). Barmé discusses his book as one of the signs of a dawning of censorship in the late 1990s. 'Advertised as (...) Peking University's second 'Wang Xiaobo,' [Yu Jie] chose as his targets the autocratic habits of traditional Chinese culture and politics, fascism in twentieth-century Europe, and the suppression of free thought.' (Barmé 1999: 352) This was not without risk. Yu Jie was jailed for a short period in 2004.

Moreover, voices like his are rare; what dominates is a picture of a generation growing up under the scrutinising, demanding eyes of their parents. A generation having to live through an anything but ideal educational system, criticised for its sole insistence on memorising rather than thinking, and for whom politics is merely an unfashionable word, belonging to a complicated past. A generation, also, which often turns to music to navigate these circumstances in their everyday lives. As we have already seen from the letters of fans to their bands, music helps them to carve out their own space. Music has the power to move away from the pressures of parents, teachers and leaders, and as such is strongly related to generational difference; rock music in particular helps to distinguish oneself from the older generation. Music operates as a technology of the self, since it creates an alternative space for the young self to reflect upon life, to fantasise about alternatives to lifestyles offered by older people, and to explore ideologies which are not articulated at home, at school or by the state.

Music Preferences and Involvement

Having outlined the broader structures within which Chinese youth navigates, in the remaining part of this chapter I want to analyse, first, the importance of genre, returning to the pop-rock distinction; and second, to scrutinise how music is used for technologies of the self related to gender, to age, to place, to subjectivity and, finally, to politics. Again, it is my aim to let the youngsters speak, to return to theory only in the concluding part of this chapter.

The guiding principle in this section is again that music operates as a technology of the self. It does not just express a mood, it 'is a resource for the identification work of "knowing how one feels" – a building material of "subjectivity."' (DeNora 1999: 41) Music helps to organise and produce the self, the shifting of moods, the control of energy level, the mode of attention and concentration; it helps one to recollect and cope with memories and it negotiates one's engagement with the world (ibid.: 44). Music is part of the care of the self. It operates as a vehicle to move out of undesired states, and as such a technology of the self, it helps to build and manage subjectivities needed to navigate a society in strong flux, and perceived as highly competitive; a society in which traditions no longer provide a sense of security and grounding. Music is a tool in the reflexive project of the self, a way to manage individuality in a rapidly changing and highly demanding society.

Preferring a specific genre can already help to ground oneself a bit. The respondents were asked to indicate their appreciation of music genres ranging from Western classical music to Chinese rock on a progressive five-point scale. Figure 4.1 shows the popularity of the different genres among male and female respondents.

Figure 4.1 *Popularity of Music Genres*

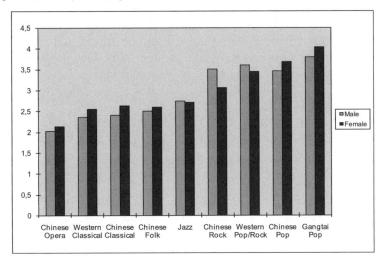

As expected, pop and rock music are most popular among Beijing youths. Female respondents tend to favour classical and pop music, whereas male respondents prefer rock. The gender difference, as indicated in Table 4.1, is striking: Rock remains predominantly a masculine genre, whereas pop is mainly favoured by females. These are statistically significant differences. Whereas in the US rock music is more popular than pop, in China, and most likely in East Asia, the roles are reversed (Hakanen & Wells 1993: 60). The gender differences between pop and rock audiences are also found in other studies.[8]

Table 4.1 *Music Preference*

Music preference	% (n = 650)	Male (%)	Female (%)
Chinese pop	36	39	61
Chinese rock	21	64	36
See no difference	23	49	51
No preference	20	55	45

A factor analysis on the question about the respondents' music preferences for nine different genres points to the coexistence of three musical territories, namely classical music (in which predominantly Chinese and Western classical music is represented); pop music from Hong Kong, Taiwan, or the mainland; and rock, in which Western pop and rock, and Chinese rock and jazz are represented (Table 4.2).[9]

Thus, the distinction between pop and rock returns in taste differences among the respondents, but a third taste ought to be included as well, namely classical music. As Figure 4.1 shows, this musical territory is least popular among Beijing youths. It can be argued that because of the stated genre distinctions in the question, this does not show that Chinese audiences group the same artists under rock as I do. However, Appendix II presents the factor analysis based on the respondents' opinions of different singers. Again, the distinction between Chinese rock and Chinese pop appeared, to which a third component (Western pop music) was added. The survey thus justifies speaking of three genre-related audiences.

To what extent do these three musical territories attract distinctive audiences? Does audience involvement differ? If by involvement we mean the time they spend listening to music, the number of cassette tapes they own, and the importance they attach to music, there appear to be differences between the different music audiences. There is a significant positive relationship between number of cassette tapes – at the time of the survey the main music medium in China – and a preference for rock music, whereas pop is slightly negatively correlated.[10] There is no significant relationship between classical music and number of cassettes. If we look at media consumption, the rock audience listens significantly longer to music compared to the pop audience, 53 minutes compared to 34 minutes respectively.[11] The audience showing no strong preference for either pop or rock spends around 34 minutes a day listening to music.[12]

Table 4.2 *Factor Analysis of Music Genres*

	Classical	Pop	Rock
Chinese classical music	0.777	-0.210	0.051
Chinese opera	0.705	-0.030	-0.036
Chinese folk music	0.778	0.143	-0.097
Western classical music	0.648	-0.193	0.225
Gangtai pop	-0.135	0.767	0.160
Chinese pop	-0.015	0.885	0.088
Western pop & rock	-0.098	0.062	0.795
Chinese rock	-0.081	0.374	0.681
Jazz	0.283	0.004	0.637

These figures present a clear picture among the three musical territories distinguished earlier. The respondents positioned in the rock territory are significantly more involved in music, in the sense that they
have more cassette tapes and spend more time listening to them. There
also is a strong and significant positive relationship between rock and
music as a topic of conversation among friends,[13] whereas such a relationship does not exist for either the classical or pop territory. Furthermore, the preference for rock is clearly gendered, and it is mainly preferred by the male respondents.

As I have shown in the previous chapters, the rock mythology is a
hard cultural force which produces distinct cultural scenes, involving articulations of musical selves enmeshed in specific imaginations and representations of authenticity and place. Rock is not that easy to listen
to; it is perceived by many Chinese to be noisy and uncomfortable, for
example by Hung Xin. She told me that rock *demands* more involvement from the audience:

> When you feel sad, or when you feel the need for something
> sweet, you can listen to pop. But you cannot have such an atti-
> tude for rock. When you listen to rock, you have to think about
> it, you have to sense what the singer wants to express, wants to
> convey to the audience – their anger, despair, hope, ambitions,
> these things.

Rock is here perceived to require more interpretative 'work' from the
listener. The rock mythology is a strong force of territorialisation, especially when compared with pop (Deleuze & Guattari 1987).[14] Thus,
especially when positioned in the rock territory, one is more likely to
talk about music. Rock facilitates stronger identification when compared to pop. It is used to articulate one's identity as well as to create
symbolic group boundaries. In his letter to Modern Sky, Li Huagang articulates the pleasure of talking about rock:

> I'm a rock and roll fan, and a lot of my friends are making rock
> music. We're all very concerned about the development of Chi-
> nese rock! The biggest pleasure in my life is to chat with my
> friends about music, about rock. You can imagine how happy I
> am to see that Chinese rock is developing so strongly ... rock mu-
> sic is our greatest love! It releases us, it satisfies us ...

He points to the pleasure of talking about rock and about his use of the
music: it releases him, the act of listening satisfies him emotionally, and
since he writes about 'us,' this is considered a communal act. Rock apparently creates a community. The stronger involvement rock demands

does, however, not imply that rock offers more, or better, or more distinctive technologies of the self. Rather, it offers a set of technologies
which partly overlaps with those of pop and classical music, while rock
partly generates a more unique set of technologies. For example, pop
speaks to feelings of romance, femininity, loneliness, ennui and sorrow,
more so than rock does (Fung &Curtin 2004; Moskowitz 2008). In
what follows, I would like to highlight five more distinct technologies of
the self enabled by rock music: technologies related to masculinity, to
age (being young), to place (coming from the mainland, perceiving
Beijing as the centre), to self-regulation and to politics. This overview is
not exhaustive, but highlights the most conspicuous technologies that
emerge from the materials.

The Gendered Self

Regression analysis shows that classical music is more attractive to
youths with a higher level of education, particularly girls, whereas pop
appeals more to youths with a lower level of education and to girls.
Rock appeals mostly to boys.[15] Within rock, there are also gender differences. In the survey, 49% of the men consider Cui Jian 'good,' in contrast to 27% of the women; for Tang Dynasty, these percentages are
40% and 14%, and for Zheng Jun 27% and 23%, respectively (see Appendix III).

Xie Wei (18) stresses his male identity by stating that he is a *rock
man*. The pop-rock distinction appears in his letter to heavy metal band
Overload:

> [My classmates] indulge themselves in their pure love for Hong
> Kong and Taiwan pop music. What pure love? It is only musical
> rubbish, catering to ignorant youth. Anyway, there're some
> young people like me who're trying hard to find the essence of
> music and to find the source of life.

Inspired by the rock mythology and related discourses of authenticity,
rock music is used as an identity marker, as a way to establish a taste
hierarchy with one's classmates, and at the same time, to link up with
other fans and the musicians.[16] Thus, a sense of both particularity and
communality is created. Along with their idol, they fight against pop, as
this fan expresses in a letter to Gao Qi, lead singer for Overload: 'Gao
Qi, you're so wild! Your scream has smashed the over-sweet sound of
pop!'

The narrative separating pop from rock intersects with the assertion
that authentic music cannot be commercial. In the words of Zhang

Min: 'In Hong Kong, people are more commercial, they might not be interested in rock music.'

It is not enough to know the language of rock; one ought to be *real*, according to Chen Li in a letter to Modern Sky:

> In this society, a lot of people turn rock'n'roll into a kind of talking capital. Someone who's humming Ling Dian [a pop-rock band] – once he notices a girl is coming over – starts talking loudly with his friends about Kurt Cobain, about London, Suede. It's ridiculous. But there are so many of this kind of people in our daily life ...

Apart from reifying the masculinity of rock by assuming that girls only like pop (and the example he uses is interesting, as Ling Dian is a pop-rock band, see chapter two), the importance of acknowledging the shared notions of authenticity is articulated by this fan. Knowledge of the global rock idiom is not a guarantee of acceptance. For Chen Li, to be considered a true rock fan one has to despise pop and be sincere when talking about rock. This sentiment is echoed in the words of 17-year-old high-school student Wei:

> Rock singers don't care about money and just play. Because of that, we distinguish them from *Gangtai* pop singers. We hate those pop fans. They're like servants, slaves that kneel before their owners. In rock, we can hear some true feelings. Pop fans admire a singer only because he has a certain style. If he were to change his style, he'd be criticised, whereas rock fans are more tolerant and open.

Value judgments are much less harsh the other way round. Pop fans indicate they dislike rock because it is too noisy, but do not downplay it in other terms, like Xue Mei, a 19-year-old woman, who told me: 'I don't like rock: I think it's disorderly. I like peaceful music, and I like to listen to music alone, not with others.'

As mentioned before, within rock there are strong gendered differences. The heroic masculinity as performed by Tang Dynasty speaks significantly more to boys than to girls; that is, boys can identify with the 'leather jacket – motorcycle' poses, whereas such articulations of masculinity appeal less to girls. The same goes for the tough pose of Cui Jian. His rebellious attitude is significantly less appealing to the female audience. 'Softer' and more innocent-looking rock singers, such as folk-rock star Zheng Jun, are attractive to both boys and girls. The regular-guy aesthetics of folk produces a masculinity that is less loud; instead, the singer creates a sphere of closeness which appeals to all audiences. The same goes for female pop singers like Faye Wong; her image – that of a modern urban girl who is in control of her life – appeals to both girls and boys. Music choices affirm dominant gender roles, rather than challenge them. This can likewise be translated into a technology of the self, in that music facilitates gendered performances of the self.

Many boys write about their desire to become friends with the heavy metal bands; they ask for telephone numbers and such items as posters. The rock singer is treated as more than just a close friend; he or she is a hero, someone to worship. The masculinity of rock, intersecting with its perceived authenticity, appears clearly in the poem written by a 15-year-old boy, Zhang Yu, and dedicated to Overload:

> Overload, you are the light in my heart that never dims
> You are the embodiment of my ancestors from a long time ago
> You are the herald of power and courage
> You give me the courage to be a man
> You teach me the truth of this world

The fan uses the music to inform his gender identity and, in line with the rock mythology, the music is considered to tell 'the truth of this world.' It shows once again the power of the music, how a band speaks to the audience. It is crucial here to realise that he is writing, just like the boy quoted earlier who states he is a *rock man*, to a heavy metal band. The chivalric aesthetics of heavy metal are addressed to boys. The harder a sound, the more it caters to masculine identifications.

Generational Differences

A preference for rock is also a performance linked to age: many respondents claim rock to be a sound for young people, in contrast to pop. I have already shown how music is used to create an alternative space separate from parents and teachers – and it is particularly rock that facilitates such generationally-driven technologies of the self. According to Qing Ming, rock is used to distinguish oneself from the older generation: 'Old people will of course not like rock. It's a kind of distinction for the young people. They want to make their own style. But I know that some of my friends' parents think Cui Jian is acceptable, but like He Yong...never!'

Hung Xin believes that rock is used to mark a certain *rite de passage*, to deal with the period of becoming adult:

We're all young people and we have the same psychological experience. Young people are eager to become mature and to become what older people want them to be, but there's still a long
time to go. During that time you have to experience fear, anger,
jealousy, you know, just something you want to express, to pour
out. And Zheng Jun is doing that very well, without imitation,
without disguise; he just cries out.

Rock is related to generational differences. It caters to the emotional,
the young, new and alternative, but also to the disorderly and unfinished. Pop is believed to be incapable of articulating generational differences. As Qu Nian put it, 'Rock is suitable for young people; pop is
liked by all people, my grandparents, my parents, and me.'

The picture that emerges so far is not that of a fleeting audience, but
rather of fairly clearly demarcated music cultures in which in particular
rock is used as a marker of distinction, which comes with an obligation
to perform one's taste. Age and gender are most strongly related to music preferences. The performance of taste is a performance of authenticity, linked to a critique of commercialisation and to an anxiety towards,
if not critique of, the ideologies promoted by the older generation.

This generational difference is articulated in a rather ironic style in a
letter to the band The Fly. Here, Wang Jinshen, a secondary-school student, draws an analogy with the Communist Party. He writes in a *dakou*
style:

I see hope, hope that the alternative will subvert the mainstream,
hope that the underground will usurp the upper ground. It's
time we learnt from the Communist Party, that is, to develop
from an underground party into the ruling party, and finally to
dictatorship. We should also leave the underground and bring
forward an earthquake and let all the structures on the ground
fucking collapse. Therefore, when finances allow, we must use
every commercial trick: packaging, promoting, and marketing.
This is not losing our dignity, but only a strategy to secure our
basis. The day when The Fly sells a million copies, when Modern
Sky is richer than Shanghai Audio-Visual, when an ordinary factory worker hums "Nirvana" [a song by The Fly], we will have
reached our goal. We won't get depressed when we're old. Don't
worry, we have a bright future. China's *guoqing* [national charac-
teristics] are changing, they're becoming more and more open.
Youth's ability to appreciate and accept is increasing. Those stu-
pid fans who believe in marketing and sales will finally be captured...

By using communist tactics for the Great Long March of rock'n'roll, the underground can overtake the mainstream, a politicised mainstream, and not only pop music, but 'all the structures on the ground [will] fucking collapse.' The future belongs to the young, in his rhetoric. Interestingly, both reviewers from Taiwan and Feng Jiangzhou of The Fly make the same analogy. The univocality of these readings is emblematic of the semiotic power of rock.

Place and Belonging

Place is a third axis through which rock audiences distinguish themselves and motivate their musical preferences. Like the musicians, the rock fans position themselves vis-à-vis pop. And pop at the same time symbolises Hong Kong and Taiwan:

> We have to admit that Chinese recording techniques are much better than those in Hong Kong or Taiwan. (...) Your emergence is the new starting point of Chinese and Asian culture. It is a great comfort to us that rock music saved us from the suffocating sea of pop music from Hong Kong and Taiwan. (Zhou Zhou, 15-year-old male student, in a letter to Overload)

Music plays an important role in the production of locality; it gives audiences a sense of place, of belonging (Biddle & Knight 2007; Chow & De Kloet 2008; Stokes 1994). The audience uses the music to negotiate place, that is, mainland China and Beijing. Pop can also be used to negotiate place; fans of Leon Lai, for example, relate to his music in ways that reveal a strong sense of belonging to Hong Kong; fans use his work 'to gain a sense of home, to become part of a community that is neither fluid nor transnational, but one that is instead profoundly rooted and quite fixed.'(Chow & De Kloet 2008: online) There is nothing peculiarly Chinese or Asian about this; the same study showed how fans of a Dutch pop icon, Marco Borsato, relate to his music in ways that betray a specific sense of Dutchness. In other words, even when sound and lyrics are by and large similar across the globe, pop icons are appropriated in intricate ways that help to produce a sense of locality, of home.

Listeners living in Beijing may prefer *Gangtai* pop for its cosmopolitan image, for example, take Olivia. When I interviewed her, she told me that life in Beijing is too slow for her, that she doesn't like the tempo of the city. She is highly critical of contemporary Chinese society: The educational system is bad, the economic reforms are too slow, and the political system is outdated. Most youth I spoke to are proud to live in Beijing, but Olivia feels differently: 'I think it's funny. Most people say that Hong Kong has no culture, but that Beijing does. Culture belongs more to the past. I think contemporary China has no culture (..) I think that Hong Kong is now better than Beijing.'

When we got around to rock music, she said she doesn't like it at all. Her appreciation of Hong Kong is articulated in her music preferences. 'I think [mainland pop singers] just want to imitate those from Hong Kong and Taiwan; they don't have their own style. And their imitation is not good, so people feel kind of disgusted. The melody is much worse than those from Hong Kong and Taiwan.'

Dissatisfaction with the current social and political realities is negotiated through *Gangtai* pop, rather than rock. Her strongest preference is for Western pop music – e.g. the Spice Girls (*La Mei*) and the Backstreet Boys – thus echoing her desire to study abroad. Others are even more specific and distinguish Beijing from other big cities in China. Huang Shan, for example, told me: 'Beijing is an ancient city with a long history, very different from Guangzhou or Shanghai. Maybe because Beijing is the capital it can produce such an angry kind of music.'

In his words, both the image of Beijing as signifying the richness of Chinese culture and its current role as the political and administrative centre of China are considered beneficial for rock music. The articulation of place, signifying culture, returns in discussions about whether or not Chinese rock can be considered a mere imitation of its Western counterpart. Qin Ming was disappointed after she heard Western rock, and felt that Chinese rock is merely a bleak imitation: 'Before I listened to Western rock, I thought Chinese rock was very good. But by and by, as I listened to Western rock, I found that Chinese rock is so much alike that I can't bear it.'

Most youths disagree with her. Although 31% of the respondents agreed with the statement that Chinese rock is a copy of Western rock, 69% disagreed. According to Zhang Ming, Chinese musicians imitate Western pop; she considers Faye Wong to be a copy of Enya. In her view, Cui Jian and Tang Dynasty do not imitate – they make Chinese music. The attempt by musicians to localise rock, being a hard cultural form, proves successful at the moment of reception. Kasper's opinion of NO's underground sound (a sound which, as I argued in chapter one, belongs to the 'harder' forms of rock), are revealing. 'NO's music has a lot of things. If you're not Chinese, you can't totally understand NO. I think NO's music is totally Chinese.'

Audiences consider Chinese rock to be more Chinese than Chinese pop is. Rock thus gains cultural legitimacy; it is accepted as it reasserts notions of cultural difference. Traditional Chinese instruments and adaptations of minority music in Chinese rock were often referred to by the respondents as signifying the Chineseness of the music. Cui Jian, Tang Dynasty, and Zheng Jun are favourite examples of how Chinese rock is not a mere imitation.

Li Tian believes that Chinese musicians do a good job in adding a Chinese flavour to Western rock. 'At first, Chinese rock learned from the West, but it has gradually created its own style. Cui Jian's music is very different from the West, especially his music style. Although he used Chinese traditional instruments, his music is very different from traditional music.'

Music preferences are connected to gender and age as well as to the production of place. Music is used to articulate a sense of both longing and belonging: in the case of rock, a longing for authenticity, for honesty, as well as a longing to be, or to become, a real man, together with a *belonging* to a specific place, Beijing. These are technologies of the self. Technologies which intersect with patterns of distinction; the masculinity of rock marginalises the feminine, and the centring of Beijing disregards Hong Kong as a plastic city.

Building Subjectivity

Music is an important tool for self-regulation in a society that seems to be in perpetual flux. My survey included two statements directly related to emotional uses of music, namely 'I listen to music to calm down' and 'I listen to music to boost my mood'. Correlations with the first statement are low. There is a negative relationship between classical music and listening in order to boost one's mood; this relation is reversed, but weaker, for rock.[17] I asked Qin Ming about when she listens to classical music. She replied, 'When I'm angry or depressed, I play classical music and by and by I feel serene. When I'm feeling too lazy or too quiet, I listen to rock.'

Others, like Zhi Yong, however, indicate they use rock to cope with depression. 'I find listening to rock an effective way to ease my depression. (..) Modern China is a competitive society, and this makes people more aggressive. Sometimes it makes me tired and I feel depressed.'

Classical music is used for calming down and concentrating, whereas rock is used to boost one's mood. Both are used to deal with depressed feelings. Bai Fan wrote to Overload to explain how they had opened up a new world for him:

> I'm very excited, a new blood came into my body (...) I want to release myself and to hide myself. I am interested not only in your music style, but also in your appearance, long hair to your

shoulders, very cool. I want to copy it, but my school doesn't permit students to have long hair.

Sometimes, however, it may annoy the family and disturb the precious harmony. In his letter to Overload, Li Zixu writes:

> This world is too hypocritical. Every time I see my depressed face in the mirror I feel helpless and at a loss. At moments like this I will listen to your songs and turn up the volume and drift away on your music. My family don't want me to listen to such music, they want me to be quiet and study hard.

Rock is supposed to disturb harmony and disrupt one's bright future, and thus has to be silenced. Rock, in his words, represents a place to hide, more than a place to fight. But for some, music does help when making important decisions, as Li Junjun wrote in his letter to Tang Dynasty:

> Tang Dynasty, how are you? By and by I became fascinated [by your music], I can even listen to your tape more than a dozen times a day. I have come to know the meaning of heavy metal and understand that this is what I had longed for for so long. (...) Last February, I resigned from my job, my mother couldn't understand, I felt very annoyed.

This boy felt strengthened by the music, and dared to quit his job. It might be fair to say that the chivalric aesthetics of the heavy metal band Tang Dynasty helped him to resist the dominant value of remaining loyal to your boss. In particular, the hard sounds of heavy metal and underground music bring out stories of emotional release and excitement. Zhang Hongbin attended a performance of The Fly and then wrote to Modern Sky in April 1999:

> Every movement of Feng Jiangzou was so unusual, especially his weird costume which was absolutely rebellious. And the silver powder sprayed all over his body and his dirty hair constructed a most punk, most rebellious musician. We have finally tasted the decadent art so rare in China, as well as the kind of sound so readily labelled 'filthy' by the media. In The Fly's music, one will never find any sound of hypocrisy and trendiness.

The music is considered authentic – as it is never hypocritical – and pure punk, which here is equated with rebelliousness. The vulgar aesthetics of The Fly, like the chivalric aesthetics of Tang Dynasty, is a strong force of territorialisation; it shocks people, and those who like to be shocked are drawn into an underground world, as expressed by the following fan:

> I have just listened to The Fly. It feels like a release, like leaving an unlit village toilet ... Two things shock me: first, Feng Jiang-zou's lyrics, and second his singing style ... Although I've been listening to Western rock and roll for more than a year, the linguistic barrier makes it difficult for us to relate to their anger. But now I've finally listened to real Chinese underground music. I'm so excited. (Cong Ling, a female secondary-school student from Beijing)

The excitement provoked by The Fly is very different from the intimate sphere that folk produces. For example, take the emotion in this letter from 18-year-old female student Xu Li to Zhang Chu:

> The day before yesterday, a very, very big event happened: Deng Xiaoping died. I feel very sad because I feel as if I have lost someone to depend on. Deng is a very important character in Chinese history. I think I will only use the word 'great' to describe him. Mao Zedong was also an outstanding man; he was talented and brave and did a lot for the founding of new China, but he was a myth, too far away from us. (...) [Deng Xiaoping] was charming and had his own principles, he knew how to grasp opportunities and did not overdo things. I feel a sense of awe, of sadness and of loss in my heart.

This girl shares her feelings of loss with Zhang Chu after the death of Deng Xiaoping. In her case, the rock star is treated as a close, personal friend with whom one discusses personal feelings. As explained in chapter two, the folk aesthetics produces a discourse of authenticity based on notions of equality and normality. Not surprisingly, this female fan writes about her personal worries rather than her admiration for Zhang Chu. Consequently, different scenes feed into different technologies of the self: in folk, the musician is transformed into a friend, the sounds are used to survive hard times, and the words inspire retrospection. Unlike the heavy metal singers, the folk singers are not heroes. Instead, they are friends with whom the audience – both male and female (in terms of gender, folk is more inclusive) – shares feelings of nostalgia, a longing for an easy life, for the tranquillity of the countryside. In the case of pop, the music cannot only be used to articulate a sense of cosmopolitan belonging, but is also used to negotiate feelings of romance, loneliness, ennui and sorrow (Fung & Curtin 2004; Moskowitz 2008).

The Political Self

When Leng Ling refers to the filthy society, she clearly shares Feng Jiangzhou's critique, and his politics of cultural pollution: 'I believe they [The Fly] are the most real and the most honest human beings. They refuse to compromise with this filthy society. They just make their own music and go their own way – their courage is admirable.' (Leng Ling from Shenzhen)

When audiences are asked about the political implications of rock, it is predominantly the name of Cui Jian that pops up. Although other bands – such as Zu Zhou, Tongue and Re-TROS – also articulate clear political views and critiques, it is Cui Jian that has reached out to a wide audience, which explains my decision to focus intently here on the response to his oeuvre. Most youths like Cui Jian for his first two albums, which were released in 1989 and 1991. Some of his songs have become part of the collective memory of Chinese youth. According to 22-year-old Qin Ming, Cui Jian is best capable of expressing political issues.

> Cui Jian is good at integrating politics into his music. It's the real situation, people are very interested in politics because of Mao Zedong, because of the Communist Party. The words to 'A piece of red cloth' [one of his songs] assert that Chinese people have been cheated, that they thought they were heading for a better life, a perfect society, yet later found that they had been wrong.

Shik Shak is the leader of a student rock group at Beijing University. The decision to adopt such a weird pseudonym indicates his attempt to be different. During their weekly gatherings, they watch music videos and discuss rock music. At times they have to fool the University authorities; for example, in order to be allowed to show a Guns and Roses video, they said the tape demonstrated how to play an electric guitar. The group has around 50 members. Cui Jian is one of Shik Shak's favorite singers:

> I think all Chinese youth felt like me, that Cui Jian expressed the things from our heart. I think his music reflects the true feelings of the common people, compared with the so-called pure love in pop music. Now I think rock in China has lost this spirit, the

spirit of the common people. Many people use rock as a way to say 'Oh, I'm different; I play rock.'

Qin Ming – the girl who identifies with the political issues Cui Jian dares to confront – shares his feelings and also speaks of the decline of Chinese rock during the 1990s. 'Singers like Wang Lei and Dou Wei don't care about national affairs, nor about this world; they only care about themselves. Yet they don't know why they're so lonely, why they're so bound by the world, so I don't like the recent rock singers very much. Their sight is limited.'

Those who identify with the political agenda of Cui Jian, who consider his music an authentic expression of the concerns of 'common people,' are critical of new bands as they are believed to be less sincere. Their narratives evoke a sense of temporality. Cui Jian brings back memories of an idealised past, when politics ranked high on the agenda, and the forces of marketisation, globalisation and individualisation were less overwhelming than they have been since the mid-1990s. However, many rock fans dislike political content. Huang Shan inverts the narrative of Shik Shak:

> Cui Jian's songs are too political. Tang Dynasty and Dou Wei just describe life, so I understand them much more. I listen to music to relax. If you add political factors, that's not relaxing; it makes me feel tired. (...) Before the 1990s, the media talked about politics all the time, so we had to pay attention to it, but now we have more things to do. We can watch TV and care about sports and music, our life is richer than before. It is natural that we care less about politics now.

Thus, there is a certain erasure of possible political interpretations of rock music, which explains why Cui Jian, as China's most political rocker, lost so much of his audience during the 1990s. For the younger generation, like 19-year-old Mei Lin, he is simply too old. 'Cui Jian is very famous, but I haven't listened too much to him; he's part of the past, he's too old.'

Finally, some criticise Cui Jian for becoming famous and losing the 'true' rock spirit, as Yin Zheng explains in his letter to Modern Sky: 'Some may say: Well, we also have punk in the Chinese market, for instance, Cui Jian. But according to me, Cui Jian is no longer punk. He has already become an accessory to commercialisation; he has betrayed the essence of punk.'

Cui Jian evokes images of the 1980s, and is the only rock singer who has reached an immense audience via his music. The political metaphors in his songs have inspired the young generation of the 1980s.

What remains today are the nostalgic memories of those days. Cui Jian is above all a politicised rock star, a predicament that has brought him fame, both in and outside China, yet constrains him. To his audience, it provides ways to articulate the political, as well as to recapture memories of a past.

Technology and Control

Listening to music is a reflexive and performative act. Sounds are integrated into lives and used as technologies of the self. The audience is engaged in a constant dialogue with musicians, and music is used as an important topic of conversation among friends, as a way to enact one's identity. Music provides 'a rich array of cultural resources for self-constitution and reconstitution over time (...) [its] properties may contribute to or colour the shape and quality of social experience, self-perception and emotion. Music is not merely a sign of existing states but is a building material of those states; it is bound up with the very weft of experience in the making.' (DeNora 1999: 53-54) Rock serves as a marker of distinction that produces a sense of identity, belonging and community; rock is portrayed as a better, more authentic, less commercial sound when compared to pop.

The preference for rock produces a taste hierarchy in which rock is positioned as better than pop: the latter is considered commercial, shallow and girlish. This resembles very much Thornton's observations on the gendered house versus pop divide. 'Among youth cultures, there is a double articulation of the lowly and the feminine: disparaged *other* cultures are characterised as feminine *and* girls' cultures are devalued as imitative and passive. Authentic culture is, by contrast, depicted in gender-free or masculine terms *and* remains the prerogative of boys' (Thornton 1995: 104-105). Rock is said to express true feelings; pop fans are looked down upon as they are mere slaves of the stars. Such taste hierarchies are increasingly being produced *within* popular culture, rather than proliferating along the high culture versus low culture axis (Thornton 1995).

Taste is a performance (Kuipers 2006), and from the interviews it seems that particularly the rock audience feels the need to perform their taste, and critique pop. This performance is linked to authenticity and gender: the rock audience becomes more real and more masculine through their taste. Music thus reinforces gender hierarchies and stereotypes. This can also be turned around, by claiming that pop can be used to negotiate femininity. In their work on pop diva Faye Wong, Fung & Curtin argue that she is highly 'influential among adolescents and young women, she has not only become a figure for textual identification but also a polysemic icon for cultural aspirations and feminist projects throughout Greater China.'(Fung & Curtin 2004: 263) In his study of Mandapop audiences in Shanghai and Taipei, Moskowitz shows how Mandapop 'provides a means of communicating more honestly than everyday speech and culture allows. The songs allow people in Taiwan to express loneliness, isolation and anomie.' (Moskowitz 2008: 379) Melancholy and loneliness are strong tropes in Mandapop. These themes speak to Chinese audiences across the straits as well as globally. Thus not only rock but also Mandapop (and similarly, other genres like Western music and classical music) is used as 'a device or resource to which people turn in order to regulate themselves as aesthetic agents (...) achieving this regulation requires a high degree of reflexivity; the perceived "need" for regulation (...) emerges with reference to the exigencies and situational "demands" made upon [the respondents].' (DeNora 2000: 62)

It is my contention that these demands are even stronger for Chinese youth, when compared to their Western peers, both for the *dakou* generation on which this chapter has focused, as well as for the subsequent generation from the 1980s. The demands imposed upon youth by the educational system, the family, and the state, in conjunction with global capitalism, produce new regimes of living in which new post-socialist if not neoliberal subjectivities are created. These subjectivities are flexible, reflexive selves which need to be able to survive in the condition of compressed modernity, in which reality seems in constant flux, and the iron rice bowl of youth has been smashed into numerous pieces and replaced by the perpetual tyranny of the new. Such uncertain times require new belongings, new spaces that youth carve out for themselves, distinct technologies of the self – for which music is of crucial importance.

The constitutive forces of rock such as the claim on authenticity (a claim constructed in different ways for different scenes within rock), the negotiation of place, its catering to masculine identifications and its articulation of generational fault lines are forces of territorialisation creating a strong sense of belonging. The rock mythology, intersecting with its arguably loud sound, is a strong force of territorialisation – rock *demands* more involvement. Audiences located in the rock territory are significantly more involved in the music compared to those located in the pop and the classical territories.

Music is used as a technology of the self; these technologies facilitate reflexivity and help to gain a sense of *control* – albeit often imaginary and only temporarily, a control moreover that often involves the sharing of experiences with peers – over life. It gives a sense of control over the political; Cui Jian can be 'used' to perform a longing for political resistance, The Fly to parody the political, and a dislike of Cui Jian often signifies a disavowal of the political. Music is used to gain a sense of control over gender, so a preference for heavy metal often indicates a strong identification with a heroic masculinity. Music preferences give a sense of control over place, and help create a sense of home and belonging. At a regional level, a preference for rock often indicates the centring of mainland China, at times together with Taiwan, vis-à-vis Hong Kong. Music helps to deal with the anxieties produced by the demands of parents and teachers, and thus gives a perceived sense of control over another generation. A preference for pop at times carries a critique of such constructions, and presents a longing for a modern, cosmopolitan, urban lifestyle in which politics is merely a word belonging to the past. Music is used to gain a sense of control over oneself; some listen to rock to release their energy, and others listen when they are depressed. Music helps to build subjectivity in a society which imposes multiple demands upon its youth. Music is used to gain a sense of control over the past; a preference for Cui Jian often signifies a longing for the 1980s.

There are multiple technologies of the self enabled by music; this chapter has only outlined the technologies that were most conspicuous in the materials under study. Though there is more, there is always more, as May argues in his introduction to Deleuze: 'However we live, there is always more. We do not know of what a body is capable, nor how it can live. The alternatives of contentment (*I have arrived*) and hopelessness (*There is nowhere to go*) are two sides of the same misguided thought: that what is presented to us is what there is. There is more, always more.' (May 2005: 172) There is more to pop, with its articulations of romance, loneliness and camp, than I have been able to show in this chapter. There is more to the live performances of music. In the case of rock, these involve an outburst of liminal energy, in which performer and audience come together to perform the almost sacred shared ritual of music making. The energy that filled MAO bar during the performance of Queen Sea Big Shark in May 2008, the pogo dance in front of the stage, the collective singing of the line 'money fucker money fucker,' these moments and spaces enable affective and bodily technologies of the self deserving of further study (see Field & Groenwegen 2008). There is more, the shared embodied performance of pop through karaoke at home as well as in karaoke bars deserves further scrutiny, as a technology of the self that seems conspicuously more popular in the Asian context as compared to the West (Otake & Hosokawa 2005). There is more, also, in the diasporic use of Chinese music worldwide. Cyberscenes emerge through which a diasporic Chinese community establishes worldwide connections mediated through their preferences for pop or rock.

Music is used to gain a sense of control over the uncontrollable. It provides ways to depoliticise a politicised life – a life in which both the educational system and the family system are politicised. Even an erasure of political interpretations is a political act in itself. I am therefore bound to conclude with a contradiction. Rock facilitates technologies of the self; rock is part of the reflexive project of the self, which is a continuous process, during which symbolic boundaries are perpetually being drawn and contested. Audiences are on the one hand trapped in the rock mythology, and on the other hand they are constantly involved in re-articulations of the same mythology. Rock simultaneously contains and liberates, and its power lies in this very ambiguity.

5   Producing, Localising and Silencing Sounds

> I pass through this city of mass production,
> through hundreds of neon lights at Jianguomen,
> through automatic teller machines and stock market terminals, ...
> through the end of the twentieth century when we are about to be thrown
> into a money blender ...
> I look at myself which is increasingly not myself,
> but I cannot find myself.
> *Baojiajie 43, Collapse, 1998*

Seductive Narratives

In this song, singer Wang Feng from the band Baojiajie 43 expresses a global concern that assumes commercialisation to be harmful to creativity. The artist collapses along with the world when thrown into the money-blender called society. This assumption is often accompanied by nostalgia for the good old days, when everything was pure, wonderful, and authentic. All that is considered authentic melts into the thin air of commercialism. Money corrupts the true rock spirit. The early rock bands of China represent the real rock spirit; their pure and authentic voices are not yet disturbed by the cruel forces of a market economy. The new bands only go for the money. The critical voice is most likely to be silenced.

Following this line of argument, Barmé writes disapprovingly that 'Cui Jian found the market, whether in political or commercial guise, to be an indulgent if fickle master' (1999: 361). The general line in his work is that commodification signifies a full stop to subversion and rebellion. According to Steen, 'the engagement towards the Long March of Rock'n'Roll evaporates, it becomes impossible to identify [rock] with provocative ideals' (1996: 237). Jones argues along the same lines, and states that 'rock music's gradual absorption into China's burgeoning market economy has defused much of its politically oppositional potential' (1994: 149). Chinese rock musicians often express similar opinions. As Cui Jian told me:

I think that companies make the star bands. It's very commercial, all about money, and they [record company Magic Stone] did
a pretty good job at that. So many bands, they used to have some
heart, but after they signed they lost their heart and only go for
the money.

The rock mythology produces a narrative – in both China and the West
– that interprets the record industry and related forces of commercialisation that are assumed to have swept over China during the 1990s as
being hostile to the 'true rock spirit.'

Over the course of the 1990s, the state was deeply implicated in the
profoundly intertwined processes of commercialisation and transnationalisation. *The people* gradually turned into *consumer-citizens*. In the
words of Jing Wang, 'Contrary to conventional wisdom, transnational
capital not only did not weaken the Chinese post socialist state, but its
intensifying presence since 1989 has rescued a regime that barely
emerged from the crisis of confidence after the Tiananmen crackdown.
It was transnationalism that opened a space for the state to intervene.'
(Wang 2001: 95; see also Fung 2008; J. Wang 2008; Zhao 2008) How
though are we to understand the assumed commercialisation and transnationalisation of the music industry, and the role of the nation-state?
This chapter engages with this question by reflecting upon market developments, the role of regional and local record companies and the
forces of censorship.

Based on an analysis of music sales, plus more than twenty interviews
with people working in the music industry, this chapter questions the assumed commercialisation of the music market. It shows how the state,
the industry and rock culture are mutually dependent upon and thus implicated by each other. I will first show how the development of the music market does not show any sign of a big or growing market, or an intense commercialisation. The particularities of the Chinese record industry, in combination with regional and global capital flows, have created,
to adopt the jargon of the Party, a market with Chinese characteristics.

Secondly, I will show how cultural considerations and imaginations
play an important role in the entry and departure of regional record
companies, and the emergence of local ones. By the end of the 1990s,
local companies had gained in importance at the expense of regional
competitors. Although regional companies are at pains to localise rock,
local companies aim to globalise the sound. This local turn signifies, I
will argue, a desire to become truly global or transnational.

Thirdly, to further probe into the relationships between the state, producers and rock culture, I will explore how censorship is both a limiting
and a productive force. I wish to move beyond a top-down, hegemonic
view in which state power is interpreted as suppressing music cultures

in China. Instead, I argue for a dialectical view on power by presenting the tactics used by musicians and the industry to negotiate their way through the regulations. Censorship is more a playground than a political battlefield.

Market Fantasies

For centuries, the size of China's population has invited an easy exaggeration of its market potential. Even if one reaches only a small part of the youth market in China, profits are bound to be huge.[1] In a time when record sales in the West are declining steadily, China triggers the fantasy of companies, as Peter Grosslight, head of music for the William Morris Agency, states. 'China is on the tip of everybody's tongue. There's 1.3 billion people there. It's becoming a much wealthier place. How can we ignore that?' (in Sisaro 2007: online) A best-selling artist might well sell millions of albums on the mainland. No wonder, then, that while witnessing the blossoming of the Chinese rock culture in the early 1990s, record companies, mainly from Hong Kong and Taiwan, became increasingly interested in the production of Chinese rock. However, reality turned out to be far less profitable, particularly regarding the production of rock, and companies which entered the market in the early 1990s, were pulling out of it by the end of the decade. Instead, local companies such as Jingwen, Scream (a subsidiary of Jingwen), Modern Sky, and New Bees gained importance in the production of rock, whereas companies like the Huayi Brothers (*huayi xiongdi*) and Music Nation (*daguo wenhua*) are important producers of pop in the Mainland.

China is more an importer rather than exporter of music, according to Keane (2007: 117); quoting 2004 copyright statistics, in 2004, China imported 331 items of audio productions, while it exported four items. In China, 40 per cent of the music has a domestic origin, while 55 per cent has a regional (45 per cent) and international origin (10 per cent); for Hong Kong these figures are 34 per cent and 56 per cent respectively, while for Taiwan these are 54 per cent and 38 per cent respectively. Taiwan thus has comparatively the strongest domestic music market of the three, whereas Hong Kong's is mostly oriented towards international music.[2] The share of domestic repertoire has declined over the years in both China and Hong Kong – in China from 51 per cent in 2001 to 40 per cent in 2004, in Hong Kong from 47 per cent in 2001 to 34 per cent in 2005, while it rose slightly in Taiwan from 50 per cent to 54 per cent. To compare, in Japan 74 per cent consists of domestic repertoire, while in the US this is 93 per cent. Yet, for the Netherlands, only 16 per cent of the music market consists of domestic repertoire –

indicating that within the more peripheral West, Anglo-Saxon music dominates much more as compared to Asia (figures from IFPI 2006).

In other words, music cultures positioned culturally closer to the An-glo-Saxon centre of popular music will develop a less vital domestic mu-sic scene when compared to music cultures positioned further away from the centre. But the increased dominance of international repertoire in both Hong Kong and China may hint at a homogenising trend, in which global music cultures are becoming more dominated by the An-glo-Saxon music world. Yet the solid and stable position of domestic mu-sic in Taiwan, Japan and South Korea (in the latter two countries, the do-mestic repertoire makes up 75 per cent and 65 per cent respectively of the market, figures that have remained stable over the years (IFPI 2006)) indicates that cultural globalisation is not that straightforward; some places – two of which are interestingly enough located on an island – have developed music cultures that seem more resistant to the forces of globalisation (in terms of repertoire, not necessarily in terms of styles, nor in terms of production). Following Chua (2004), it seems more ac-curate to consider popular music as an important force in the emergence of a pan-Asian cultural sphere, with Taiwan as its key production site.

Seventy per cent of the global music industry is in the hands of four record companies (IFPI 2006),[3] i.e. EMI, Sony-BMG, Universal, and Warner. Their important regional competitors in the 'Greater China' re-gion are Rock Records from Taiwan and the Emperor Group (EEG) and East Asia in Hong Kong.[4] The case of EMI is interesting. In 2008 they decided to pull out of the East Asian market and delegate their activities to Gold Label Records in Hong Kong. This indicates that local produ-cers have gained in importance in the production of Mandapop and Cantopop. With the exception of a few releases, the local Beijing-based rock companies are too small to be considered substantial competitors.

Still, global capital plays an important role in the production of local and regional music cultures, particularly in pop music (Fung 2006; Weber 2003). Global record companies recognise the need to localise their products in order to gain a considerable market share. They also play on specific local sentiments and thus produce nationalistic narra-tives. For example, Channel V (part of Murdoch's Star TV) has the fol-lowing slogan: 'A composite portrait of mankind today: 7 per cent Black, 36 per cent Caucasian, 57 per cent Asian, the face of the earth is Asian. Channel V – Star TV Music.'

A 'Western' company is consciously marginalising the West and cov-ering up global power imbalances under a disturbing blanket of cultural essentialism. The deification of Asian culture is employed here as a marketing tool.

The US and Japan are the world biggest music markets. Table 5.1 presents an overview of various countries, including their ranking on the 2005 sales list.

The retail value of 'Greater China' – that is, the total retail value of China, Taiwan, and Hong Kong put together – amounted to US $ 308 million in 2005, in a market that is even smaller than the Dutch one![5] China's market amounts to only 28 per cent of the Dutch and 0.97 per cent of the US market. For the time being, although the mainland music market might be huge in terms of potential customers, it is less so in terms of its retail value. Furthermore, resonating with a global decline in retail value – between 1996 and 2002, the retail value of global sales dropped from US $ 39.8bn to US $ 31bn, with an average annual decrease of 3.5 per cent (Liang 2004: 84) – the market in Greater China also declined steadily, as Table 5.2 shows.

Table 5.1   *2005 World Music Sales Ranking (IFPI 2006)*

Country	US$m Retail Value	Ranking
USA	12,269	1
Japan	5,448	2
UK	3,446	3
Germany	2,210	4
France	1,990	5
The Netherlands	431	12
India	156	21
Taiwan	109	23
China	120	27
Hong Kong	79	31
Indonesia	67	35

Table 5.2   *Retail Value Recorded Music Sales (US$m) 1995-2005 (IFPI 1999, 2000, 2005)*[1]

	1995	1996	1997	1998	1999	2000	2001	2002	2003	2004	2005
China	(178)	(188)	127	103	94	101	134	165	200	133	120
Hong Kong	(183)	231	175	118	99	108	109	99	93	81	79
Taiwan	336	415	427	320	307	240	192	174	150	148	109
Greater China	(697)	(834)	729	541	500	449	435	438	392	318	268
US	12,100	12,298	11,906	13,193	14,251	14,805	13739	12,609	11,847	12,506	12,269
Japan			6,741	6,510	6,033	6,445	6,272	5,689	5,164	5,360	5,448
Netherlands	716	660	607	561	522	455	623	584	550	516	430

[1] For China, the 1996/1997 figures and for Hong Kong the 1995/1996 are not comparable, which is why these figures are put between brackets. Chinese figures are estimates, they are at most an indication. The 2004 figures are reported on a different basis to previous years, which explains the sudden drop. Figures up to 1999 are based on IFPI (1999, 2000), the 2000 figures are based on IFPI (2004), while the figure from 2001 to 2005 are based on IFPI (2006).

The Hong Kong market reached its peak in 1995 and then declined, but the Taiwanese market underwent gradual growth until 1997.[6] The mainland market also went down. Celine Cheung, manager of the publishing unit of Rock Records Hong Kong, explained to me how Canto-pop sales figures decreased in Hong Kong during the 1990s. 'There is a great difference between now and the past. When I entered this industry in 1988, I worked with the company of Anita Mui. A good album would sell 200,000 copies. Now a top one like Leon Lai sells only 50,000 to 80,000. Most artists sell around 2,000 to 3,000.'

Since then, the figures have only declined further. By now, it is generally understood that the CD is a product meant to market a star, to create his or her market value. This value can in turn be capitalised on through acting in commercials and movies, or selling ringtones of the hit song, and the star can attract large audiences during performances. Rather than CD revenues, most record companies depend on other sources of income to survive, not only through live shows, merchandise and ringtones, but also through the publishing of magazines, as a (web) design consultancy and book publisher (Sisaro 2007).

Apart from the institutional drawbacks that prevent the big four record companies from fully entering the market, the market itself is less appealing to transnationals, as indicated by the withdrawal of EMI already mentioned. According to Negus (1997: 2), 'Since the end of the 1980s, the music industry has been continually reorganising to deal with the world on a more regional basis.' Thus, rather than only licensing music to Asia, during the 1980s transnational record companies decided to set up local offices and become the owner of a record company that gave direct access to the local market (Laing 1998: 339). This process of the globalisation of the music industry is uneven, and reflects an exclusion of certain markets. 'So-called global markets tend to be those which have strictly enforced copyright legislation and highly priced CDs rather than cheaply priced cassettes (so Japan is an important global market, whereas India is not). Hence (...) the global is imagined in terms of a series of very particular criteria.' (Negus 1997: 2) One reason why China is excluded relates to the role of music publishers.

In the global market, record companies consist of a production and a publishing unit. The latter contracts bands, composers and lyric writers and sells their work to the production unit. They record the master tape, take care of the production of the units (CD, DVD or LP), market the product, and arrange distribution to retailers. In the case of a band that writes its own songs, it is contracted by the publisher for the intellectual property rights and by the record company for the mechanical reproduction rights, and receives royalties from both business units.

The role of publishers in China, however, is entirely different and can best be compared with the role of a book publisher. In China, the publisher decides to release a music product, often arranges the duplication of the master tape, and is responsible for its distribution throughout the country. What, then, are the roles left for the record companies? A record company contracts the artist and records the master tape. It takes care of the design and is responsible, sometimes together with the publisher, for the marketing. In China, there is no copyright collection society; copyright revenues usually do not exist, and artists receive a fixed sum, although they may get royalties if sales exceed a certain limit. Usually, a record company sells the master tape to the publisher for an amount that guarantees a fixed number of releases. If more units are sold, the publisher pays an additional amount to the record company. Foreign record companies are not allowed to set up an independent office in China; only joint ventures are legal (Chen 2002; Huang 2007; Winfield & Peng 2005). Publishers are, by definition, state-owned enterprises, which is crucial as this strongly affects the 'openness' of the Chinese music market. The consequence of the continued involvement of the state is obvious, the 'state feels safe about the localisation process of global capital, and meanwhile, by partnering with the global capital, it opens a new epoch for China's national cultural policy: they explore economic, cultural, and political interests out of the global-state synergy.' (Fung 2008: 13) According to Gene Lau of ZOOM music, a Hong Kong company with an office in Beijing:

> For the international record companies, if they cannot handle the distribution directly, they are not really interested. Many foreign companies now have an office in China, but they are working on a very small budget and trying to learn how to manage a company in China. Their main purpose is to sell their foreign products to China.

Instead of seriously entering the market, foreign record companies choose to license their products to a local publisher. All sound carriers in China are released by one of the 250-300 publishing houses. 'These are centrally monitored by the Audio-Visual Office of the Ministry of Culture, while the News Publication Office controls all the licensing of publications and duplication rights. The music business is still regarded as a subset of the publication business.' (Fung 2008: 56) The publishing houses are thus powerful and relatively independent entities, in that they are state-owned companies looking to gain a firm position on the music market. Their primary goal is to be, or to become, a profitable enterprise.[7] According to Gene Lau, the competence of publishing houses depends largely on their relationship with the ministries they belong to. If that relationship is good, their products are more likely to be approved. The official approval of one of the ministries is necessary to release a foreign product. According to Song Zufen, who works for CMSP, one of China's major publishing houses:

> The difference is that if we work with a domestic record company, we just reach an agreement and they send the master tape. But a foreign record company has to get official permission, they have to get the right from the copyright bureau, then we go to the broadcast and TV bureau to get the permission.

Although there are different ways to set up a local business, in all cases companies depend on local music publishing houses to release their products. The exclusion of China from the global music market shows that while it is easy to *imagine* the Chinese market as being both huge and open to the West, the reality is more complex: Local particularities – such as the legal system, the prevalence of copyright infringement and the dominant role of the government – in combination with the market-led considerations of transnational companies, prevent the mainland music market from having access to the global music industry.[8] It is thus too simple to summarise developments in the 1990s under the concept of commercialisation and opening up. The development of the Chinese music market during the 1990s, and up to 2007, actually presents a rather gloomy financial picture. The narrative goes that in the 1990s the spirit of money took control in China, yet it proves to be a fairly fragile spirit when it comes to the record industry.

Edward Ko, manager of Rock Records Shanghai, predicted to me that everything would change after China entered the WTO in 2001. 'Promotion, publishing, everything will change. The market will become a normal one and piracy will be reduced.' But did it? Aside from the question what a 'normal market' signifies, the changes have proven to be much more complicated. WTO accession has merely resulted in a change from a market socialism model to a state-controlled capitalist corporation model with the state as major shareholder (Huang 2007: 441). As Winfield and Peng state, 'There appears to be a convolution of the Party line and the bottom line, a Chinese media system moving from totalitarianism to market authoritarianism.' (2005: 256) Neither commercialisation, nor the entry into the WTO, has resulted in a retreat of the state; quite the contrary. 'The paradox of China is that micro-freedoms co-exist with illimitable political power.' (Ong & Zhang 2008: 11)

Neither the state nor capital are external to each other. Instead, both are mutually implicated (Fung 2006, 2008; Wang 2001). Following Ong, the Chinese state employs the twin modalities of neoliberal governmentality: 'neoliberalism as exception' and 'exceptions to neoliberalism.' (Ong 2006) In embracing the influx of foreign capital, and in allowing the emergence of small relatively 'independent' local record companies, the state follows a neoliberal route. *Simultaneously*, in retaining control over publishing and distribution, as well as through the censorship apparatus, the state also makes 'exceptions to neoliberalism.' (see also Zhao 2008: 6) As Fung (2006: 84) observes, 'It is not that global capital kowtows to Chinese authorities; or that the state backs down to allow their entry. (...) Nowadays, transnational media corporations and the Chinese authorities work in tandem to produce a state-global media complex.' This complicity of the state with global and regional capital challenges dominant notions of capitalism (as inherently liberal and free from the nation-state)[9] as well as prevailing assumptions about the communist nation-state (as being at odds with a capitalist logic). Global capitalism and the Chinese nation-state can work very well together, producing depoliticised articulations of cultural forms that constitute a hybrid mix of cosmopolitanism and neo-nationalism, a mix which serves as the lubricant for the shared accumulation of capital. Yet, whereas Fung (2008: 61) points out that 'the state's receptive attitudes towards these transnational music records are just miniature testing grounds and rehearsals for more extensive fusion and collaboration between the state and global capitals,' the decline of the market in tandem with the rather weak position of the big four in the Mainland hints at the uncertain and shaky road that lies ahead for this fusion. This becomes clearer when we look at the developments in the production of rock since the early 1990s.

Cultural Be/Longings

What motivated producers in the early 1990s to enter the market, and what made them stay for all these years? An obvious reason is, of course, that companies hope for better times. In the words of Leslie Chan from Red Star:

> Maybe in three years the market will be open, and if we hadn't started two years ago, we wouldn't have a chance to survive. If we can produce one classic album a year that people will still buy ten years later, we just hope ... (...) Nobody wants to give up the Chinese market, you know, because it's so huge, but to survive will be a long march, it isn't easy.

Sometime later, Red Star did actually pull out of the market. Apart from their desire to fill the vacuum left by the absence of the big companies, discontent with the pop music they grew up with was often quoted as a consideration:

> I don't like Hong Kong music, although I am a Cantopop lyric writer. (Gene Lau, ZOOM Music)

> The more time I spend in China, the more I realise that Canto-pop has a big problem; it has no spirit, the music is not music. (..) It's like drinking water, it has no taste at all. (..) But for the music in China, especially the Beijing artists, they really come up with something. (Leslie Chan, Red Star)

It is interesting that those who mainly deal with pop music pointed out in the interviews that they are committed to other music genres:

> My favourite is of course rock, I like the songs from your heart, I don't like the commercial thing. (...) Pop music depends on market needs, so there is no difference between songs. (Eric Kwok, Polygram)

The 'favourite is *of course* rock' was said in an apologetic way, as though his involvement in the promotion of pop should be excused. For both Red Star and ZOOM music, the perceived authenticity of Chinese rock music and their discontent with 'commercial' Cantopop comprise important reasons to enter the market. Added to the perceived authenticity of the music is the image of Beijing as the cultural centre of 'Greater China'. The appeal of Beijing rock to regional record producers can be interpreted as an imagined cultural pilgrimage. The Hong Kong and Taiwan producers return to their imagined cultural roots and thus merge with 5,000 years of history. Both the perceived authenticity of rock music and the notion that Beijing is the cultural centre, support Negus' argument that 'what are often taken to be straightforward business decisions are actually based on a number of culturally specific beliefs and assumptions' (Negus 1998: 367). These beliefs and assumptions are not necessarily shared by all the parties involved. Musicians are often highly critical about record companies, and smoothly retreat to the grounds of cultural essentialism in order to make their point:

> I don't know how a record company should be, but to me, the Taiwanese like to cheat people. The Taiwanese are good at making fake things. (Gao Wei from Underground Baby, signed by Taiwan-based company Magic Stone)

> Red Star gives me very small royalties; it's very unfair, but they are Hong Kong people, you know. (Zhang Qianqian, female singer contracted by Red Star)

These opinions show that the commercial and cultural links established by Hong Kong and Taiwan record companies with the Beijing rock scene do not imply the emergence of a common culture. Cooperation between regional record companies and Beijing musicians ignites cultural struggles between companies and artists, struggles in which 'national characteristics' are articulated in order to explain perceived differences and strengthen one's own position. In turn, producers often react in a similar manner. Rock Records manager Celine Cheung from Hong Kong complained about how lazy Chinese rock singers are, and that they constantly had to visit Beijing to inquire about the progress of Dou Wei. Others consider them simply brainwashed by communist propaganda. In the words of Hong Kong manager Dickson Dee: 'After so many years of communist education [the musicians] are actually kind of brainwashed already and they do not know how to be against the government.'

The production of rock can thus be interpreted as a struggle over and for culture. Boundaries – that is, markers of cultural difference – are both drawn and contested. The commitment of producers to Chinese rock can be traced to a complex and contradictory set of factors. It is a cultural pilgrimage, yet for producers the final destination of this pilgrimage – Beijing – simultaneously signifies repression and unpredictability; the market refuses to get any better. As a result, regional record companies – Magic Stone from Taiwan and Red Star from Hong Kong – gradually pulled out of the Chinese rock market, leaving a gap filled by local companies. The production of rock is characterised by a decrease rather than an increase in economic ties between China, Hong Kong, and Taiwan.[10]

The local turn in the production of rock is considered in the popular mainland press to have resulted in the emergence of the New Sound Movement. Modern Sky plays an especially pivotal role, with at least ten new titles a year in what is perceived to be the rebirth of Chinese rock, following the crisis discussed in the introduction. New Bees is another local independent company that operates in a style similar to that of Modern Sky, where Scream, a subsidiary of Jingwen, generally focuses on the more extreme genres.[11] Shen Lihui, manager of Modern Sky, has set a trend in the music business of China. Modern Sky is run by young people and is housed in a chaotic office where the most recent computers (i-Macs, of course) are used. Shen Lihui is profiting from what he calls 'a relaxed attitude towards music publishing on the part of political authorities' (in Steen 2000: 46), a relaxation most certainly linked to the waning of government control after the 15th Party Congress in September 1997. Guo and Su (in Steen 2000: 47) label Modern Sky a 'typical postmodern PRC paradox' because it uses different tactics to circumvent and work in line with the regulations. Following my earlier observations on the state-capital nexus, it is actually not that paradoxical by now. The rise of small independent local companies ties in well with the rhetoric and policies – initiated by the state but mainly promoted by the local Beijing government – to establish a 'creative industry' in the city, as to facilitate a move from the 'made in China' label to a 'created in China' paradigm (Keane 2007). The words of Bo Lu, manager of Scream, are indicative of the current state-creative industry nexus, producing a market with Chinese characteristics:

> I always have confidence in the government. It's true, as they say, that China has its own characteristic. And they have known from the very beginning that China is going to walk the road of capitalism anyway, for they simply knew that capitalism is more human-oriented. We're on our way there, no matter what they call it in the future.

Following the arguments of Ong (2006), as pointed out earlier, China operates on the dual logic of 'neoliberalism as exception' and 'exceptions to neoliberalism.' Bo Lu's view too easily ignores the particularities of the Chinese state-market constellation. As Zhao (2008: 341) observes, 'Various socialist discourses have re-emerged to serve as a powerful ideological and moral constraint on the further capitalistic development of the Chinese political economy.' Both capitalism and neoliberalism are at most unfinished projects, and there are no reasons to believe this will change in the near future – neoliberal practices of regulation – such as opening up a space for the emergence of local record companies – 'coexisting with illiberal forms of industrial and state controls.' (Ong & Zhang 2008: 9)

Rather than pointing the finger at these, manager of local companies cite cultural factors to explain why the regional ones never really got a foothold in the Chinese rock market. In the words of Fu Chung from New Bees, 'The problem is that the managers were not Beijingnese, so they had little knowledge of how to operate in the mainland market, and operated as they do in Hong Kong and Taiwan.'

Modern Sky is extremely clear in positioning its products vis-à-vis the earlier rock bands. Shen Lihui constantly stresses that he wants more diversity. Steen (2000: 55) quotes Shen Lihui from the website of his band, Sober:[12]

> One irresponsible shouter is leading a group of headless shou-
> ters; this is today's situation of Chinese rock music. At present,
> the irresponsible shouter has already turned into a chattering old
> woman. Today, without understanding anything, he is still reco-
> vering from the complaints of his childhood. In fact, apart from
> affirming Freudian science, this doesn't say anything to us. This
> world has already started to change, and the things he is talking
> about don't have anything to do with us. (...) I think, he or they
> should go into a museum and get some sleep.

Clearly Shen Lihui is talking here about Cui Jian and his generation.
Cui Jian responds to this by labelling the new generation as 'charlatans
without culture' (Yan & Ou 1999: 31). With the depoliticisation of everyday life, Cui Jian is framed as a voice from the past; the bands from
Modern Sky have taken over his role. The early generation is downplayed as comprising screaming, long-haired individuals. This is merely
a marketing device, to be turned upside down when deemed profitable.
For the Modern Sky music festival of 2008, the organisers proudly an-
nounced the staging of He Yong and Zhang Chu, two of the voices
from the past.

The new generation is said to reflect contemporary urban life; more
playful and less rebellious. New Bees boss Fu Chung gives similar descriptions of the new generation and refers to his company's band The
Flowers as one of its examples.[13] Such characterisations of the New
Sound advocated by Modern Sky cover up the fragmented state of Beijing's rock culture already analysed. In employing such a chronological
framework, Modern Sky positions, or better, brands itself as the new
brand name for rock. Shen Lihui provides more markers with which to
distinguish today's generation from the previous generation (in Steen
2000: 56):

> New Music's function is to link up. In the past, the temperament
> of [bands like] 'Tang Dynasty' was very local. The new bands are
> much more international. We are preparing to spread much
> more Chinese new wave music to Taiwan, Hong Kong, and Eur-
> ope. Not to make contact and not to exchange is impossible. The
> Indians also had culture, but they failed to make contact. There-
> fore, their influence weakened day by day.

Fu Chung from New Bees voiced a similar ambition:

> I think that if we can produce music that can meet the standard
> of international music, many overseas Chinese will be proud of

it. (..) [Taiwan and Hong Kong rock musicians] lack an idea or spirit in their music.

Which brings us back to the negotiation of place. The local turn signifies a desire to become global, which corresponds to my earlier observation that just as the local travels well globally, the global travels well locally. What interests me here is not the validity of such a desire – it is easy to think of bands who are still eager to Sinify their sound – but more how regional companies motivate their activities in terms that reflect a cultural pilgrimage, whereas a local company aims to conquer the world by adapting to the perceived global (that is, Western) standards of rock. Fu Cheng's remarks on the attempts to make rock with Chinese characteristics are indicative:

> I feel it makes no sense. When I listen to a Dutch band, I don't question what its Dutch characteristics are. What matters is whether the music moves you. Since rock comes originally from the West it is obvious that musicians play Western instruments. If they insist on integrating Chinese elements, the music becomes unnatural and is not successful. Music is all about authenticity and sincerity.

What links the motivations of regional and local record companies is that both express a desire for a strong Chinese culture, a desire that that is packaged in the sound of rock.

Silencing Sounds

According to the ancient Chinese philosopher Confucius, there are two dangerous kinds of music. The first is loud and jarring music, which stimulates chaos. The second is pleasing but lewd music. Both are supposed to disturb the harmony he considered crucial for society (Tuan 1993: 89). If Confucius were to enter a music store in Beijing today, he would most likely classify rock as the loud music, and pop as the pleasing but lewd kind. Confucius might be pleased to know that the current authorities in China share his view and do their best to censor popular music, in particular rock.

A case in point is Cui Jian. He expressed his annoyance to me after fifteen years of struggling with official authorities: 'I think the Chinese government plays a child's game that I can't play. Maybe you can treat them as kids, or maybe worse, maybe you should lie, or be patient, only then you can win.'

Over the years, for reasons even unknown to Cui Jian himself, he became more acceptable to mainstream media. He is now allowed to perform on TV and in big concert halls. In 2008, he appeared in a talk show on CCTV after having organised a concert to raise money for the Sichuan earthquake victims. On the question how he, who used to be rebellious, was now driven by a wish to help his fellow Chinese, he carefully challenged the reference to 'fellow Chinese' by insisting he wanted to help *people* who are in need. The acceptance of Cui Jian may hint at the increased openness of media culture in China. A Hong Kong producer told me in 2008 how he feels this is not quite the case:

> Elderly people have always been assigned to be the person in charge and as a result the standard of censorship is not getting more open, on the contrary, it is getting more conservative. For example, the Hong Kong and China versions of Joey Yung's *Close Up* album are different, one track has been deleted from the album due to the sensitive lyrics.

The banned song contained lyrics that were considered too sexual. In general, as another music producer explained to me in 2009, 'any wording relating to politics/sexually implicit/obscene/wild fantasies is immediately banned.' In this final part of this chapter, I aim to discuss this 'child's game,' as Cui Jian terms it, of the Chinese government, and to map out the impact of censorship on the production of music in China.[14] I argue against generalisations that depict the artistic circle in China as being completely suppressed by, or in complete compliance with, the communist state. In other words, the artist is neither fully a victim nor fully an accomplice. I will first briefly describe a model of censorship – that of the 'velvet prison' – and the censorship regulations currently in place. After that I will discuss how and where rock is directly confronted with state regulations, and how the actors involved navigate their way through the regulations.[15] The focus will in particular be on lyrical content, since lyrics appear to be the nodal point from which to scrutinise popular music; only once did a singer – Anthony Wong – tell me his music was banned from TV because the sound was considered too disorderly.[16] Censorship proves to be more of a playground than a political battlefield. In the final section I will show how censorship is productive for the proliferation of Chinese rock culture.

Velvet passions

How can we interpret censorship policies under a communist system? To answer this question, Barmé (1999) adopted the idea of the velvet prison from Haraszti (1987), who analyzes the relationship between artists and the communist Hungarian authorities during the post-Stalinist period. In post-revolutionary China, Barmé argues, the Party cannot scrutinise and control artists as it did during the Cultural Revolution (1966-1976). Instead, by co-opting artists into its bureaucratic system, a system of top-down control has been replaced by the self-imposed compliance of the artist (Barmé 1999: 1-19). According to Barmé (7): 'Technocrats reformulate the social contract, one in which (...) consensus replaces coercion, and complicity subverts criticism. Censorship is no longer the job of a ham-fisted apparatchik but a partnership involving artists, audiences, and commissars alike.'

Through the state's co-opting of artists, Barmé believes self-censorship has become the major form of ideological control. Only a few artists – the naive heroes – dare to speak out against self-censorship, whereas others – the maverick artists – work independently and are, in the case of China, generously funded by regional and global capital (Barmé 1999: 12-13). Interestingly, neither author draws the obvious link between their work and that of Gramsci, who already in the 1930s argued that state hegemony had moved from coercive control – manifested through direct force or its threat – to consensual control, in which individuals 'voluntarily' assimilate the view of the state (Fernia 1987: 23-60; Gramsci 1971).[17]

Although I consider the Gramscian idea of a velvet prison an appealing analogy, as analogy goes, it unfortunately runs the danger of easy generalisations and oversights of peculiarities that are at odds with broad similarities. It is at best frayed velvet, with holes and signs of wear. As I will show, the idea of a velvet prison is at times an accurate way to describe how musicians deal with the authorities. However, the idea can be considered a rather violent, paternalistic and overpoliticised narrative.

It is violent, as it imprisons artists in a position of compliance with the authorities. It is paternalistic, as the subtext reads that true artists ought to resist any cooperation with state institutions. And it is overpoliticised, as it reduces complex cultural realities to a stereotypical dichotomy of artist vs. the state, a reduction I consider to be emblematic of the Western gaze on China. Kraus, in his critique of the velvet prison analogy, ends with the observation that 'like their counterparts in other nations, Chinese professionals sometimes find it difficult to maintain their ideals against material blandishments from the powerful. They must often cautiously keep their heads low, doing little better to act boldly against authority than professionals elsewhere.' (Kraus 2004: 174) As in other societies, the relationship between state and rock in China is neither that of full compliance, nor that of plain opposition. It is necessary to release Chinese artists from the discursive construction of the velvet prison, and to search for understandings that interrogate the political by highlighting the tactics used by bands, companies, and state-owned publishers within the system, in order to circumvent the system.

Regulations

According to Article 102 of Chinese criminal law, it is an offence for any person 'to confuse right and wrong, to poison people's minds, to incite the masses and create chaos, to undermine socialist revolution and construction, and to achieve the final goal of overthrowing the people's democratic dictatorship and socialist system.' (Fu & Cullen 1996: 145) Such a statement offers a fine glimpse of a strong feature of Chinese law: ambiguity. What is meant by right and wrong? What is most poisonous in popular music? Song Zufen from one of China's biggest publishers concisely summarised their policy: 'There should not be any sexual content, or anti-China, anti-government content. We just cut out these inappropriate parts.'

The issues deemed most sensitive – or, to retain the jargon of the law, most poisonous to the minds of the people – when it comes to the contents of popular music, are politics and sex. One can distinguish laws directed against cultural expressions inciting sedition, subversion, and defamation (thus focused on the political), and those against obscene and indecent expressions (thus focused on the moral).

In China, there is a wide array of regulations and laws on which officials can fall back when they want to censor cultural expressions. In October 1997, in a law passed regulating live performances, the third article reads: 'Performances should be held in order to serve the people and serve socialism; to put social benefits foremost, to improve the excellent culture of our nation, and to enrich and improve the people's spiritual life.' (Anonymous 1997c) Most items deemed sensitive returned in a law issued to control online video content which became effective on 31 January 2008. Most ambiguously, all content that might disturb social harmony was considered illicit. This item was mentioned among a list of other topics related to, for example, the position of minorities, sovereignty of the nation-state, religious sects, sexuality, gambling, and terrorism and security (de Kloet 2008).[18]

Two overall interpretations of these sets of rules and regulations seem equally plausible. First, despite the lack of belief in the rules among policy makers and enforcers, and despite the inherent ambiguity of the rules, they do allow for selective enforcement. The state has the legal tools to censor anyone at any time for just about anything. Over the years, this power has not diminished. 'China's elaborate regime of party-state power in public communication has few parallels in the contemporary world. What is apparent is the party's determination to sus-

tain this regime at all costs and by all means, its ability to constantly re-
vamp and perfect this regime, and its progressive amplification and
modernisation since the early 1990s.' (Zhao 2008: 61) Yet, such a reading very much resembles a view in which China is imagined as an
overtly politicised space, a view predominant in the West. Moving away
from the staticism of such a view, I would say that the ambiguity in the
regulations confines and yet offers the space for those involved, including the state-owned publishers, to negotiate their own way through
them. This negotiation may take the form of self-censorship, circumvention, intentional disregard, or other tactics as creative as the music
itself. To substantiate this claim, I will deal with some of the ways the
regulations are being negotiated.

Negotiations

Although all publishers in China are state-owned enterprises, and operate under the production regulations outlined above, they are far from
identical. Besides establishing and maintaining good relations with the
authorities, a good publisher knows the right tactics to employ when
negotiating the rules. Dickson Dee from the Sound Factory, an independent record label in Hong Kong, explained how he succeeded in releasing an album by Wang Lei, a Guangzhou-based rock singer:

> The publisher knew that some of the lyrics might lead to pro-
> blems, but then they also knew how to play the game. They sim-
> ply did not send anything to the censorship department, they just
> released it, and so far there has been no problem.

This is a clear example of how the state is directly involved in circumventing its own rules (as publishers are state-owned companies), and
how ambiguous the enforcement of the law is. Such ambiguity is in
turn traceable among the publishers themselves; some are more conservative than others.

An often-used tactic employed by record producers and music publishers is 'linguistic camouflage'. Wang Yong's release by Magic Stone
is a case in point. Magic Stone's Beijing manager Niu Jiawei explained
how they changed the lyrics on the jacket in order to circumvent censorship:

> We never put restrictions on the singers, in order to give them
> the freedom to perform the best they can. But we have to use
> some tricks to evade censorship. Usually we coin some words to
> replace the prohibited lyrics on the jackets which are similar in
> pronunciation. For example, Wang Yong's lyrics *wo jiu cao ni*

made – 'Fuck your mother' – was changed to *wo jiu qu ni ma?* –
'Shall I marry you soon?'

Linguistic camouflage was also applied to the printed lyrics of The Fly's
'Gun or Bullet,' which appeared on a compilation album in 1994. 'Sex'
(*xing*) was turned into 'heart' (*xin*), and 'making love' (*zuo ai*) into 'loving wrongly' (*cuo ai*). On Zu Zhou's third album, the name Jiang Zem-
ing appears in the English version on the jacket, but is left out in the
Chinese version, to be replaced by empty boxes. Through the publishing houses, the state not only increases its control over the market, but
also ensures a share of the revenue. The latter function of publishing
houses helps explain why the tactics of linguistic camouflage are at
times applied with the state's direct involvement. The urge to make
money often outweighs the need to censor. Niu's assertion of giving absolute freedom to their singers corresponds with the romantic myth of
the individual artist, and as such resonates well with the rock mythology. Louis Chan from Red Star told me: 'We warn them to avoid having
any political content in their lyrics. They are pretty clever in this, they
usually don't write about politics but more about personal issues.'
   In 1999, Modern Sky released the second album by NO. The lyrics
of four of the nine songs are not given on the jacket. One of these four
songs ('Injustice') contains the following words:

   You have taken action to feel easy, feeling easy is freedom
   Freedom is human rights
   But human rights is politics!
   Comrade, you have foolishly entered the stage of politics

Audiences are aware of the tactics employed by the industry. Zhang
Weiyun complained in his letter to The Fly that the lyrics on the jacket
had been censored:

   Was the publisher too careless, or was it because of the strict
   censorship system? Whatever the reason, when releasing this album officially, I believe it should have been done in a responsible way vis-à-vis us rock fans.

Other fans were more understanding, and simply asked for the correct
version of the lyrics, or expressed their admiration that the band had
managed to pass through the censorship system. In any case, audiences, at least some of them, are aware of the restrictions and are able
to read between the lines of the sung and the written (or non-written)
version.

Often, companies simply drag their feet in order to pass the censors, others change the lyrics on the sheet, as Bo Lu from Scream records explains. 'I never ask the artists to alter their works. But when I submit the work to the censors, I'll alter the lyrics on the inside sheet of the record. I do this without lying to them. I let them know that what the artists sing is not exactly what is on the lyrics sheet.'

Again, the state is complicit in the censorship, the publisher knows the tricks, and is even told, yet agrees to play the game all along. But not always; Zi Yue's song 'Traffic Accident' did not pass censorship. Its lyrics run:[19]

My ass keeps on moving up and down
Accompanying you into yet another orgasm
You boast of the unique odour on your body
Suggesting that I come, and laugh like you

A song that undoubtedly would have had a parental warning attached to it in the United States has never been released in China. The same happened to Cobra's '1966', a song with the Cultural Revolution as its theme. Record company Red Star tried their utmost to get the full CD accepted. The first publisher they went to rejected four songs, so they searched for another one. They finally found one who wanted to omit 'only' this song.[20]

It is important to note that regulations are interpreted differently in different places. As Jing Wang observes, 'Even within a single province, the multi-layered, sub-governing structure (e.g. metropolis, country, township) makes generalisations about administrative infrastructure difficult to draw.' (2001: 4) When He Yong made fun of model worker Li Xuli on TV in late 1996, he was forbidden to perform for three years – so he went to Kunming in South-west China and performed there. Even within Beijing there are differences, as more is possible when one has established good relationships with the local police. The timing is also important: conforming to the idea of the velvet prison, bars sometimes close during sensitive periods (such as around 4 June), or no live performances are staged when a Party congress is being held. Former bar owner Fei Fei clearly had not established good relations with the police:

The police come unexpectedly to the bar to make sure no one is dancing and that the audience is not too large. If you have 15 seats in the bar, then you can only have 15 guests. If you have more than that, you might get into trouble. But you can never tell: sometimes they do not allow it, sometimes they do.

His last remark is characteristic; the only thing everyone knows is that one never knows, and the only thing one is sure of, is that no one is sure of anything. The strategy crucial to organising performances is to establish good relations with the local authorities, yet even this does not guarantee an untroubled future. Good relations remain important today, as one rock artist told me in 2008: 'I bribe the officials. That is the way it is in this country, I know their rules. I treat them for dinner, I offer money.'

Nevertheless, things have improved considerably since the late 1990s. Many CDs have been released with clear political content. Also, the increased popularity of singing in English has most likely make it easier to pass censors, even with songs like 'Hang the Police' from Re-TROS, a song that comes with a highly political music video in which images of exploding buildings, marching crowds, war and violence are intermingled with the band wearing white masks, making them face-less, and with TV monitors in the background. At the end, the line 'We are watching you' appears. The politics of the song are quite explicit in both text and image, but Modern Sky was able to release both the CD and a DVD with this clip. It is likely that the choice of language helped. Numerous venues, like 2 Kolegas, Mao Live house, D-22, Star live house and Yugong Yishan, host concerts regularly, all of which are an-nounced on websites and in magazines. Compared to the 1990s, the rock infrastructure has improved considerably, as has its openness. Even then, during sensitive periods like the Beijing Olympics, the situa-tion has become more tension-filled and bands are under greater scru-tiny. Shou Wang from Carsick Cars explained how some bands mana-ged to circumvent the rules: 'Before the Olympics, if you wanted to play in some big places like Yugong Yishan, you had to send them your ly-rics, but even then, you could send them the songs that you don't want to play.'

Large-scale concerts are somehow more problematic, particularly in Beijing, mainly because the Chinese authorities are scared of large gath-erings, and particularly those of young people. Such a fear is not specifi-cally Chinese or communist; there is a whole body of literature discuss-ing the 'problems' of large gatherings of youths (Cohen 1980; Hebdige 1988). For example, the MIDI festival, an open-air festival often com-pared to Woodstock, has been postponed or cancelled several times. The last cancellation was in May 2008, most likely because of the Olympics. However, in October of the same year, the Modern Sky festi-val took place in Haidian Park, whereas the MIDI festival was organised on its own MIDI school premises (see Figure 5.1). Such festivals were quite unthinkable in the mid-1990s, attesting to a relaxation of control over the past decade.

Figure 5.1   *Audience at the Modern Sky Music Festival in 2008 (photo by the author)*

Shortly after He Yong was banned from performing in the capital in 1996, a concert by pop-rock singer Zang Tianshuo was cancelled. Neither his music nor his lyrics, which reflect on such issues as friendship and love, are particularly sensitive. It was simply bad timing, as the authorities had been alarmed by He Yong's provocative act. Zang Tianshuo complained to me that artists like He Yong frustrate the development of Chinese rock. Here, the idea of the velvet prison is rather accurate: those who transgress the boundaries of the velvet prison and do not comply with the authorities (in the case of He Yong, by making fun of a model worker), are criticised by those musicians who opt for compliance. He Yong's rebelliousness is held responsible for frustrating future chances of performing. In the words of Zang Tianshuo:

> The most important thing is that the bands and the government should cooperate with each other. For example, both I and Cui Jian got the government's cooperation and then we became successful, but many new bands are not famous; if they cooperated more, people would get to know them.

A certain level of compliance is expected in order not to upset the system, and Zang Tianshuo considers this crucial for the further development of the rock scene. He was able to perform six months later in a fully-booked Workers' Stadium; after all, He Yong's act only stirred up the political waters for a brief time. The success of this performance, in

turn, annoyed Niu Jiawei, who faced so many problems while organising the Magic Stone concert. He told me: 'Zang Tianshuo applied for
this concert for a whole year. What's more, he keeps on saying in public
that he is not making rock'n'roll and that he only wants to do something for the government and the common people.'

Thus, people within the rock scene deal with the velvet prison in different ways. Zang Tianshuo argues in favour of it, whereas He Yong
chooses to transgress its boundaries. All are involved in exploring the
limits of what is permissible in China. At times, transgressions of
boundaries occur, after which the state becomes stricter for a while.
The velvet prison is always there, and though it is omnipresent, it
would be wrong to assume its omnipotence.

Proliferations

Finally, I will move beyond the two restrictions that have so far limited
my discussion of censorship; that is, a bias toward singling out its
restrictive silencing force at the cost of discussing its productive power,
and the reification of the state by presenting censorship as basically a legal issue, whereas it can also be seen as a way in which language is con-
strained. Censorship is also a productive cultural force. According to
Butler (1997: 128), 'Censorship precedes the text (...) and is in some
sense responsible for its production.' Censorship precedes the text because it first has to define what is and what is not acceptable speech,
which in itself is a speech act. 'Censorship is implicated in its own re-
pudiated material in ways that produce paradoxical consequences.' (130)

By pointing out that sex and politics are sensitive issues, the law
draws attention to sex and politics; it *produces* them as dangerous discursive zones. Censorship is very much a constitutive force for the subject; to move outside the domain of speakability implies risking one's
subjectivity (133). Such a view of censorship broadens the issue toward
what can and what cannot be said; it rests on a Foucauldian idea in
which power is considered productive, and guides Butler to the observation that 'censorship is at once the condition for agency and its necessary limit, [(...) such] agency is implicated in power' (141).

By censoring rock, the Party is at the same time intricately involved
in the production of rock as a distinct music world, because it not only
focuses attention on a specific music genre, but it also corresponds well
with the marketable image of rock as a suppressed and therefore rebellious sound. The zone of unspeakability becomes a site of subjectivisa-
tion for those who aim to perform in line with the rock mythology. The
case of punk band 69 is illustrative. Together with three other hard-core
punk bands, they released their first album in 1999. When I asked vocalist Peter about censorship problems, he told me:

Before we released it we expected problems, we *hoped* we'd get problems. You know why? Because if we had problems we'd get famous, everybody'd know: 'Oh, this band had problems. What's the problem, let's buy it!' You know what I mean? We hoped, but nothing happened and we were disappointed.

Here, censorship ties in neatly with the rock mythology, a mythology which has proven to be so powerful for hardcore punk. The importance of government restrictions for the proliferation of the Chinese rock culture cannot be ignored. The censorship of rock in China can be interpreted as both restrictive and productive: It confines the space of rock, yet simultaneously creates space for it. Censorship thus both silences *and* produces culture.

It is equally important to note that censorship is not solely defined and imposed upon citizens by the state. Regulations governing the domain of sexuality are neither typically Chinese nor confined to the state. On the contrary, parents, educators, and official censors are involved in governing the boundaries of the sexually permissible. By singling out the official laws, one runs the danger of reifying the state and thereby covering up the other sites of censorship, most notably the music industry, which excludes sounds deemed unprofitable. Furthermore, it is at times futile to retain the dichotomy of censor-censored, as though these were two different entities. As discussed above, censorship is implicated in all discursive domains; it produces zones of unspeakability that not only operate at an explicit, and often juridical, level, but are also very much implicit: They are etched into the discourses constituting everyday life. In other words, the forces of censorship reside as much inside us as they operate outside us.

Commercial Complexities

My study of the record industry shows that the complex processes of commercialisation during the 1990s have led neither to the disappearance of the state nor to a financial boom. The combined music market of Mainland China, Hong Kong and Taiwan turns out to be a marginal one when compared to other markets. State capital (global, regional and local) and rock culture are deeply implicit with one another. Neither the processes of commercialisation nor China's entry into the WTO have resulted in the retreat of the state. On the contrary, even today, in the midst of the maelstrom of capitalism, the Chinese state has held a firm grip on, or better, is part and parcel of, the media industry. What has emerged in the past two decades is a state-global media complex (Fung 2006: 84). The post socialist state has, through its complicit coexistence with the market, 'rejuvenated its capacity (...) to affect the agenda of popular culture, especially at the discursive level.' (Wang 2001: 71; see also Fung 2008; Zhao 2008) Chinese socialism has become enmeshed in, rather than superseded by, global capitalism.

Consequently, as Xudong Zhang argues, 'the fact that the global capitalist context and the Chinese state-form fully interpenetrate and depend on each other does not mean that there is a well-synchronised, homogenous historical time by which to measure and evaluate things everywhere, or that the political economy of global capitalism is now solely responsible for explaining the totality of human history.' (2008: 10) The case of rock culture provides a case in point. First, steadily declining revenue figures show that it is too easy to speak of commercialisation. Second, the frequent juxtaposition or combination of global capital with a local state runs the danger of ignoring local and regional flows of money and people. Against a general picture of a rise in global investments in China (Curtin 2007), rock culture's production witnesses a retreat of global and regional companies, in favour of local labels. It is hence not quite possible to speak of the production of rock in terms of commercialisation and transnationalisation – reality turns out to be much more messy and contradictory.

In the 1990s, regional record companies entered what was considered a promising market, where apart from financial factors, cultural considerations also played a role – a discontent with the pop music these producers grew up with, and a longing for what is perceived to be the epicentre of Chinese culture, Beijing. Both financial and (generally ignored) cultural considerations resulted in the gradual retreat of regional producers, giving way to an emergence of small local labels. The local turn signifies a move away from a focus on making rock with Chinese characteristics, toward making rock that meets assumed global – that is, Western – standards. It reflects a desire to become truly cosmopolitan.

The final section of this chapter delves deeper into the relationships between state, market and rock culture by exploring the issue of censorship. This might best be interpreted as a playground where cats and mice play a game in which the former do not care to seriously enforce the rules, while the latter want to avoid them as much as possible. A top-down, hegemonic model of power in which the state suppresses culture ignores their mutual dependence and, again, complicity (Kraus 2004). Self-censorship – the main bars of the velvet prison – proves to be only one of the ways for artists and producers to deal with ambiguous censorship regulations in China. I have presented the tactics used by musicians, producers and, most interestingly, state-owned publishers, such as linguistic camouflage, circumvention of rules and delaying the date of release, to negotiate their way through the regulations.

Furthermore, censorship produces zones of unspeakability, and such zones are fertile ground for those who want to perform in line with the rock mythology.

The state, the market and rock culture are all implicated in the silencing as well as the productive power of censorship. As such, not only does the production of rock force us to rethink the assumed commercialisation and transnationalisation of the Chinese media, it also helps to unpack the mutual dependencies between state, market and culture. The metaphor with which this chapter opened, that of a country thrown into a money blender, has by now lost its rhetorical appeal. The combined workings of capitalism and communism are much more subtle and refined. They do not throw China into a money blender, rather, they render the omnipresence of the state merely invisible, and produce the simulacrum of perpetual progress in a market free from any cultural (be)longings.

Conclusion: Paradoxical Performances

'Are five nights warmer than one night, then?' Alice ventures to ask.
'Five times as warm, of course.'
'But they should be five times as *cold*, by the same rule –'
'Just so!' cried the Red Queen. 'Five times as warm, *and* five times as cold.'
Lewis Carroll, Through the Looking Glass *(1992 [1871]: 188-189)*

Mirrors

The rock culture in China does not exist, as such. Rock is not dead; as a genre, it is falling apart into separate scenes that are supposedly different, temporarily stable, and – at the same time – held together by the same beliefs in rock. Rock is not dead, given the sustaining power of the rock mythology. It is this mythology which produces the crucial, spatially and ideologically inscribed divide between rock from Beijing and pop from predominantly Taiwan and Hong Kong. Whether it is folk, underground music, or pop-punk, rock musicians seem to agree on one thing: they are *not* making pop. In contrast to what is often perceived by musicians, record companies, journalists, and academics as the fake, commercial sound of pop, rock musicians express their 'true feelings' in their music. Pop is rock's most conspicuous constitutive outside.

Authenticity is of crucial importance in the rock mythology, especially when this mythology travels to places outside the West. Whereas musicians in the West are literally born in the imagined centre of rock, their counterparts in China constantly have to prove themselves in order to gain the right to make rock music. Compared to the Western claim to the origins, and therefore to the continual making, of rock, Chinese rock musicians must bear the burden of providing authenticating proof in order to avoid being labelled mere copycats. The production of a scenic authenticity involves an exploration of different aesthetic tracks. I have analysed the Dadaistic, vulgar, and metaphorical aesthetics coupled to the lo-fi recording techniques of underground bands; the chivalric aesthetics of heavy metal; the regular-guy aesthetics of folk-rock; the rhythmic DIY aesthetics of hardcore punk to which pop-punk adds a spontaneous mischievous pose; the urban, keeping it real aesthetics of hip-hop; and, finally, the eclectic, electronic, and cosmopolitan aesthetics of the fashionable bands.

The articulations of Chineseness (ancient China, communist China) are particularly significant for those scenes more closely tied to the 'typical' rock idiom, such as the rebellious sound of Cui Jian, the heavy metal of Tang Dynasty, the hardcore punk of 69, and the underground sound of Zu Zhou. The 'harder' the sound, the stronger the urge to localise it. Bands positioned in scenes operating on the boundaries of the rock mythology – such as pop-rock, folk-rock, pop-punk, and the fashionable bands (the recurring hyphen already indicating the hybridism of these scenes) – are less involved in attempts to localise their sound. Sometimes they even choose to articulate their global aspirations. For instance, the fashionable bands, which are emblematic of the New Sound Movement of Beijing, clearly voice their wish to be as global as possible. Consequently, and despite their current popularity among Chinese youths, they receive less attention from the Western press, since they appear and sound less Chinese. Though the soft sells locally, it is the hard that makes it to the West. In a related way, the global travels well locally, and the local travels well globally.

Most accounts of Chinese rock treat the music and the lifestyles surrounding it as reflecting the zeitgeist of Chinese urban youth culture. It is an appealing idea to interpret rock as a mirror of society. However, in this book, I have tried to walk through the mirror, as Alice did in Wonderland, and look for the paradoxes, taking a paradox as a 'seemingly absurd though perhaps actually well-founded statement' (OED 1984). As May writes in his introduction to Deleuze, a 'paradox involves the bringing together of disparate elements into a convergence that neither reduces one to the other nor keeps them apart.' (2005: 104)

Throughout this exploration, we have come across many seemingly absurd statements. If we are to grasp the meanings of rock and the dynamics of Chinese society, we ought to take these paradoxes seriously, rather than cover them up under a comforting blanket of fixed theoretical preoccupations that force us to say rock is either this or that, and not both. In the previous chapters, I laid bare the paradoxes (but without labelling them as such) that underlie the music industry, the making of music, the listening to music, and the governance of music, and showed how readings that appear to be contradictory are in fact complementary. To foreground the deparadoxicalising force of the rock mythology is to acknowledge its productive, creative, and generic power on the one hand, and its confining, suppressive, and violent power on the other. By positioning rock as a cultural form hardened by the deparadoxicalising force of its mythology, it becomes necessary to include all domains related to rock: its constitutive outsides, the audiences, the producers, and the state.

Deparadoxicalisation

Rock is a dynamic, sonic field with the rock mythology as a powerful deparadoxicalising force. This force produces rigid binary relationships and informs univocal readings. This production of binaries resonates uncomfortably with a more general tendency to frame late-socialist societies in terms of rigid dichotomies. The question I want to pose in this conclusion is how to reconnect the poles of these binaries, how to recuperate the cacophony of voices, how to move towards a language that does not reduce the complexities of everyday life to fixed binaries that betray a Cold War rhetoric in which, for example, the official and the unofficial or the state and the people are opposed to each other.

Readings of rock in China often either stress that it is a copy of Western music, or point out its specific Chinese characteristics. The paradox here is that popular cultures in China, and elsewhere, are as local as they are global. The local and the global are complementary rather than contradictory. To perceive this as a contradiction misses the point as much as singling out either one of them. However, due to the deparadoxicalising force of rock mythology, the Western focus is often on the Chineseness of Chinese rock, whereas at times in China, its Chineseness is emphasised, and at other times, its globality. Popular cultures are, I believe, profoundly *dakou*, if not polluted (De Kloet 2007). They are both global and local, constantly involved as they are in articulating the differences from and sameness with the perceived 'origins' of, in this case, rock. Given the historically dominant West to East cultural flows, cultural 'origins' are, more often than not, perceived to be located in the West.

Although communist ideology evaporated during the years of reform, the CCP is increasingly relying on nationalist sentiments as a unifying ideology. This often invokes a celebration of both ancient China and communist China. In its eagerness to localise the sound of rock, so as to avoid copying the West, Beijing musicians employ related articulations of Chineseness. At times their references are overtly subversive; some bands transform the peaceful sound of 'traditional' instruments in order to challenge the underlying myth of China's rich cultural past, while others simply express their pride in Chinese culture. All, however, reify the idea of China's uniqueness and in so doing come close to the dominant ideologies of the CCP. Simultaneously – and it is crucial to erase the notion of time here, since I am no longer talking about moments of compliance and moments of rebellion, as both happen at the same spatial and temporal juncture – these dominant ideologies are subverted.

It is time to unhook the rebellious rock star, and unravel the complementary – rather than the contradictory – politics of rock. Readings that
stress the 'subversive' side of, for example, Madonna's gender performances, are as inadequate as those that point out the ways in which
she reasserts dominant gender roles. Madonna does both. Only if we
position such paradoxes at the heart of our analysis, can we grasp the
politics of popular culture and its complex dynamics in society at large.

The politics of rock function, as all politics do, as a force of both inclusion and exclusion. One needs an outside to constitute an inside;
hence the importance of studying the sounds excluded by the rock
mythology. This has resulted in a discussion of what I have called the
subaltern sounds. In its masculinity, rock marginalises the feminine. In
its reification of Beijing as the cultural centre of China, rock marginalises voices from places outside the capital. By constantly criticising and
ridiculing *Gangtai* pop, rock excludes those sounds that are not packaged by the rock mythology. The female voices employ their own tactics
to negotiate the masculinity of rock, some by a denial of gender, some
by a dramatisation of it, and some by a cosmopolitanisation of gender,
whereas others inscribe gender into punk ideology. The sounds from
places outside Beijing voice a critique of the centre, which they consider
arrogant and corrupted by the spirit of money. In Shanghai and
Guangzhou, bands claim to have subverted the commercial positioning
of their city, and therefore to have become even more authentic, more
real, than rock from the centre.

If we are to interrogate the rock mythology, a journey through *Gangtai* pop is most promising. The often-heard critique that pop can never
be rebellious or politically subversive proves easy to debunk; there are
numerous examples of the political use of pop. Of course, the focus on
the political in the strict sense of the word is itself questionable; the
opacity of pop, along with its banality and artificiality, creates a multivocal and intertextual musical space that dramatises the present. Pop both
relies upon and toys with notions of authenticity. In its extravagant display of inauthenticity, pop challenges the idea of the authentic musician
(or the unique artist) who composes his or her immortal songs (or
makes his or her unique art). It is pop's ambiguity and fluidity, indeed
this opacity, which makes it such a difficult sound to grasp.

Three music territories can be distinguished – classical, pop, and rock
– through which audiences move in and out. In particular, audiences located in the rock territory are strongly involved in the music; rock, as a
hard cultural force, demands more involvement from the audience. The
rock mythology is a strong territorialising force, but the territory becomes swampy at the moment of reception. Audiences are both passive
and active. They employ technologies of the self highly dependent upon
the bands and sounds such technologies are built on. These technolo-

gies help to negotiate gender, to articulate generational fault lines, or a sense of spatial belonging, to build one's subjectivity, and to explore political beliefs or disbeliefs. Reception is not just defined by context, but also by the text itself. In the reflexive project of the self, sonic technologies play an important constitutive role – not only for the *dakou* generation but also, and maybe even more so, for the subsequent generation of the 1980s. To fully comprehend the complex and intersecting nature of these technologies making up the self *and* social reality, structure and agency are to be perceived as mutually constitutive.

Processes of commercialisation in China are anything but univocal. For instance, the state remains a key player in the music industry and in the commercial sector as a whole, while amidst all the worries over commercialism, the music market, both in China and in 'Greater China,' declined during the 1990s and thereafter. Furthermore, regional cultural and economic flows are uneven; *Gangtai* pop travels particularly well to China, whereas only rock travels back, and does so on a far smaller scale. The investments made by companies from Hong Kong and Taiwan can be interpreted as a failed commercial and imagined cultural pilgrimage due to the harsh economic climate. The subsequent local turn signifies the emergence of Beijing companies which are now the key producers of rock music. It coincides with the rise of the *dakou* generation and the New Sound Movement. This again shows how processes of production, music-making, and music consumption are closely intertwined, rather than hostile toward one another. The deparadoxicalising force of the rock mythology generates readings in which commercialisation is considered harmful, while its productive force is ignored; to put it bluntly, commercialisation is a necessary prerequisite for any popular cultural form to emerge in a contemporary society.

A complex package of regulations governs the production of rock, its mediation on TV, and live performances. The rock mythology directs attention to the restrictive nature of censorship. Not only does it reaffirm the perceived totalitarian character of the CCP, but it also ties in well with the framing of rock as a rebellious sound. To point out the creative negotiations artists and industry employ in order to circumvent, subvert, or ignore the rules, again runs the danger of feeding the idea of the creative artist fighting his or her way through a harsh political landscape for the freedom of his or her thoughts and sounds. By censoring rock, the CCP actively produces it as a specific music world. Censorship produces speech; it necessarily has to say what cannot be said, which in itself is a speech act. By pointing out that art may or may not be pornographic, the censors themselves draw attention to sexuality, thus inspiring rock bands to include on jackets, or exclude from jackets, images that are deemed to be 'pornographic.' Censorship forms both the necessary condition for and the limitation of agency; it both contains and produces culture.

Sonic Hierarchies

The rock mythology as a deparadoxicalising force directs people's gaze. It encourages them to follow ready-made narratives and to experience a flattened world. Assuming the eyes of Alice in the land of mythology, we are confronted with a wide range of paradoxes that together constitute the world of rock; paradoxes that are too often turned into opposing binaries. If we view these paradoxes seriously, as I argue, we are bound to acknowledge the generic and productive power of the rock mythology, while at the same time refusing to be contained by fixed readings of rock culture. My insistence on listing the range of binaries does not lie in a need to present a piece of neat and tidy discourse that produces rock as a music genre. On the contrary, throughout this book I have analyzed the complex sonic, political, commercial, and cultural processes behind the world of rock in China. But time and again, we are confronted – in both popular and academic discourse, in both the West and China – with these binaries. The discourse on rock, and, I repeat, on popular culture, is very much framed by the paradoxes that are turned into opposing binaries.

The harder a sound rocks, the more difficult it is to escape from a univocal reading in which one has to choose. In particular 'hard' scenes, such as hardcore punk and underground music, are loud (literally and metaphorically) in denouncing commercialisation, and eager to assume a rebellious image – one readily picked up by journalists and academics alike. Indeed, these scenes provide ample evidence of the creative, generic power of the rock mythology. I must admit it is these scenes, along with the hoarse sound of Cui Jian, that make me feel at home in Beijing. They point to the most quintessential sonic power of rock. Yet, in their univocal attitude to such issues as authenticity, rebellion, and commercialisation, they allow little space for the paradoxes; consequently, they show us how the hard force of the rock mythology both produces *and* confines culture.

When we return to the crucial dichotomy rock versus pop, we are confronted with both the generic productivity and the silencing capacity of the rock mythology. How should we grasp the sonic varieties of the opaque sounds of pop? Why are we so silent when it comes to discussing the generic subtleties of pop, and the different modalities of karaoke culture? Both the univocality of the harder scenes within rock and the silencing power of the rock mythology as a whole require further critical interrogation.

As a first step, it will help, I think, to try to live with the paradoxes – to try to grasp their subtleties, their fluidity, their ambiguity – rather than to lose ourselves in a one-sided reading of popular music, in which we either downplay pop or accuse rock of betraying its spirit. If we trace both sides of the paradoxes and take them as complementary rather than contradictory, then the organising binaries produced by the rock mythology will dissolve – at least theoretically speaking. By asking ourselves time and again who says what from which perspective, and what mythology is at work here, which productive and creative forces are propelled by this mythology, and which paradoxes are flattened out by the mythology, we negotiate an idealism that tends to take sides, gliding toward a more subtle, more fluid, and ultimately more dynamic way to narrate 'reality'. This study presents an attempt to liberate the paradoxes of reality. Not to change reality as such, which is why I speak of negotiating ideology; but to interrogate its imaginations, to articulate the stories too often silenced, sidetracked, and ignored. Stories which, along with other stories that are anything but silenced, sidetracked, and ignored, constitute the cultures of, in this case, popular music (and thus not necessarily rock) in China.

There is no need to deny the power of rock as a generic label, as long as this does not result in the silencing or ridiculing of pop, just as there is no reason to celebrate the high arts at the expense of popular culture, or vice versa, or the hard cultural form at the expense of the soft. What happens when we take the binaries outlined above – binaries which are so pervasively present in discourses that frame popular cultures – as paradoxes rather than contradictions, is that we create a space for a dialogue as we subvert cultural hierarchies. Beethoven and the Spice Girls, rock from the West and rock from China, rock and pop, literature and pulp, the sixth-generation Chinese cinema and Hollywood, serious drama and soap operas, the high and the low, the divine and the banal, the hard and the soft. All coexist, very often, with heavily guarded boundaries, so real and authentic. What need to be resolved are not so much the boundaries, as the implicated hierarchies and assumed oppositions.

Binary Socialism

This step holds the potential to reflect further upon the links between culture and politics. In an attempt to describe contemporary Chinese realities, Wang refers to a statement made by Lu Xun in 1927, who proclaimed that 'China is currently on the verge of entering a momentous era. But "momentous" doesn't necessarily mean it will bring life, it can also mean death.' (Wang 2003: 585) The changes taking place are so manifold and complex, of which the increased gap between the haves and have-nots may be the most alarming one – that the future of society appears merely as murky and indeterminate (598). He warns against the incredible persistence among intellectuals 'to think in terms of binaries like traditional/modern, closed/open, conservative/reformer, market/planned, socialism/capitalism, and communism/anticommunism.' (598) The binary mode of thinking is neither specific to China nor specifically new nor recent. In a book with the wonderful title *Everything was forever until it was no more*, on life in the Soviet system between the 1950s and the 1980s, Yurchak (2005) refers to the predominance of dichotomies in analyses and descriptions of late socialism in the Soviet Union. The predominance of what he terms 'binary socialism' obscures rather than clarifies, in his view, everyday realities of those living in the Soviet Union. He argues against the 'use of binary categories to describe Soviet reality such as opposition and resistance, repression and freedom, the state and the people, official economy and second economy, official culture and counterculture, totalitarian language and counter-language, public self and private self, truth and lie, reality and dissimulation, morality and corruption, and so on.' (2005: 5) Such language seems equally pervasive in accounts of Chinese realities. The perpetual reproduction of binaries can be traced back to a Cold War rhetoric. Chow refers to the portrayal of China as the King Kong syndrome, 'producing "China" as a spectacular primitive monster whose despotism necessitates the salvation of its people by outsiders.' (1998c: 94) Indeed, judging from the abundance of stories on China, both in academic and popular discourse, what China needs is exposure, discipline, and punishment – in order to be contained, if not freed, and move towards a 'liberal' and 'democratic' society.

What we need to look for, then, is a language that insists on the continuous interweaving of what are generally perceived as opposites. How to force an implosion of the regime of language that produces binary tropes of knowledge, in which one loses sight of everyday lived realities? Not to return to the fantasy of the Real, as if that were a solid and uniform, unmediated constellation of experiences existing outside the domain of representation. More to unleash the *heteroglossia* of everyday life in China, to account for the complexity and ambivalence of living in a system both communist and capitalist, a system that resists any easy classification scheme.

Earlier in this book, following Bakhtin, I referred to the rock mythology as an authoritative discourse, whereas the sound of pop holds the power to unfold the *heteroglossia* of everyday life. The danger of this observation lies in its reification of the pop-rock binary, just like a West versus Rest dichotomy haunts the discourse on cultural globalisation – also in this book. Just as binaries such as official versus unofficial ought to be taken as paradoxes rather than opposites, so do dichotomies like rock versus pop and The West versus China. For Bakhtin, authoritative discourse operates as an 'a *prior* discourse,' (1981: 342), one that precedes other discourse, and one that is clearly demarcated and cannot easily be changed, resonating with Appadurai's description of hard cultural forms. It permits 'no play with its borders, no gradual and flexible transitions, no spontaneously creative stylising variants on it.' (Bakhtin 1981: 343) Not only the mythology, but also the related East versus West distinction can be read as an authoritative discourse. Yet, as Yurchak explains, drawing on Bakhtin, even the utterances that are made in full support of these authoritative discourses – by rock bands, by critics, by analysts – may perform a different role than just a reification of the discourse. Utterances are always 'dialogised'; everything anybody ever says (or, in the case of music, plays) always exists in response to things said before and in anticipation of things that will be said in response. We never speak in a vacuum. Utterances are performative, they make things happen, while at the same time, 'the meaning of any given speech act is never completely determined in advance.' (Yurchak 2005: 20)

The ubiquitous juxtaposition of the West versus China that propels the politics of authenticity in Chinese rock constitutes an assumed geopolitical division. It is simultaneously a performative authoritative discourse that reproduces alleged cultural differences, relations, histories, etc. As such, just like the rock mythology produces sounds, so does this geopolitical distinction enable the emergence of diverse, multiple and unpredictable meanings that may run counter to the meanings of the authoritative discourse. The ironic references to Western icons of rock music by Sober, and the playful references to disco imagery and sounds by The New Pants, and more generally, the ubiquitous gesturing elsewhere (Baulch 2008) – are all enabled by, first, the globalised idiom of rock and, second, by an assumed division between China and the West. Such performances can slide into unpredictable directions. Popular culture is thoroughly hybridised and polluted, it builds and borrows from hegemonic, authoritative discourses, to fragment endlessly into different forms, voices and sounds, unfolding into a *heteroglossic* discourse in which Party rhetoric can be parodied and neoliberal ideologies can be accommodated and challenged at the same time.

This raises questions about the potential political and social power of popular culture. For sure it is too easy to lament the rise of the 80's generation as a generation without any ideals or political zeal. The multiple voices included in this book – from musicians, audiences, producers, critics, academics – attest to the complexity and ambivalence of popular culture in China. All these voices operate within a complex set of predominantly authoritative discourses of, for example, global capitalism in tandem with the nation-state. Yet at the same time, they give twists and turns to this already mongrel mix of communism and capi-

talism. Neither a utopian narrative of change and revolution nor a dys-
topian account of the rigid eternal status quo can account for the workings of culture and politics. Let me for the last time return to the Soviet
Union, of which Yurchak writes: 'The unanimous participation of Soviet
citizens in the performative reproduction of speech acts and rituals of
authoritative discourse contributed to the general perception of that system's monolithic immutability, while at the same time enabling diverse
and unpredictable meanings and styles of living to spring up everywhere
within it. In a seemingly paradoxical twist, the immutable and predict-
able aspects of state socialism, and its creative and unpredictable possibilities, became mutually constitutive.' (Yurchak 2005: 29) Today's realities
may further complicate the matter of politics, as we have to include globalisation and global capitalism as important accomplices of authoritative
discourses – be it the discourse of the nation-state, of democracy, or the
rock mythology and its entrenchment in a West-East divide. '[B]etween
the West and the East a certain segmentarity is introduced, opposed in a
binary machine, arranged in State apparatuses, overcoded by an abstract
machine as a sketch of a World Order.' (Deleuze & Parnet 1987: 131) To
take a binary as a paradox may offer a potential line of flight – to stay in
Deleuze's discourse – out of the binary machine.

The crux here is to insist on the possibility of a politics taking place
within and *based on* authoritative discourses. As we are living in a world
characterised by an absence of a utopian outside (Hardt & Negri 2000),
it becomes all the more urgent to think through the political and social
possibilities emerging from within the systems in which we are living,
to use them as the building blocks for a cultural politics that is not
caught in fixed binaries but instead explores rather than debunks paradoxes. A cultural politics that resists the deparadoxicalising force of
authoritative discourse and instead may help to produce new cracks and
fissures in discourse. When we acknowledge the paradoxes we live in,
and resist the hierarchical fault lines that propel cultural production, we
may seize the potential to realise social and political change. Indulging
ourselves in the hardest sounds we can find in Beijing may help
achieve that, just as immersion in the opaque yet shiny world of pop
may work. They may open up a world of differences, of possibilities;
show that there is always more to life; that we can move further than
the actual, towards the virtual, the field of endless possibilities that may
unfold in the future; *also* as mutations and amplifications of authoritative discourse. 'Actualised difference constitutes the present. The return
of difference constitutes the future.(...) Whatever we see, whatever we
say, there is more – always more' (May 2005: 62, 95) The possibility of
change lies in the actualisation of the virtual – of that what is already
there, yet remains contained, sanitised or immobile.

Notes

Introduction

1   See Zhu (2006) for an elaborate analysis and genealogy of *liumang* culture.
2   Baranovich (2003: 48) also notes the danger of sweeping statements when he writes
      that 'the impact of rock, nevertheless, should not be underestimated. It still constitu-
      tes a viable subculture in China, especially in Beijing, and although marginal, still ex-
      erts, even if only indirectly, some degree of influence on the wider culture.'
3   At www.guangzhou.elong.com/theme/themei48.html, accessed 12 July 2000.
4   Other examples in which he all too sweepingly critiques Chinese artists are, for ex-
      ample, his critique of writer Wang Shuo (1999: 97), of film director Chen Kaige
      (Barmé 1999: 194) and of film director Zhang Yuan: '... Zhang Yuan's work, with un-
      swerving entrepreneurship, had hit on an issue [homosexuality] sure to appeal to the
      international art-house world and its attendant critics. (...) [The gay scene] was being
      depicted partly for its sensational value by a director who had an established record
      of overcoming his filmic deficiencies by pursuing the controversial.' (196) Unfortu-
      nately, he fails to make explicit what precisely, for example, Zhang Yuan's 'filmic defi-
      ciencies' are.
5   Qiu Ye speaks with a likeminded nostalgia about the *dakou* era: 'The mid-1990s were
      really exciting, I felt very fulfilled at that time, now the cultural environment is much
      better that those days in terms of material conditions. My personal feeling is that the
      environment of rock music is more embarrassing than Chinese soccer. The latter is
      too lazy, they go to sleep after dinner, the former was too hungry, it pleases whoever
      serves food.' (in Anonymous 2008: 107)
6   But both Carsick Cars, and some of their contemporaries like PK14, attest to the fal-
      lacy of framing the new generation as overtly apolitical, as both bands integrate
      clearly political themes in their work. Carsick Cars, for example, has one song titled
      'No Future Square' – allegedly a reference to Tiananmen and the June 4th crackdown.
      Both Carsick Cars as well as PK14, along with Joyside, Hang on the Box, Shazi, T9/
      Hanggai band, New Pants, SUBS, Xiao He and Cui Jian feature in the documentary
      Beijing Bubbles that offers an illuminating insight in Beijing rock culture; also avail-
      able on YouTube (Messmer & Lindt 2008).
7   http://dystopia.blogbus.com/logs/14428275.html, 1 January 2008, accessed 29 Sep-
      tember 2008.
8   http://blog.sina.com.cn/twocold, 16 April 2008, retrieved 20 August 2008, see also
      Siemons 2008: 79-81.
9   The pop-rock divide is thus anything but a Chinese invention; instead, it is a globa-
      lised dichotomy that has its (imagined) origin in the West (Frith 1996). Rock verse is
      said to be poetry. Rock is believed to be sincere and authentic. The desperate screams
      from Kurt Cobain signify a truly tormented soul, ultimately verified by his suicide,
      whereas the plastic voice, face, and body of Britney Spears carries a mass-produced
      product. See also Regev (2007b).

10   It is easy to continue giving examples; in a review of a documentary on Chinese rock
     music, a Dutch journalist translates the perceived Western origin into a sense of
     superiority: 'China is lagging behind in popular music and will never be able to make
     up for it. It is unclear whether Chinese youth actually wants such music.' (Kamer
     1997) Another example comes from a rock singer – Daan Stuyven – from Belgium.
     When he made a trip to Guangzhou for a Belgian television documentary series, he
     expressed his discontent with Chinese music scenes (Canvas, *China voor Beginners*, 13
     March 2008), that to him were shallow and lacking any sign of rebellion: 'Pop music
     here is a disaster (...) Music should be a counterculture, there is no such thing here,
     at most some copies from the West. I was most intrigued by the conductor of the tra-
     ditional Chinese orchestra. This guy started as a rock musician, went to the West,
     discovered classical music and then moved on to discover traditional Chinese music.
     This is what I wish for all cultural domains in China, if necessary through the con-
     tact with the West, that they return to themselves.' Apparently, in this musician's
     view, this 'self' can only be actualised through evoking assumed 'unique Chinese tra-
     ditions,' a return to the imagined purity of a cultural, oriental essence. The sole pos-
     sible mode of music production comes from a return to a 'traditional musical past.'
11   Both magazines are in Chinese, their names appear in English as well as Chinese on
     the cover. Whereas *Modern Sky Magazine* applies a more fashionable style, and is di-
     rectly linked to the record company, *Music Heaven* is more sober in its style. By 2009
     both titles were defunct, two new magazines have replaced them, entitled *So Rock!*
     Magazine and *Rock*. Interestingly, *So Rock! Magazine* reserves a lot of attention for
     bands from outside Beijing. Like their predecessors, the covers of both magazines
     present Chinese and English bands and an accompanying CD introduces both Wes-
     tern and Chinese rock music (see Stokes 2006 for a review of Chinese rock press).
12   Examples are: underground punk (*dixia pengke*), punk pop (*liuxing pengke*), trash me-
     tal (*bianchi jinshu*), hardcore punk (*yinghe pengke*), and drum'n'bass as listed in Yuen
     (1999: 2021).
13   For an overview over time of articulations of place on CD jackets of Chinese rock
     CDs, see Steen 2008.
14   Indicative of this combination of the cosmopolitan and the national are the words of
     the vocalist of Muma, who discusses their CD *Yellow Star*: 'I am yellow and we are
     all young. When facing the raising of the flag, we look at the shining yellow stars
     printed on the flag but deeply feel our incapability to the nation. (...) When I listened
     to Joy Division, I would like to figure out my own position, a kind of music that is
     sympathetic to me. Did anyone sing before me in my language? No. Therefore I sing
     for myself.' (Johnson 2004: 10)
15   Combining the *Gang* of *Xiang Gang* (Hong Kong) with the *Tai* of *Taiwan*. Given its
     inclusion of both Cantopop and Mandapop I have chosen to use this term through-
     out this book, since my argument as well as the positioning of rock singer vis-à-vis
     pop is generally applicable to both styles.
16   As explained to me by the creative director of Sony Taiwan (interview on 8 June
     2004).
17   See for analyses of Chinese rock for example Baranovitch 2003; Brace 1992; Chong
     1991; Chow 1993; Efird 2001; Field & Groenewegen 2008; Huang 2001, 2003; Huot
     2000; Jones 1992, 1994; de Kloet 2000, 2005; Lanning, 1991; Lee, 1996; Qian
     2007; Steen, 1996, 2000, 2008; Stokes 2006; Yan 1999, 2004; for studies on pop,
     see Chan 1997; Chu 1998; Erni 2001, 2007; Fung & Curtin 2004; Fung 2008; Ho,
     2000, 2003; Khiun 2003; Lee 1992; Mitchell 2006; Moskovitz 2008; Witzleben
     1999.

18 Here I refer to a contamination of both culture and theory. As I explain elsewhere (De Kloet 2007), in times when longings for cultural purity abound, the insistence on impurity and pollution is a decidedly positive and timely move for me.

19 Given my limited musicological knowledge, the balance is rather uneven, as the focus is more on lyrical than on musical content.

20 A distinction can be made between the official press – i.e. newspapers and magazines directly linked to the CCP, such as the *People's Daily* (*Renmin ribao*) and the *People's Music* (*renmin yinyue*) – and the semi-official or popular press, which operates more independently (Bax 1998). Stokes (2006) makes a further distinction for the semi-official press between pop magazines aimed predominantly at teenagers – such as *Current Scene* (*Dangdai gequ*), *Fan's World* (*Gemi dashijie*), and *Pop* (*Qing yinyue*) – and the 'critical' pop magazines, such as *Audio and Video World* (*Yinxiang shijie*), *China Broadway* (*Zhongguo bailaohui*), *Music Heaven* (*Yinyue tiantan*), and *Modern Sky Music Magazine* (*Modeng tiankong*) (see also Steen 2000). The articles from the official press at times contain a propaganda-like critique of popular music, labelling it as spiritual pollution from the West; the pop magazines contain short features on the lives of pop stars, whereas the critical magazines are more focused on the music itself, often expressing an aim to educate the readers in issues related to popular music, with a special focus on rock. These latter pop magazines have been a valuable source of information for this study.

21 All interviews were taped and transcribed. I chose not to use a standard questionnaire, but worked with an array of sensitising concepts in the back of my mind, such as 'Chineseness,' 'politics,' and 'gender.'

22 Due to my limited knowledge of Chinese, interpreters were enlisted for the interviews and to translate both lyrics and articles. It goes without saying that this has affected the data, making, for example, a participatory observation in bars quite impossible. In any case, my Western appearance made me more of an outsider, which has its advantages as well as disadvantages. Musicians, record companies, and youths were always very helpful and open, and were quite eager to talk about their life and work. Their goodwill – and the rapport developed during the years of relating to them and their music – helped me to move into the rock culture quite easily. Articles on the rock culture I published in Dutch, English and Chinese journals and magazines added to my status and made bands and record companies more eager to help me.

Chapter 1

1 This resulted in a new regime of table manners – the defiling hand should be kept on the table – and advice on the best sleeping positions, going as far as advising one to tie one's hands to the sides of the bed (Dikötter 1995: 172).

2 For a comprehensive overview of China's rock culture, see the Japanese online database at www.yaogun.com and for an English source, including a wiki, see www.rockinchina.com/ as well as the countless MySpace sites of the bands.

3 The frequently used label 'avant-garde' to describe contemporary art in Beijing is problematic in that it imposes a temporality on Chinese art that denies its coevalness with 'Western' art worlds, where the avant-garde refers to the past (early 20th century).

4 The same goes for their Western counterparts, like the German industrial band Einstürzende Neubauten, which also participates in other cultural fields such as theatre. Both NO and The Fly admit to having been strongly influenced by Einstürzende Neubauten.

5   www.zuoxiaozuzhou.com/

6   Quoted in www.keepmakingsense.com/ACF_bio.htm

7   Feng Jiangzhou of female punk band Hang on the Box and the electronic duo Panda
     Twins, Zu Zhou of Yunnan folk singer June.

8   As he explained to me in June 2004, in China it is very easy to be the first in some-
     thing, such as, in his case, noise music and digital hardcore.

9   He Li also quotes critic Sun Mengpu, who describes the music of NO as: 'A soul is
     bleeding in butchery. A man, cursing the cultural garbage, cruelly exposes his anger,
     his tears and his despair. Rock and roll is music beyond limits. I see, in the darkness
     of fear, a pair of eyes, stunned, and a heart, floating in the air, dying.'

10   On the release for the mainland these scenes were replaced by pictures of the band
     to avoid censorship (see also chapter five).

11   Western musicians also claim technology to be falsifying, a notion that can be traced
     back to the Romantic critique of industrial capitalism in the 19th century. For a con-
     cise overview of this critique, see Negus (1992: 27-37). The popularity of MTV's un-
     plugged series in the 1990s can be seen in this light, and might be considered a re-
     action against the ultimate technologised aesthetics of electronic dance music.

12   Baranovich (2003: 54-107) elaborates on the link between ethnicity and rock, suggest-
     ing that rock serves as an empowering tool for China's ethnic minorities. The pre-
     sence of non-Beijingers within the Beijing rock culture indeed indicates that rock cul-
     ture is a cultural domain that enables musicians to move from the margin towards
     the centre, but this margin does not necessarily have to be defined in terms of ethni-
     city, as it can also apply to simple geography.

13   For a wonderful analysis of the work of Tongue, see Jeroen Groenewegen's 2004 the-
     sis, available online at www.keepmakingsense.com.

14   For an analysis of the importance of humour in Chinese rock music, see Groenewegen
     2008.

15   An interesting case in point is the music of Sister Drum (DaDaWa). Her 'world mu-
     sic', presumably strongly influenced by Tibetan folk songs, is one of the rare exam-
     ples of Chinese voices that have succeeded in entering the Western market. Its popu-
     larity outside China (both in East and South-East Asia as well as in the West) can
     partly be explained by its strong exotic flavour, which corresponds well with stereoty-
     pical images of Tibet as a mythical place with a long and rich history. Both the music
     and the imagery (the jacket depicts a veiled, mysterious woman) construct an exotic
     place, one far away from the modern world. The following critical review, which ap-
     peared in China, is interesting: 'The singer does not express the spirit and philoso-
     phy successfully (...) this music copies a lot from Tibetan folk music in an unnatural
     way. In some songs, the background vocals are more unstable than mysterious. The
     electronic instruments merely belong to superficial and snobbish modern culture'
     (Dai 1995: 22). Instead of questioning the exoticism in the music, this critic refers to
     the incompatibility of folk songs and pop music. Of course, the adjectives he uses to
     describe modern culture and the related mystification and celebration of either the
     past or other ('traditional') places are not unfamiliar. Rather than agreeing with his
     accusation that Sister Drum is a cheap cultural adaptation, I see her as being a self-
     orientalising musical act that is part of a carefully planned commercial strategy.

16   Death metal is one of the most extreme subgenres of heavy metal. Its lyrics often fo-
     cus on death, decay, and destruction, the sound tends to eschew the melodic charac-
     ter of mainstream heavy metal, and in the West the death metal scene is surrounded
     by biased stories of fights between bands which, in some cases, have resulted in mur-
     der (Kahn-Harris 1999).

17   For example, the androgynous poses in heavy metal (e.g. Kiss' makeup and Axl
     Rose's long hair) render the celebration of masculinity profoundly ambiguous.

According to Walser (1993: 120), 'the sexual politics of heavy metal are (...) a conflicted mixture of confirmation and contradiction of dominant myths about gender.' Their chivalric aesthetics turn the musicians of Tang Dynasty into male heroes, thus confirming a dominant gender myth (which equates heroes with real men). At the same time, the band constructs a space where Chinese youth can play with gender. Boys experiment with hairstyles that until then had signified the feminine, and female groupies in the heavy metal scene play the same game by appropriating masculine signs, e.g. dressing up in tough leather clothes and wearing their hair short. Through its *performance* of masculinity, heavy metal shows that gender is above all a construction, one that is constantly being forged (cf. Walser 1993: 136). There are no real men; we can at most act like one.

18 Together with Barmé (1992), Jones was the first to analyze the complicity of rock with CCP politics. He refers to an article in *China Youth News* (1991), which stated that the government should tolerate rock in order to oppose the dominance of Cantopop. 'There is not just a little irony here: an oppositional subculture based on an Anglo-American musical form that originally sprang from a repudiation of traditional Chinese culture is nationalistically invoked in the official press as a domestic alternative to foreign products' (Jones 1994: 161).

19 Jones (1994: 160) quotes Lao Wu: 'I've been Westernised almost my whole life. I spent twenty years absorbing anything Western that I could get my hands on. I never knew anything about my own tradition. And now I really hate anything from the West. I resent its influence... modern Chinese culture has never lived up to the tradition because it's been ruined by all the Western influence. We have to get back to our roots; (...) that's what the mission of [Chinese rock] should be all about.'

20 However, the rumour within the rock culture was that the conflict was far less related to ideology than to conflicts within the personal sphere.

21 Yet, one can question the validity of this distinction between public and private; following Butler, the intention of one's utterances is not what is important, nor whether statements are ironised in the private realm, the words themselves can still be violent interventions in public discourse, and may sustain the status quo in China.

22 Interestingly, their celebration of Chineseness, which is predominantly confined to their lyrics, does not cater well to the Western gaze: when Tang Dynasty performed (together with Cui Jian, Wang Yong, and Cobra) in Berlin in 1993, the audience started to leave, disappointed by what it considered to be an old-fashioned sound. The reception of Cui Jian, with his use of Chinese instruments, was much better (Steen, personal conversation, 27 August 2000).

23 According to Lawrence Grossberg (1986: 58), punk challenged the control of the major record companies, returned the single to the centre of music production, rejected criteria of aesthetic and technological expertise, rejected the star system, and it consciously sought the most minimal musical conditions of rock.

24 But, as he explains, 'The significance of rhythm for African music and culture lies not in its simplicity and 'directness' but in its flexibility and sophistication, not in its physical expressivity but in its communicative subtlety' (Frith 1996: 135).

25 The line in italics was sung in English; the lyrics come from an underground punkzine I will discuss further on in the text.

26 www.myspace.com/subsband, accessed 8 September 2008.

27 www.scream-records.net, accessed 20 July 2006.

28 www.myspace.com/yintsang, accessed 8 September 2008.

Chapter 2

1   The importance of one's hometown can hardly be overestimated in China. Migrants in cities associate with other migrants from their hometown, and employers allocate jobs to workers from their own hometown; even emigration routes can be traced between a particular town and another country (the citizens of Wenzhou, for example, have strong ties with the Netherlands, given the emigration figures (Li 1999)). So-called campus songs (*xiaoyuan gequ*) comprise a folk-rock subgenre popular among college students. The songs give voice to their angst about leaving home for an unknown future.

2   Yi Sha later accused Zhang Chu in the popular media of becoming too intellectual (Hou 1996). Cui Jian had to apologise in public after spreading the rumour that Yi Sha had written lyrics for Zhang Chu (thereby accusing Zhang Chu of not being a true musician) (Zhu 1996). Yi Sha replied: 'I have never set a single word to music for him,' and added that Zhang Chu never liked his poems (Yi 1996). Gossip is certainly an understudied theme in popular music studies, and in cultural studies in general. It requires further study given its links to politics and aesthetics (see Besnier 2009).

3   Indicative of the mobility of cultural identities in China is Hu Mage's move towards electronic music in his second album – an album which was generally not well received.

4   On 8 December 1994, a theatre caught fire in the middle of a performance, causing 325 deaths and 132 injuries. Among the dead, 288 were students under 18. When they were trying to escape from the theatre, an official from the local education bureau stopped them, shouting, 'Let the officials go first!'

5   On 10 June 2005, the town of Shalan, in Heilongjiang Province, was struck by a flash flood without warning. 105 children were killed, due to the malpractice of the local government both in forecasting the flood and in rescuing the victims.

6   On 21 June 2003, the body of a three-year-old girl was found decomposing at her home; the cause of death was starvation. Her mother, a drug addict, had been taken to the rehab centre by the police 17 days before her daughter's body began to decompose.

7   The illegal blood-trading business in Henan caused numerous HIV positive diagnoses. Some villages became 'HIV villages', where many infants tested HIV positive.

8   It is not surprising that the feminine travels especially well to the West, as women (more than men) articulate the exotic, authentic China. Examples can be found in both authorship – a number of female (overseas) Chinese writers have appeared on the Western market (Jung Chang, Amy Tan, Lulu Wang) – and in content, not only in books by these authors, but also in Zhang Yimou's movies (*Red Shorgum, Ju Dou*, and *Raise the Red Lantern*) portray the female star Gong Li (Zhang's ex-wife) in a predominantly rural setting from the past – see chapter three.

9   Yet in 2008, Zang Tianshuo was imprisoned for alleged involvement in a murder case.

10 Interestingly, his critique of the negative impact of rebellious behaviour was also voiced after Icelandic star Björk expressed her opinions on China's Tibet policies during a concert in Shanghai in early 2008. Such actions have a negative impact on the cultural scene in China: since then concert regulations have been implemented more strictly, and for organisers of festivals it has became more difficult to get official permission. It was generally believed that this was not only caused by the forthcoming Olympic Games, but also by Björk's performance.

11 See http://australianetwork.com/nexus/stories/s2203734.htm. Accessed 10 June 2009.

12 Both the record company and some youths I asked are aware of the reference to the T-shirts; what they did not know is that these T-shirts were officially banned. The slogan itself can be read at face value; that is, as the utterance of a teenager who does not want to be disturbed. It signifies a desire to resist surveillance, a refusal to act in line with the dominant images of 'youth as hope – youth as fun – youth as trouble,' as discussed in chapter one. But there is more to it, due to its intertextual reference. The audience derived a lot of pleasure from decoding the reference to the summer of 1991. When I heard them singing these lines I felt great pleasure, not only because of the intertextual reference, but also by my 'ability' to pick up this reference. This pleasure lies in the active use of one's popular cultural capital, a capital so much ignored by academics (Frith 1996).

13 From http://en.wikipedia.org/wiki/The_Flowers, accessed 9 September 2008.

14 Ibid.

15 What I leave out here is the DJ scene, which since 2000 has gained momentum with raves organised on the Great Wall, and many parties throughout the city. With the strong support of DJ Zhang Youdai, the dance scene has gained momentum with other DJs like DJ Mickey and DJ Weng Weng. However, this scene is very different from the more rock oriented scenes discussed in this book, and would require quite a different approach, focusing for example on party culture, nightlife and its political economy and the role of technology. For rare studies of dance culture in China see Basile Zimmerman (2007) and Anouska Komlosy (2008).

16 The possibility of grouping Feng Jiangzhou, Chen Dili (both of whom are now grouped as underground), and Supermarket together as an electronic scene indicates once again the inherent fluidity of the scenic approach.

17 Which made the interview a difficult exercise, as I was rapidly running out of questions. This shows how my own position remains framed by the rock mythology.

Chapter 3

1 Translated by the lyricist Chow Yiu Fai. The song is a response to the Tiananmen 1989 protests. It alludes to post-massacre China and questions the ideology of silence, of acceptance, conveniently assigned to be Chinese values and traditions, popularly known as 'the heaven' (*tian*) or destiny. The title and major theme of the song was borrowed from a poem written by Qu Yuan (±340 B.C. – ±278 B.C.) whose honest but bitter advice to the regime of his time earned him a life of frustrations, pain and finally suicide. Legend has it that his poem was originally titled *wentian*, literally 'ask heaven', but the authorities worshipped, or feared *tian* to such an extent that it would be total disrespect to place *tian* at the end of the title – it had to come first (see Chow 2009).

2 See http://english.cri.cn/4026/2007/10/29/1361@288815.htm, accessed 16 June 2008.

3 It is worth noting that female diasporic authors like Jung Chang and Amy Tan tend to attract more international attention and reputations than their male counterparts.

4 Spivak writes: 'The Woman from the South is a particularly privileged signifier, as object and mediator; as she is, in the market, the favoured agent-as-instrument of transnational capital's globalising reach' (1999: 200-201).

5 These are not all the female voices in the Beijing rock culture; for reasons of space I leave out, among others, Wei Hua, Ai Jing (who borrows her power from the discourse of folk) and Zhang Qianqian (who has moved more toward the high arts, e.g. by performing as a vocal artist in a multimedia production of Wu Wenguang.

6   The music, however, is criticised for being old-fashioned. Illustrative is the review of
     their second album by a Beijing critic (Java 2000: 29): 'Contrary to clothes, musical
     choices for women are very, very limited. In China, this problem is even more promi-
     nent. All female artists seem to have only one face: gentle, feminine. It's the same in
     rock. I am not saying all women should get crazy. But I think their character is flat,
     and too old-fashioned.'

7   See www.youtube.com/watch?v=qLiLmkog-LI, accessed 10 October 2008.

8   In the 1991 World Values Survey, China ranks highest of all countries with 96% of
     respondents agreeing with the statement "taking the drug marijuana or hashish is
     never justified" (in the Netherlands, this figure was 66%). (Inglehart *et al* 1998:
     V301)

9   This despite the fact that at a certain point Wang Yue exclaimed provocatively that
     'foreigners are very shit' (*laowai tebie shi*).

10   Tian Yuan was invited to perform at the 'Global City, Global Youth' music festival in
     Sweden in June 2002, and Channel 4 went to China to make a documentary on her
     (Qian 2007: 234).

11   See www.thebeijinger.com/blog/2008/10/06/Video-of-the-Week-Top-Floor-Circus-per-
     form-Shanghai-Huanying-Ni-at-Modern-Sky-Festiv, accessed 20 February 2009.

12   www.coldfairyland.com/album/2002.htm, accessed 9 February 2009.

13   All bands are at pains to point out their difference from Beijing rock, rather than
     from *Gangtai* pop, which shows how such organising dichotomies are anything but
     fixed. The primary constitutive outside for a music scene depends on the context.

14   Of course there are exceptions to this observation. The so-called 'China Winds' songs
     constitute a sub-genre within *Gangtai* pop in which elements of Chineseness are
     clearly integrated, with Jay Chow as one of the main protagonists.

15   For the magazine's motivation, see www.timeout.com.hk/music/features/15236/1-an-
     thony-wong.html, accessed 20 February 2009.

16   'People Mountain People Sea' is a Chinese idiom used to describe mass events where
     the people form – figuratively speaking, mountain and sea. It refers in this context to
     Hong Kong and to pop culture, but in the case of Anthony Wong it has also a critical
     aspect in that it refers to the disastrous effects such events can have, like the Cultural
     Revolution, and how the voices of minorities are too often silenced by the masses.

17   Translated by the lyricist Chow Yiu Fai.

18   I am indebted to Giselinde Kuipers for this observation, which certainly deserves
     further study.

19   The interpretation of the song is based on an interview with its lyricist, Chow Yiu Fai
     (3 March 2003).

20   Translated by the lyricist Lin Xi.

Chapter 4

1   As Tia DeNora writes (2000: 45), 'Non-musical materials, such as situations, biogra-
     phical matters, patterns of attention, assumptions, are all implicated in the clarifica-
     tion of music's semiotic force. Conversely, though, and simultaneously, music is used
     to clarify the very things that are used to clarify it.' The crux is thus to combine a so-
     ciological approach with a more textual or musicological take on audiences.

2   A study by Van Alphen (1992) of Francis Bacon's work makes a similar point. Its cov-
     er text runs: 'Most analyses of Bacon actually neutralise his work by discussing it as
     an existential expression, and as the horrifying communication of an isolated indivi-
     dual – which simply transfers the pain in the painting back to Bacon himself. This
     study is the first attempt to account for the pain of the *viewer*.'

3   Admittedly, this definition remains rather esoteric and resonates uncomfortably with
    the self-help discourse that permeates contemporary life, as McGee observes: 'Despite
    Foucault's dismissal of the vernacular self improvement culture of self-discovery and
    authenticity, there are surprising similarities between some non-Socratic Greek ethi-
    cal practices circa 380 BC that Foucault seems to advocate and the practices proposed
    by contemporary self-help culture.' (McGee 2005: 95)
4   As becomes clear from my terminology used throughout this chapter, rather than
    taking a behavioural, effect-oriented approach to audience studies, this chapter is in-
    spired by an approach in which media reception is read as a struggle over and for
    meaning (Alasuutari 1999; Ang 1985, 1991, 1996; Dickinson *et al* 1998; Fiske 1988;
    Hall 1980; Hartley 1987; Hermes 1995, 2006, Morley 1992, 2006; Nightingale
    1996, Webster & Phalen 1997). The range of possible interpretations of a certain text
    is limited by hegemonic structures in society, that is, certain readings of a text are
    preferred (Hall 1980). The 'active audience' approach runs the danger of celebrating
    agency and ignoring structure; in particular, the work of Fiske (1988) and Jenkins
    (1992, 2006) reflects a quite astonishing belief in the decoding and creative poten-
    tials of audiences. Work in this vein also tends to think of audiences as constantly
    fleeting, never fixed and utterly fragmented (Ang 1996). Meaghan Morris, taking the
    work of John Fiske and Iain Chambers as an example, pointed already in 1988 to the
    danger of banality in cultural studies, when she wrote that 'I get the feeling that
    somewhere in some English publisher's vault there is a master-disk from which
    thousands of versions of the same article about pleasure, resistance, and the politics
    of consumption are being run off under different names with minor variations.'
    (Morris 1988: 15) The outcome of such analyses is too often, in her view, banal, pro-
    blematic and tautological, generating endless variations on: 'people in modern media-
    tised societies are complex and contradictory, mass cultural texts are complex and
    contradictory, therefore people using them produce complex and contradictory cul-
    ture.' (Morris 1988: 19)
5   The survey was carried out among youths aged between 15 and 25 years old by a Beij-
    ing-based agency, Diamond Consultancy, and was financed by Philips Sound & Vi-
    sion. The sample is representative of the variables age, education, and sex. Figures
    from the real population were obtained from the China Population Statistics Year-
    book 1995 (regarding age) and were calculated by the Beijing Bureau for Statistics
    for this survey (regarding education). Figures from the sample differ at most 5%
    from official figures. The survey was carried out in five different districts in Beijing;
    thus different neighbourhoods are represented. The ten research assistants worked
    with a quota when selecting their respondents. Given the involvement of both local
    consultants and Philips, it was impossible to include political questions. The issue of
    class remains obscure given the turbulent recent history of China, which makes it
    difficult, if not impossible, to develop reliable indicators; both the parent's education
    and salary are inaccurate given the impact of the Cultural Revolution and of the wage
    distribution of the working units.
6   This group comprised 11 middle-school students, 18 university students, and three
    youths who had already started working. Sixteen were male and sixteen were female,
    and they ranged in age from 16 to 25. For reasons of privacy, the respondents were
    asked to use a pseudonym. See appendix 1 for further demographic details of this
    group.
7   The importance of the family ideology stretches beyond the actual family, toward the
    political domain. For example, the Chinese word for country (*guojia*) incorporates the
    word family (*jia*). When Hong Kong was handed back to China, it was frequently de-
    scribed as a child going back to its motherland The desire to rebel against one's par-
    ents can be interpreted in a more political way. The personal is political, perhaps

even more so in China, where the political borrows its power from the sanctified ideology of the family.

8   In the US, female listeners were over-represented in the cluster 'mainstream music,' and males were over-represented in the clusters 'music lovers', 'indifferents,' and 'heavy rockers' (Hakanen & Wells 1993, 66). Research carried out in The Netherlands shows similar gendered patterns (Mulder et al 2007; for the US, see Christenson & Peterson 1988: 298; for the UK, see Thornton 1995: 103-104). Given the increased generic blurring, related to the emergence of dance, hip hop and R&B, due to which the differences between rock and pop are becoming less prominent (Regev 2007a), such gendered differences may slowly change and eventually fade out.

9   Rotated component matrix, extraction method: principal component analysis, rotation method: varimax with Kaiser normalisation. The principal component analysis (PCA) is an analysis of many variables. Its main aim is data reduction by lumping together variables that are closely correlated. It first measures correlations between each variable with each of all other variables, after which it searches for clusters of connected variables that are maximally independent from the other clusters. The variables within one cluster are merged into a metric component/variable. These clusters are shown in the table by the gray shading. In this case, the PCA has reduced the total variance of nine variables to three independent components. The first component (classical) explains 24.8% of the variance, the second (pop) explains 17.9%, and the third (rock) explains 17.8%. Thus, in total 60% of the variance of the nine variables can be explained with three components. The inaccessible terminology of quantitative research is worth a separate study, as it produces an aura of truth as though we were dealing with so-called 'hard sciences'.

10   Pearson correlation = 0.195 and -0.102 respectively. Unless otherwise indicated, the bivariate correlation figures presented in this chapter are all Pearson correlation coefficients.

11   Both a t-test (which compares the means of two groups) for the separate pop and rock audience, as presented in Table 4.1, and a correlation analysis show significant differences.

12   Indicative is also that my survey showed a relation between the statement 'For me, lyrics are important when I listen to a song' and rock (0.135), whereas this relation was weaker for the pop zone.

13   Pearson correlation = 0.281.

14   In the words of Deleuze & Guattari: 'Now we are at home. But home does not preexist: It was necessary to draw a circle around that uncertain and fragile centre, to organise a limited space. (..) Sonorous or vocal components are very important: a wall of sound, or at least a wall with some sonic bricks in it. A child hums to summon the strength for the schoolwork she has to hand in. A housewife sings to herself, or listens to the radio, as she marshals the anti-chaos forces of her work. Radios and television sets are like sound walls around every household and mark territories (the neighbour complains when it gets too loud). (...) The territory, and the functions performed within it, are products of territorialisation. Territorialisation is an act of rhythm that has become expressive...' (Deleuze & Guattari 1987: 311, 317; see also: Grossberg 1993b; Boomkens 2000). It is the arguably loud sound of rock, intersecting with the discourses that frame this sound (the rock mythology), which marks the territory. The listener can enter the territory, but only if he or she takes the musician seriously; in other words, only if he or she accepts the terms set by the musician and producer, terms embedded in the hard force of the rock mythology. Thus, the label 'rock' produces a potential closure of interpretative possibilities, a closure not only encoded in the sound itself, but – more so – generated by the territorialising force of the rock mythology. People hide for a moment in the seemingly safe grounds of a

music territory, only to be deterritorialised by the forces of distinction *within* that territory. In the words of Grossberg (1993: 207): 'Rock is constantly producing lines of flight which can challenge not only specific territorialisation, but also the very desirability of territoriality. (...) Rock operates with a necessary contradiction: territorialising and deterritorialising, lines of articulation and lines of flight.' This de/territorialising force of the rock mythology is related to the 'reflexive' project of the self, as it produces technologies that help listeners feel at home – albeit temporarily.

15   Unless otherwise indicated, the three factors presented in Table 4.1 are used in the analysis to measure differences between different audiences. In some cases, the groups as distinguished in Table 4.2 are compared as an extra check. All predictive indicators are rather low. In the case of rock, only sex proves to be a predictor (beta= -0.143, R^2=0.020). As to pop, education as well as sex are related. Female respondents (beta=0.119, R^2=0.033) and those with a lower level of education (beta=-0.136, R^2=0.033) are more likely to prefer pop music. In particular, girls (beta=0.131, R^2=0.036) with a higher level of education (beta=0.153, R^2=0.036) prefer classical music.

16   I use the term 'fan' rather loosely for audiences with a comparatively strong involvement. I do not wish to draw a sharp distinction between 'fans' and those who are less involved. But I am aware of and hope to avoid the potential negative connotations attached to fandom. Fans caught up in the Beatlemania of the 1960s, or fans of the Spice Girls in the 1990s, are often depicted as screaming, crazy girls and boys who have lost their minds. I agree with Jenson (1992: 123), who states, 'Defending fandom as a deviant activity allows (individually) a reassuring, self-aggrandising stance to be adopted. It also supports the celebration of particular values – the rational over the emotional, the educated over the uneducated, the subdued over the passionate, the elite over the popular, the mainstream over the margin, the status quo over the alternative.' However, I do not see the theoretical need to essentialise audiences in such fixed categories as fan and non-fan. See also De Kloet and Van Zoonen, 2007.

17   Pearson correlation = -0.181 and 0.133 respectively.

Chapter 5

1   This image of the Chinese market is not restricted to post-1978 China. Already in 1842, when the Sino-British Treaty of Nanjing was signed to end the opium war and open up China, Sir Henry Pottinger, who drew up the treaty, assured the textile factories of Manchester that their capacity would be insufficient to make even one pair of stockings for each Chinese citizen in only one province. Thus the business opportunities were considered to be extremely promising (Osterhammel 1989: 171). I am grateful to Frans Paul van der Putten for this reference.

2   Unfortunately, the IFPI does not indicate whether Mandapop from Taiwan falls under the domestic market or not, but judging from the presentation of the Chinese figures it does. The international repertoire in Hong Kong is likely to consist partly of Mandapop from Taiwan.

3   According to Laing (1993: 22), 'The Christian Church was Europe's first transnational institution and its liturgy gave music an international dimension as early as the Middle Ages.'

4   The 'Greater China' concept is predominantly used to describe the economic ties between mainland China, Taiwan, Hong Kong and sometimes also Singapore and the overseas Chinese communities. It also refers to the importance attached to Chineseness when doing business; in these cases, the financial flows from overseas Chinese to China are highlighted (Harding 1995). At the cultural level, the spread of a com-

mon popular culture is an additional driving force for the formation and integration of a 'Greater China' (Gold 1993). 'Popular culture of Hong Kong and Taiwan has a growing audience on the mainland, and exchanges of artists, performers and writers between Taiwan, [Hong Kong] and the mainland are steadily increasing' (Harding 1995: 20). The 'Greater China' concept can easily become a signifier for an uncritical celebration of a transnational Chinese identity, resonating with the work of Tu Wei-Ming and his concept of Cultural China (1994). See also Callahan (2004) for an analysis of how different actors – including hooligans – are involved in the production of a 'Greater China' through networks of relations in local, national, regional, global, and transnational space.

5   Copyright income from, for example, karaoke or radio airplay is not included in these figures. Also not included in these figures are the piracy market, and the informal recording and circulation of music. Sales figures thus present a distorted view of musical activity in 'Greater China' (see also: Negus 1992: 12-13).

6   The figures of the Chinese market over time are especially problematic. Figures in China dropped from 388.7 in 1992 to 241.0 in 1994 (based on official – that is, unreliable – government figures) and from 178.4 to 279.6 from 1995 to 1997 (based on industry estimates). Hong Kong increased from 96.5 in 1991 to 183.2 in 1995, after which it decreased to 167.3 in 1996 and to 148.6 in 1997. Taiwan increased from 223.9 in 1991 to 427.8 in 1997 (all figures in US$ millions). In 2004, the China figures dropped again as the system based on which the IFPI calculated the estimated number changed.

7   To maximise profit, some go as far as producing piracy copies.

8   Space does not permit an extensive discussion on the issue of copyright, but it is important to note here that copyright is with good reason seen by many as an imperialistic discourse, and as merely ceremonial and catering to the benefit of global companies rather than artists (Dolfsma 2000; Fung 2008; Halbert 1997; Hugenholtz 1999; Laing 2004; Mertha 2005; Pang 2006; Vaidhyanathan 2003). Furthermore, as testified by *dakou* culture, piracy has also been clearly beneficial for the music culture in China. To provide an alternative to the rigid and neoliberal copyright regime that dominates the global entertainment sector, the Creative Commons movement has emerged as an alternative, which has also its supporters in China (see http://creative-commons.org/ and Lessig 2001).

9   A problematic fiction in itself given the important role the nation-state also plays in Western economies; the prominent role nation-states played during the credit crisis that started in 2008 serves as a good example.

10 Interestingly, this is different for the ownership of rock venues: Mao Live house is owned by a Japanese, Yugong Yishan by a Frenchman, and D-22 by an American Tsinghua professor.

11 Whereas Jingwen, another local company, resembles more the old working unit, their subsidiary Scream, a label focusing on the more extreme genres, has a very different identity – like Modern Sky, young, hip and trendy. Scream is a case of portfolio management, a common practice in the record industry. By dividing the company into discrete units, surveillance of its performance is ensured (Negus 1998: 360). At the same time it gives the artist the illusion of dealing with a small label.

12 Here, the distinction between rock culture and record industry becomes extraordinarily blurred; these quotes could also have been used to discuss the positioning of the fashionable bands.

13 Because The Flowers sold well in Taiwan (50,000 copies in one month), where it was released under the Magic Stone label, New Bees managed to earn a lot more money than they did in China.

14 It is worth noting that in Chinese, there is no real equivalent for the word censorship. The Chinese expression is generally taken to be *shencha*, meaning to inspect or to check. The emphasis thus lies on the act of inspecting, rather than on the item to be inspected. Its connotation is arguably less strong than in English.

15 For reasons of space, I confine my analysis to practices directly related to music. I leave out coercion tactics related to the personal lives of musicians. Sometimes singers are charged under the law against hooligans (*liumang*), but this is only rarely the case. More often bands (Tang Dynasty) or singers (Luo Qi) are taken into custody under the charge of drug use.

16 I have also heard of a case where the Ministry of Culture even subsidised a taped compilation of revolutionary classics, because of its lyrics. They were certainly not aware that these were used in punk songs; as such, the government subsidised a musical parody of itself.

17 The idea of a velvet prison positions artists vis-à-vis the state. Such politicisation of art and popular culture is not restricted to China alone; it can also be found in writings on other communist/post-communist societies. Interpretations of the role of rock music in such societies differ among academics, most of whom are highly informed by the rock mythology. Wicke, for example, argues that 'rock music contributed to the erosion of totalitarian regimes throughout Eastern Europe long before the cracks in the system became apparent and resulted in its unexpected demise' (Wicke 1992: 81). In his discussion of rock in Czechoslovakia, Mitchell makes a similar statement, saying that 'rock music has represented probably the most widespread vehicle of youth rebellion, resistance and independence behind the Iron Curtain' (Mitchell 1992: 187). Ramet draws less on a fixed hegemonic model in her writing on Russian rock in the 1980s. She points out that the authorities politicised rock, and that the music itself is not intrinsically political. The erosion of the political order badly affected the rock scene, which, according to Ramet, has lost energy now that the fight with communism is over (Ramet 1994: 10, 209). Ramet's study shows that, in contrast to what the quotations from both Wicke and Mitchell suggest, there is little ground to uphold the idea that rock and socialism are natural enemies. On the contrary, the East German state used rock as one of its propaganda tools (Rauhut 1998: 343). However, I do not know of such a direct use of rock by the Chinese authorities. In her critique on the often assumed political role of rock in socialist societies, Peckaz concludes, in line with the narrative of the velvet prison sketched above, that 'relationships between the socialist state and rock were more often symbiotic than contradictory, hence many rock musicians were more interested in adapting to the *status quo*, rather than destroying it' (1994: 48).

18 The implementation of profoundly ambiguous regulations like these – with their focus on the political and the moral, and their element of national protectionism – is far from consistent with the actual text. Also, those who wrote them or are supposed to enforce them often do not believe in the regulations. As such, it can partly be considered a discursive masquerade, meant to legitimise the Party, yet not really taken seriously by anyone. According to Fu and Cullen (1996: 274), compared to other countries, it is not so much the law texts that are 'problematic', as their enforcement.

19 The reason was more the enraged mother of one of the band's members (Zhang Yue), who works in the media industry herself, who thought vocalist Qiu Ye was a bad influence on her son, and asked the censors to pay extra attention to this release.

20 Of course, not only rock faces censorship; pop does as well. Yet given the often more explicit political and/or sexual contents of its lyrics, it can be assumed that rock faces stronger restrictions than other music genres.

Chinese Glossary

Ai Jing	艾敬
Audience	听众
Authenticity	真实性
Backdormitory Boys	后舍男生
Badhead	坏脑唱片
Bai Guang	白光
Balinghou	80后
Baojiajie 43	鲍家街43号乐队
Bei Dao	北岛
Bianjibu de gushi	编辑部的故事
Black metal	黑金属
Bo Lu	吕玻
Brain Failure	脑浊乐队
Carsick Cars	晕车的车乐队
Catcher in the Rye	麦田守望者乐队
Censorship	审查
Chen Dili	陈底里
Chen Kaige	陈凯歌
Cheung, Jacky	成龙
Cheung, Leslie	张国荣
"China Broadway"	中国百老汇
Chinese Communist Party	中国共产党
Chow Yiu Fai	周耀辉
Chun Sue	春树
Cobra	眼镜蛇乐队
Cold Blooded Animals	冷血动物乐队
Commercialisation	商业化
Compass	指南针乐队
Convenience Store	便利商店乐队
Cool Fairyland	冷酷仙境乐队
Crystal Butterfly	水晶蝴蝶乐队
Cui Jian	崔健
Cultural T-shirts	文化衫
Dadawa (Sister Drum)	朱哲琴
Dai Jinhua	戴锦华
Dakou	打口
Dance music	跳舞音乐

Danwei	单位
Death metal	死亡金属
Deng Lijun (Teresa Teng)	邓丽君
Deng Xiaoping	邓小平
Dee Dickson	李劲松
Ding Wu	丁武
Douban 9	豆瓣九点
Dou Wei	窦唯
Electronic music	电子音乐
Erhu	二胡
Face	面孔乐队
Fang Lijun	方力钧
Fashionable bands	时髦乐队
Feng Jiangzhou	丰江舟
Flowers, the	花儿乐队
The Fly	苍蝇乐队
Folk	民歌，民谣
Folk Rock	民谣摇滚
Future sound	未来之声
Gangtai pop	港台流行音乐
Gao Qi	高旗
Gao Xiaosong	高晓松
Globalisation	全球化
Gong Li	巩俐
Gray Wolf	灰狼乐队
Guzheng	古筝
Han Han	韩寒
Hang on the Box	挂在盒子上乐队
Hardcore Punk	硬核朋克
He Yong	何勇
Heaven	天堂乐队
Heavy metal	重金属
Hei Bao	黑豹乐队
Hip Hop	嘻哈音乐
Hopscotch	跳房子乐队
Hou Dejian	侯德建
Hu Mage	胡吗个
Hui, Sam	许冠杰
Grey Culture	灰色文化
"I'm pissed, leave me alone"	烦着呢，别理我
Iron Kite	铁风筝
Jia Zhangke	贾樟柯
Jiang Zemin	江泽民
Jiang Wen	姜文

Jingwen	北京京文唱片有限公司
Kewang	渴望
Kuo, Kaiser	郭怡广
Kungfoo	功夫乐队
Kwok, Aaron	郭富城
Lai, Leon	黎明
Lao Wu	老五（刘义军）
Lau, Andy	刘德华
Lau, Gene	刘卓辉
LazyMuthaFucka (LMF)	大懒堂
Lee, Coco	李玟
Lei Feng	雷锋
Li Peng	李鹏
Li Suli	李素丽
Li Yuchun	李宇春
"Life is a bore"	真累
Ling Dian (Point Zero)	零点乐队
Liumang	流氓
Lo, Candy	卢巧音
Localisation	本地化
Long Kuan	龙宽
Luo Dayou	罗大佑
Luo Qi	罗琦
Ma Yoyo	马友友
Magic Stone	魔岩
Marketisation	市场化
Mao Zedong	毛泽东
Massage Milk	按摩乳
Meteor Garden	流星花园
Mian Mian	棉棉
MIDI Festival	迷笛音乐节
Ministry of Culture	文化部
Modern Sky	摩登天空
Mok, Karen	莫文蔚
Mu Zimei	木子美
Mui, Anita	梅艳芳
Music Heaven	音乐天堂
Nameless Highland	无名高地
Nan xun	南巡
The National Broadcasting, Film & TV Bureau	国家广播电影电视总局
New Bees	新蜂唱片
New Pants	新裤子乐队
New Sound Movement	新声运动

New wave	新浪潮
Noise	噪音
Ou Ning	欧宁
Overload	超载乐队
Peng Lei	彭磊
People Mountain People Sea	人山人海
Punk	朋克
Pop music	流行音乐
Pop Punk	流行朋克
Pop Rock	流行摇滚
Qing Dao	青岛
Qiu Ye	秋野
Queen Sea Big Shark	后海大鲨鱼
Rap metal	说唱金属
Red Star	红星乐队
Reestablishing the Rights of Statues	重塑雕像的权利乐队
Reflector	反光镜乐队
River Elegy	河殇
Rock music	摇滚音乐
Rock Records	滚石唱片
San Mao	三毛
Scream Records	嚎叫唱片
Senseless Contingent	无聊军队
Shen Lihui	沈黎晖
Sketch krime	李俊驹
Sober	清醒乐队
Sony	索尼
Southern Muddy Bay	南泥湾
Still Life	三峡好人
Subculture	亚文化
Sun Yat-sen	孙中山
Supergirl	超级女生
Supermarket	超市乐队
Swordsman novels	武侠小说
Tan, Amy	谭恩美
Tan Dun	谭盾
Tang Dynasty	唐朝乐队
Tatming Pair	达明一派乐队
Thin Men	瘦人乐队
Tian Zhen	田震
Tianjin Audio Visual Company	天津音像公司
Tongue	舌头乐队
Tsai Ming-liang	蔡明亮
Tudou	土豆

Twisted Machine	扭曲机器乐队
Underground	地下
Underground Baby	地下婴儿乐队
Urban folk	城市民歌
Voodoo Kungfu	零壹乐队
Wang Lei	王磊
Wang Shuo	王朔
Wang Xiaobo	王小波
Wang Xiaofeng	王小峰
Wang Xiaofang	王晓芳
Wang Yong	王勇
Wei Hua	蔚华
Wong, Anthony	黄耀明
Wong, Faye	王菲
Wong Kar-wai	王家卫
Wooden Horse (*Muma*)	木马乐队
The World	世界
Wu Wenguang	吴文光
Xia hai	下海
Xiao He	小河
Xintiandi	新天地
Yan Jun	颜峻
Yi Sha	伊沙
Yi wu suo you	一无所有
Yin Ts'ang	隐藏乐队
Youth culture	青年文化
Yu shijie jiegui	与世界接轨
Yugong Yishan	愚公移山
Zang Tianshuo	臧天朔
Zhang Chu	张楚
Zhang Qianqian	张浅潜
Zhang Yimou	张艺谋
Zhang Youdai	张有待
Zhang Yuan	张元
Zheng Jun	郑钧
Zhou Ren	周韧
Zhou Yunpeng	周云蓬
Zi Yue	子曰乐队
Zuoxiao Zuzhou	左小祖咒

Appendix I   Interviews

Musicians

1. Coco, male, 22 years old, jazz singer, studied at the Shanghai conservatory, English spoken, 30 July 1999
2. Cui Jian, male, 36 years old, studied music, Chinese and English spoken, 26 August 1997, more meetings in 2001, 2004, 2007 and 2008
3. Ding Wu, male, 34 years old, studied art, vocalist for Tang Dynasty, Chinese spoken, 13 July 1997
4. DJ Michael (Ni Bing), male, 32 years old, studied architecture in Shanghai, English spoken, 12 April 2000
5. Fei Fei, male, 21 years old, ex-bar owner and musician, Chinese spoken, 21 September 1997
6. Feng Jiangzhou, male, 33 years old, studied art, vocalist for The Fly, Chinese spoken, 18 September 1997, 24 April 2000, more meetings in 2004, 2005, 2007 and 2008
7. Gao Wei, male, 24 years old, vocalist for Underground Baby, Chinese spoken, 13 October 1997
8. Gu Yujin, female, 33 years old, studied classical piano, plays keyboards in Cobra, English spoken, 21 November 1997
9. He Yong, male, 26 years old, singer, Chinese spoken, 2 October 1997
10. Hu Mage, male, 27 years old, studied art, Chinese spoken, 5 April 2000
11. Kuo, Kaiser, male, 31 years old, American-born Chinese, studied Chinese in the US and played in Tang Dynasty, English spoken, 7 September 1997
12. Lei Jian, male, 26 years old, singer, Chinese spoken, 1 October 1997
13. Li Wei, male, 24 years old, ex-soldier turned singer, Chinese spoken, 28 October 1997
14. Li Weiyun, male, 21 years old, singer for Shanghai band Seven and university student, English and Chinese spoken, 4 August 1999
15. Liang Heping, male, 43 years old, musician, active in the rock culture since its start, Chinese spoken, 8 November 1997

16. Lin Di, female, 29 years old, vocalist and Su Yong, bass player, members of Cold Fairyland, Chinese spoken, 10 June 2004

17. Liu Wei, male, 27 years old, ex-businessman and ex-activist, now singer, Chinese spoken, 28 October 1997

18. Long Kuan, female, female, English spoken, 20 June 2004

19. Luo Qi, female, 22 years old, singer, Chinese spoken, November 1997

20. MC Webber, Foenix XIV, Sbazzo, Heff, members of Yin Ts'ang, English spoken, 19 June 2004

21. Pang Pang, male, 24 years old, guitar player Shanghai band Crystal Butterfly, Chinese spoken, 31 July 1999

22. Peng Lei, male, 23 years old, vocalist for The New Pants, studied art, Chinese spoken, 4 April 2000

23. Peter (Liang Wei), male, 24 years old, studied art and advertising at Beijing University, vocalist for 69, English spoken, 14 October 1997 and 18 April 2000

24. Qiu Ye, male, 33 years old, vocalist for Zi Yue (now Yaoshi), Chinese spoken, 21 July 1997, 4 December 1997, 26 April 2000, more meetings in 2004 and 2008

25. Shen Lihui, male, 30 years old, Manager of Modern Sky record company and vocalist for Sober, Chinese spoken, studied art and design, 7 August 1999 and 2 April 2000

26. Shou Wang, male, 22 years old, vocalist for Carsick Cars, English spoken, 20 September 2008

27. Wang Feng, male, 26 years old, graduated from the Beijing conservatory, vocalist for Baojiajie 43 [the address of the conservatory], Chinese spoken, 10 September 1997

28. Wang Lei, male, 26 years old, studied Sichuan opera, Guangzhou rock musician, interviewed in Hong Kong by Chow Yiu Fai on 21 May 1997

29. Wang Xiaodong, Zhou Xiaoan, Da Mao, Can Luomeng and Er Mao, male, studied at the music academy of Inner Mongolia, formed the band Ling Dian (Point Zero), interviewed in Hong Kong by Chow Yiu Fai, Chinese spoken, 20 June 1997

30. Wang Yong, male, 34 years old, studied music, (*guzheng*) musician and bar owner, Chinese spoken, 14 October 1997, December 1999

31. Wang Yue, female, 21 years old, vocalist for Hang on the Box, Chinese spoken, 13 April 2000

32. Wong, Anthony, male, 36 years old, Cantopop singer, vocalist in Tatming pair, English spoken in Hong Kong on 4 July 1997 and Berlin on 31 July 2000, more meetings in subsequent years

33. Xiao Wei, Liu En, Su Yang, Da Yue, male, 24 years old, all students of technology and science, formed the band Catcher in the Rye, Chinese spoken, 29 October 1997

34. Yu Shan, male, 30 years old, vocalist & musician for Supermarket, Chinese spoken, 11 April 2000
35. Zang Tiansuo, male, 33 years old, musician and bar owner, studied music, Chinese spoken, 2 December 1997
36. Zhang Qianqian, female, graduated from Qinghai art school, Chinese spoken, 28 October 1997
37. Zheng Jun, 30 years old, singer, studied foreign trade at Xi'an University, English spoken, 2 July 1997
38. Zhou Ren, Huang Kejing, Qing Dao, male, 4 August 1999, members of Shanghai band The Maniacs all graduated from Shanghai University, English spoken, 4 August 1999
39. Zu Zhou, male, 26 years old, studied art, vocalist for NO, Chinese spoken, 17 September 1997, 16 April 2000, more meetings in 2004, 2005, 2007 and 2008

Audience

1. Cao Chi, male, 17 years old, high school student, Chinese spoken, 23 November 1997
2. Chu Jianli, female, 21 years old, office worker for a joint venture, Chinese spoken, 23 November 1997
3. Di Ba, male, 22 years old, studying Chemistry at Beijing University, English spoken, 15 September 1997
4. Frank, male, 16 years old, high school student, Chinese spoken, 25 November 1997
5. He Jiang, female, 23 years old, studying English at Beijing University, English spoken, 15 September 1997
6. He Jin, male, 21 years old, studying Biochemistry at Beijing University, Chinese spoken, 20 October 1997
7. Huang San, male, 22 years old, BA student of English, Chinese spoken, 19 August 1997
8. Hung Xin, female, 25 years old, studying English and International Communication at Beijing University, English spoken, 25 August 1997
9. Li Tian, male, 23 years old, studying Japanese at the Institute for International Relations, Chinese spoken, 22 August 1997
10. Liu Fangfang, female, 17 years old, high school student, Chinese spoken, 16 November 1997
11. Liu Jiayue, female, 22 years old, studying History at Beijing Normal University, Chinese spoken, 19 October 1997
12. Liu Xin, female, 23 years old, studying English at Beijing University, English spoken, 10 October 1997

13. Liu Yansong, male, 17 years old, high school student, Chinese spoken, 16 November 1997
14. Mei Liu, female, 19 years old, studying administration at Chinese Geology University, Chinese spoken, 26 October 1997
15. Olivia, female, 21 years old, studying International Journalism at Beijing Broadcasting Institute, English spoken, 19 August 1997
16. Qin Ming, female, 22 years old, English teacher at a middle school, Bachelor's degree in International Relations, English spoken, 17 August 1997
17. Qu Nian, male, 17 years old, high school student, Chinese spoken, 25 November 1997
18. Sabrina, female, 16 years old, high school student, Chinese spoken, 17 November 1997
19. San Shui, male, 20 years old, MA student of Chinese at Beijing University, Chinese spoken, 20 August 1997
20. Shik Shak, male, 20 years old, management student at Beijing University and chairman of the university rock discussion group, Chinese spoken, 4 November 1997
21. Shu Ren, male, 24 years old, studying Chinese literature at Beijing University, Chinese spoken, 18 October 1997
22. Wan Mao, male, 21 years old, studying Japanese at the Institute of International Relations, Chinese spoken, 20 September 1997
23. Wang Hong, female, 24 years old, teacher of English at a high school, graduated from the Science and Technology university in English (BA), English and Chinese spoken, 23 August 1997
24. Wei Wei, male, 16 years old, high school student, Chinese spoken, 16 November 1997
25. Wen Jin, female, 16 years old, high school student, Chinese spoken, 29 November 1997
26. Xiao Wei, male, 24 years old, studying philosophy at Beijing University, German and Chinese spoken, 13 September 1997
27. Young, female, 16 years old, high school student, Chinese spoken, 25 November 1997
28. Zhang Min, female, 22 years old, studying French at Foreign Language Institute, Chinese spoken, 27 August 1997
29. Zhao Yu, female, 21 years old, studying at the Institute for International Relations, Chinese spoken, 18 August 1997
30. Zhi Yong, male, 21 years old, studying at the Institute for International Relations, Chinese spoken, 18 August 1997
31. Zhou Xuemei, female, 19 years old, middle school student, Chinese spoken, 20 August 1997
32. Zuo Dan, male, 20 years old, studying Chinese, Chinese spoken, 27 August 1997

Industry

1. Chan, Leslie, male, chief manager of Red Star, Hong Kong, English spoken, 5 July 1997
2. Chan, Louis, male, manager of Red Star Beijing office, English spoken, 28 August 1997
3. Cheuh-hung, Lee (Francis), male, managing director for Rock Records – Twister Music, English spoken, 30 June 1997
4. Cheung, Celine, female, director of Rock Records Publishing Hong Kong, English spoken, 19 July 1999
5. Dee, Dickson, male, 30 years old, manager of Sound factory, an independent Hong Kong label, ex-manager of Tang Dynasty and Wang Lei, Chinese and English spoken, 6 July 1997
6. Fu Chung, male, 27 years old, manager of New Bees, Chinese spoken, 11 April 2000
7. Ko, Edward, male, manager of Rock records Shanghai, English spoken, 27 July 1999
8. Kwok, Eric, male, marketing manager for Polygram Hong Kong, English spoken, 27 June 1997
9. Lao Ge, male, music producer in Beijing, Chinese spoken, 2 December 1997
10. Lau, Gene, male, manager of ZOOM music, lyricist for Cantopop and manager of Ai Jing, English spoken, 5 November 1997
11. Lo, Monpris, male, marketing executive JVC Hong Kong, Chinese spoken, 27 June 1997
12. Mui, Steve, male, manager JVC Hong Kong, Chinese spoken, 27 June 1997
13. Niu Jiawei, male, production coordinator Magic Stone Beijing, Chinese spoken, 16 September 1997
14. Shen Lihui, male, 30 years old, manager of Modern Sky record company and vocalist for Sober, studied art and design, Chinese spoken, 7 August 1999 and 2 April 2000
15. Song Xiaoming, male, art director at Jingwen, Chinese spoken, 31 October 1997
16. Song Zufen, female, manager of Music Sound & Picture Publishing House, Chinese spoken, 24 October 1997
17. Vlaar, Olav, male, marketing at NVPI, Dutch spoken, March 1999
18. Wang Xiaojin, male, 40 years old, manager of Luo Qi and owner of Xiendie company, Chinese spoken, 4 December 1999
19. Dana Burton, male, organiser of Hip Hop events, English spoken, 25 May 2004
20. Himm Wong, male, late 20s, manager of Urban Magazine, Chinese spoken, 30 May, 2004

21. Bo Lu, male, manager of Scream Records, Chinese spoken, 20 June 2004
22. Two Hong Kong music producers, anonymous, English spoken, 5 November 2008

Critics

1. Casper, female, 22 years old, organiser of rock parties, assistant to Kika, music fan, English spoken, 28 July 1999
2. Chan Fai-hung, male, 33 years old, director of commercial radio Hong Kong, Chinese spoken, 25 June 1997
3. Dai Jinhua, female, cultural critic at Beijing University, Chinese spoken, 13 October 1997
4. Law, Roddy, male, production & promotion director for Channel V, producer of 'Very China', English spoken, 26 June 1997
5. Wang Xiaofeng, male, 30 years old, Beijing rock critic, author of *The Guide to Occidental Music*, Chinese spoken, 16 October 1997
6. Yan Jun, male, 27 years old, critic, poet and novelist, author of 'Beijing New Sound', Chinese spoken, 9 April 2000
7. Yuen Chi-chung, male, manager for Music Colony Hong Kong, English spoken, 19 July 1999
8. Zhang Youdai, male, 30 years old, studied at drama school, radio DJ and organiser of rock parties, English spoken, 16 July 1997, December 1999
9. Zheng Fan, male, director of the Beijing Rock Academy, graduated from trade school in foreign trade, English and Chinese spoken, 18 October 1997
10. Xu Zhiyuan, male, blogger and cultural critic, English spoken, 20 May 2008.

Appendix II   Factor Analysis of Singers

	Rock	Pop	Western
Leon Lai	-0.288	0.403	0.154
Leslie Cheung	-0.295	0.634	0.242
Jacky Cheung	-0.183	0.641	-0.270
Faye Wong	0.017	0.574	-0.191
Beyond	0.095	0.605	-0.353
Zheng Jun	0.514	0.293	0.125
Cui Jian	0.712	0.098	0.165
Dou Wei	0.742	0.147	-0.087
Tang Dynasty	0.756	0.078	0.024
George Michael	-0.066	0.223	0.731
Madonna	0.048	0.135	0.561

Explained variance rock: 19.8%; explained variance pop: 16.4%; explained variance Western: 11.8%. Total explained variance: 48.0%

Appendix III   Popularity of Singers and Bands

Singer	Scene	Popularity	Male	Female	Significance	% Doesn't Know
Jacky Cheung	Cantopop	1.34	1.43	1.24	0.000**	3.7
Beyond	Hong Kong pop-rock	1.42	1.41	1.44	0.555	12.9
Faye Wong	Cantopop	1.55	1.56	1.54	0.646	11.4
Leslie Cheung	Cantopop	1.60	1.71	1.48	0.000**	3.4
Cui Jian	Chinese rock	1.69	1.57	1.82	0.000**	7.7
George Michael	Western pop	1.72	1.77	1.66	0.034*	43.8
Dou Wei	Chinese rock	1.80	1.73	1.88	0.001**	20.0
Zheng Jun	Chinese folk-rock	1.80	1.79	1.82	0.427	18.8
Tang Dynasty	Heavy Metal	1.81	1.66	1.97	0.000**	13.7
Leon Lai	Cantopop	1.91	2.02	1.81	0.000**	2.0
Wang Lei	Guangzhou rock	1.92	1.98	1.86	0.036*	51.2
He Yong	Chinese rock	1.94	1.91	1.98	0.112	29.5
Madonna	Western pop	1.95	1.90	1.99	0.093	11.2
Anthony Wong	Cantopop	1.99	2.02	1.98	0.348	40.8

Scale: three point scale, good (1) – average (2) – bad (3).
T-test:
*: significance < 0.05
**: significance < 0.01
N = 650

Bibliography

A, S. Review of Underground Baby. *Yinyue Shijie (Music World)* 54, April 1999.

Alasuutari, P. (1999). *Rethinking the Media Audience: The New Agenda*. London: Sage.

Allen, L. (2004). 'Kwaito Versus Crossed-Over: Music and Identity During South Africa's Rainbow Years', 1994-1996. *Social Dynamics, 30*(2), 82-111.

Alphen, E. v. (1992). *Francis Bacon and the Loss of Self*. London: Reaktion Books.

Ang, I. (1985). *Watching Dallas: Soap Opera and the Melodramatic Imagination*. London: Methuen.

Ang, I. (1991). *Desperately Seeking the Audience*. London: Routledge.

Ang, I. (1996). *Living Room Wars: Rethinking Media Audiences for a Postmodern World*. London: Routledge.

Ang, I. (2001). *On Not Speaking Chinese: Living Between Asia and the West*. London: Routledge.

Ang, Z. (2008). 'Lingyi Siwei Shashou de Xiaoxiang: He Li Nan Yitong Ruqing Naoxibao' (Voodoo Kungfu: The Portrait of a Mindkiller, Invidae Braincells with Li Nan), *Zhongxing Yinyue (Heavy Metal)*, *28*, 43-45.

Anonymous. (1996). *China Statistical Yearbook 1996*. Beijing: China Statistical Publishing House.

Anonymous. (1997a). Review of Ling Dian (Point Zero). *Yinxiang Shijie (Audio and Video World)*, September, *119*, 34.

Anonymous. (1997b). Luo Qi. *Yinyue Shenghuo (Music Life)*. 24 October.

Anonymous. (1997c). Yingyexin Yaochu Guanli Tiaoli (New Regulations For Performances). *Renmin Ribao (People's Daily)*. 21 August.

Anonymous. (2008). Interview with Qiu Ye. *In Music (Yinyue Shikong)*, September, *390*, 107-109.

Appadurai, A. (1996). *Modernity at Large: Cultural Dimensions of Globalisation*. Minneapolis: University of Minnesota Press.

Babcock, B.B. (1978). Introduction. In B.B. Babcock (ed.), *In The Reversible World: Symbolic Inversion in Art and Society*. London: Cornell University Press, 13-38.

Bakhtin, M. (1981). *The Dialogic Imagination*. Austin: University of Texas Press.

Bakhtin, M. (1986). *Speech Genres and Other Late Essays*. Austin: University of Texas Press.

Bakken, B. (1994). *The Exemplary Society: Human Improvement, Social Control and the Dangers of Modernity in China*. Oslo: Oslo University.

Bal, M. (2002). *Travelling Concepts in the Humanities*. Toronto: University of Toronto Press.

Baranovitch, N. (2003). *China's New Voices: Popular Music, Ethnicity, Gender, and Politics, 1978-1997*. Berkeley: University of California Press.

Barmé, G. (1992). 'The Greying of Chinese Culture'. In H. C. Kuan & M. Brosseau (eds.), *China Review 1992*. Hong Kong: Hong Kong University Press, 13.11-13.52.

Barmé, G. (1999). *In the Red: On Contemporary Chinese Culture*. New York: Columbia University Press.

Barmé, G., & Jaivin, L. (1992). *New Ghosts, Old Dreams: Chinese Rebel Voices*. New York: Times Books.

Barthes, R. (1957). *Mythologies*. New York: Hill and Wang.

Baulch, E. (2003). 'Gesturing Elsewhere: The Identity Politics of the Balinese Death/Trash Metal Scene', *Popular Music, 22*(2), 195-215.

Baulch, E. (2008). *Making Scenes: Reggae, Punk, and Death Metal in 1990s Bali*. Durham: Duke University Press.

Bax, J. (1998). Verhaal Uit Beijing: Jongeren en Rockmuziek in China. MA Thesis, Leiden University.

Bei, S. (2004). "Kunjing" Zhong Gundong – "Fengguncao" Yuedui Zhuchang Shen Yan Fangtan (Interview with Shen Yan, Lead Singer of Feng Gun Cao). *So Rock!, 28,* 12.

Bennett, A. (1999). 'Subcultures or Neo-Tribes? Rethinking the Relationship Between Youth, Style and Musical Taste', *Sociology, 33*(3), 599-617.

Bennett, A. (2004). 'Consolidating the Music Scene Perspective', *Poetics, 32*(3-4), 223-234.

Bennett, A., & Kahn-Harris, K. (eds.) (2004). *After Subculture: Critical Studies in Contemporary Youth Culture*. New York: Palgrave MacMillan.

Bentoni. (1999, 13 March 1999). Interview with Luo Qi. Retrieved 30 September 2000, from www.bentoni.com/deutschstunde/new-tips/ddstip101.html

Besnier, N. (2009). *Gossip and the Everyday Production of Politics*. Honolulu: University of Hawai'i Press.

Bhabha, H.K. (1994). *The Location of Culture*. London: Routledge.

Boomkens, R. (2000). *$ign of the Times*. Amsterdam: Amsterdam University Press.

Bourdieu, P. (1979). *Distinction: A Social Critique of the Judgement of Taste*. London: Routledge.

Brace, T. & Friedlander, P. (1992). 'Rock and Roll on the New Long March: Popular Music, Cultural Identity, and Political Opposition in the People's Republic of China', in R. Garofalo (ed.), *Rockin' the Boat: Mass Music and Mass Movement*. Boston: South End Press, 115-128.

Butler, J. (1990). *Gender Trouble: Feminism and the Subversion of Identity*. London: Routledge.

Butler, J. (1997). *Excitable Speech: A Politics of the Performative*. New York and London: Routledge.

Caldwell, J.T. (2008). *Production Culture: Industrial Reflexivity and Industrial Practice*. Durham: Duke University Press.

Callahan, W.A. (2004). *Contingent States: Greater China and Transnational Relations*. Minneapolis: University of Minnesota Press.

Carroll, L. (1992 [1872]). *Through the Looking Glass*. Hertfordshire: Wordsworth Classics.

Cen, G., & Li, D. (2006). 'Social Transformation and Values Conflict Among Youth in Contemporary China', in C. Daiute, Z.F. Beykont, C. Higson-Smith & L. Nucci (eds.), *International Perspectives on Youth Conflict and Development*. Oxford: Oxford University Press, 156-172.

de Certeau, M. (1984). *The Practice of Everyday Life*. London: University of California Press.

Chan, J. (2003). Punk No More, from www.thebeijinger.com. 30 November 2005.

Chan, S. (ed.). (1997). *Qinggan De Shijian: Xianggang Liuxing Geci Yanjin (The Practice of Affect: Studies in Hong Kong Popular Song Lyrics)*. Hong Kong: Oxford University Press.

Chen, A. (2002). 'The Structure of Chinese Industry and the Impact from China's WTO Entry', *Comparative Economic Studies, 44,* 72-98.

Chong, W.L. (1991). 'Young China's Voice of the 1980s: Rock Star Cui Jian', *China Information* (6, no.1), 55-74.

Chow, R. (1993). *Writing Diaspora: Tactics of Intervention in Contemporary Cultural Studies*. Bloomington: Indiana University Press.

Chow, R. (1995). *Primitive Passion: Visuality, Sexuality, Ethnography, and Contemporary Chinese Cinema. Film and Culture*. New York: Columbia University Press.

Chow, R. (1998a). *Ethics after Idealism: Theory – Culture – Ethnicity – Reading.* Bloomington: Indiana University Press.

Chow, R. (1998b). 'On Chineseness as a Theoretical Problem', *Boundary 2, 25*(3), 1-24.

Chow, R. (1998c). 'King Kong in Hong Kong Watching the "Handover" from the U.S.A.', *Social Text, 55*, 93-108.

Chow, R. (2006). *The Age of the World target: Self-Referentiality in War, Theory, and Comparative Work.* Durham: Duke University Press.

Chow, R. (2007). *Sentimental Fabulations: Contemporary Chinese Films: Attachment in the Age of Global Visibility.* New York: Columbia University Press.

Chow, Y.F. (2008). 'Martial Arts Films and Dutch-Chinese Masculinities', *China Information, XXII*(2), 331-359.

Chow, Y. F. (2009). 'Me and the Dragon: A Lyrical Engagement with the Politics of Chineseness', *Inter-Asia Cultural Studies, 10*(4), 544-564.

Chow, Y.F., & de Kloet, J. (2008). 'The Production of Locality in Global Pop: A Comparative Study of Pop Fans in The Netherlands and Hong Kong', *Particip@tions, 5*(2), online.

Christenson, P., & Peterson, J.B. (1988). 'Genre and Gender in the Structure of Music Preferences', *Communication Research, 15*(3), 282-301.

Chu, Y. (2000a). *Guanghui Suiyue: Xianggang Liuxing Yuedui Zuhe Yanjiu (1984-1990) (Glorious Days: Study in Pop Groups in Hong Kong (1984-1990)).* Hong Kong: IP Publishing.

Chu, Y. (2000b). *Xinggang Liuxing Geci Yanjiu (A Study of Pop Lyrics in Hong Kong).* Hong Kong Joint Publishing Co.

Chun, A. (1996). 'Fuck Chineseness: On the Ambiguities of Ethnicity as Culture as Identity', *Boundary, 2*(23), 111-138.

Chun, S. (2004). *Beijing Doll.* New York: Riverhead Trade.

Cohen, S. (1980). *Folk Devils and Moral Panics: The Creation of the Mods and Rockers.* Oxford: Martin Robertson.

Cohen, S. (1997). 'Men Making a Scene: Rock Music and the Production of Gender', in S. Whiteley (ed.), *Sexing the Groove: Popular Music and Gender.* London: Routledge, 17-36.

Condry, I. (2000). 'The Social Production of Difference: Imitation and Authenticity in Japanese Rap Music', in H. Fehrenbach & U.G. Polger (eds.), *Transactions, Transgressions and Transformations.* New York: Berghan Books, 166-184.

Condry, I. (2006). *Hip-Hop Japan: Rap and the Paths of Cultural Globalisation.* Durham: Duke University Press.

Cooper, C. (2000). 'Rockin' in the Mainland: China's Sonic Uprising', from www.papermag. com/paperdaily/paperclips/00paperclips/Chinese_Rock/index.html

Curtin, M. (2007). *Playing to the World's Biggest Audience: The Globalisation of Chinese Film and TV.* Berkeley: University of California Press.

Dai, C. (1995). 'Miandui Xinling (Face the Heart)', *Zhongguo Yinxiang (China Audio-Visual Monthly)*, 12, 22-23.

Dai, J. (2002). 'Gender and Narration: Women in Contemporary Chinese Film', in J. Wang & T. E. Barlow (eds.), *Cinema and Desire: Feminist Marxism and Cultural Politics in the Work of Dai Jinhua.* London: Verso, 99-150.

Danny, D., & Hang, F. (2004). 'Hip-Hop Shili (The Power of Hip Hop)', *Channel [V] Magazine*, 100.

Dao, Z. (1997, 27). Wuyue Huainian Zhangju (Remember Zhang Ju in May). *Dangdai Getan (Modern Music Field)*, 5.

Deleuze, G. & Parnet, C. (1987). *Dialogues.* New York: Columbia University Press.

Deleuze, G. & Felix Guattari (1987). *A Thousand Plateaus: Capitalism & Schizophrenia.* London: The Athlone Press.

DeNora, T. (1999). 'Music as a Technology of the Self', *Poetics, 27*, 31-56.

DeNora, T. (2000). *Music in Everyday Life.* Cambridge: Cambridge University Press.

Dickinson, R., Harindranath, R., & Linne, O. (1998). *Approaches to Audiences: A Reader*. London: Arnold.

Dikötter, F. (1995). *Sex, Culture and Modernity in China: Medical Science and the Construction of Sexual Identities in the Early Republican Period*. London: Hurst & Company.

Dolfsma, W. (2000). 'How Will the Music Industry Weather the Globalisation Storm?', *First-Monday 5, 5*.

Dundee. (1999). 'Beijing Yaogun: Smells Like Teen spirit (Beijing Rock: Smells Like Teen spirit)', *Yinyue Tiantang (Music Heaven), 31*, 26-28.

Dutton, M. (1998). *Streetlife China*. Cambridge: Cambridge University Press.

Efird, R. (2001). 'Rock in a Hard Place: Music and the Market in Nineties Beijing', in N.N. Chen, C.D. Clark, S. Gottschang & L. Jeffery (eds.), *China Urban: Ethnographies of Contemporary Culture*. Durham: Duke University Press, 67-88.

Erni, J.N. (2001). 'Like a Postcolonial Culture: Hong Kong Re-Imagined', *Cultural Studies, 15* (3-4), 389-418.

Erni, J.N. (2007). Gender and Everyday Evasions: Moving with Cantopop. *Inter-Asia Cultural Studies, 8*(1), 86-108.

Evans, H. (1997). *Women and Sexuality in China: Female Sexuality and Gender since 1949*. New York: Continuum.

Evans, H. (2008). 'Sexed Bodies, Sexualised Identities, and the Limits of Gender', *China Information, 22*(2), 361-386.

Fabian, J. (1983). *Time and the Other: How Anthropology Makes its Object*. New York: Columbia University Press.

Fang, H. (1997, October). 'Zang Tianshuo Bu Yan "Dimi" (Zang Tianshuo Doesn't Say 'It Goes Down'), *Huangsheng Monthly*, 93-95.

Farrer, J. (2002). *Opening Up: Youth Sex Culture and Market Reform in Shanghai*. Chicago: University of Chicago Press.

Farrer, J. (2008). 'Play and Power in Chinese Nightlife Spaces', *China: An International Journal, 6*(1), 1-17.

Fernia, J.V. (1988). *Gramsci's Political Thought: Hegemony, Consciousness and the Revolutionary Process*. Oxford: Clarendon Press.

Field, A. (2007, 26 July 2007). China's Primal Scream. *www.policyinnovations.org/*.

Field, A., & Groenewegen, J. (2008). 'Explosive Acts: Beijing's Punk Rock Scene', *Berliner China Hefte, 34*, 8-26.

Fiske, J. (1988). *Television Culture*. London: Routledge.

Fong, V. (2004). 'Filial Nationalism Among Chinese Teenagers with Global Identities', *American Ethnologist, 31*(4), 631-648.

Forman, M. (2000). *The 'Hood Comes First: Race, Space, and Place in Rap and Hip Hop*. Middletown: Wesleyan University Press.

Foucault, M. (1983). 'The Subject and Power', in H.L. Dreyfus & P. Rabinow (eds.), *Michel Foucault: Structuralism and Hermeneutics*. Chicago: The Haverest Press, 208-226.

Foucault, M. (1984). 'What is an Author?', in P. Rabinow (ed.), *The Foucault Reader*. New York: Pantheon Books, 101-120.

Foucault, M. (1984 [1971]). 'Nietzsche, Genealogy, History', in P. Rabinow (ed.), *The Foucault Reader* (pp. 76-100). New York: Pantheon Books.

Foucault, M. (1997 [1982]). Technologies of the Self. In P. Rabinow (ed.), *Michel Foucault: Ethics, Subjectivity and Truth*. New York: The New Press, 223-252.

Foucault, M. (1997 [1983]). 'On the Genealogy of Ethics', in *Michel Foucault: Ethics, Subjectivity and Truth*. New York: The New Press, 253-280.

Freud, S. (1930). *Civilisation and Its Discontents[Das Unbehagen in Der Kultur]*. New York: Norton and Company.

Frith, S. (1996). *Performing Rites, On the Value of Popular Music*. Oxford: Oxford University Press.

Fu, H.L., & Cullen, R. (1996). *Media Law in the PRC*. Hong Kong: Asia Law & Practice Publishing.

Fung, A. (2006). '"Think Globally, Act Locally": China's Rendezvous with MTV', *Global Media and Communication*, 2(1), 71-88.

Fung, A. (2008). *Global Capital, Local Culture: Transnational Media Corporations in China*. New York: Peter Lang.

Fung, A., & Curtin, M. (2002). 'The Anomalies of Being Faye (Wong): Gender Politics in Chinese Popular Music', *International Journal of Cultural Studies*, 5(3), 263-290.

Gans, H. (1999). *Popular Culture and High Culture: An Analysis and Evaluation of Taste*. New York: Basic Books.

Geist, B. (1996). 'Die Modernisierung der Chinesischen Kultur: Kulturdebatte und Kultureller Wandel im China der 80er Jahre', in B. Staiger (ed.), *Mitteilungen des Instituts für Asienkunde Hamburg* (Vol. 263). Hamburg: Calling P.O.D.

Giddens, A. (1990). *The Consequences of Modernity*. Cambridge: Polity Press.

Giddens, A. (1991). *Modernity and Self-Identity: Self and Society in the Late Modern Age*. Cambridge: Polity Press.

Gilroy, P. (2000). *Between Camps: Nations, Cultures and the Allure of Race*. London: Penguin.

Gold, T.B. (1991). 'Youth and the State', *The China Quarterly* (127), 594-612.

Gold, T.B. (1993). 'Go With Your Feelings: Hong Kong and Taiwan Popular Culture in Greater China', *The China Quarterly* (136), 907-925.

Gramsci, A. (1971). *Selection from the Prison Notebook of Antonio Gramsci*. London Lawrence and Wishart.

Gries, P.H. (2004). *China's New Nationalism: Pride, Politics, and Diplomacy*. Berkeley: University of California Press.

Groenewegen, J. (2004). *Tongue: Making Sense of the Underground Rock Community Beijing 1997-2004*. Leiden University, Leiden.

Groenewegen, J. (2008). *Humour and Parody in Chinese Popular and Rock Music*. Paper presented at the East Asian Popular Music, Small Sounds from Big Places? Conference, Leiden.

Grossberg, L. (1986). 'Is There Rock After Punk', *Critical Studies of Mass Communication* (3), 50-74.

Grossberg, L. (1993). 'The Framing of Rock: Rock and the New Conservatism', in T. Bennett, S. Frith, L. Grossberg, J. Shepherd & G. Turner (eds.), *Rock and the Popular Music: Politics, Policies, Institutions*. London: Routledge, 193-209.

Hakanen, E. & Wells, A. (1993). Music Preference and Taste Culture Among Adolescents. *Popular Culture and Society*, 1(17), 59-73.

Halbert, D. (1997). 'Intellectual Property Piracy: The Narrative Construction of Deviance', *International Journal For the Semiotics of Law* 10(28), 55-78.

Hall, S. (1980). 'Encoding-Decoding', in S. Hall, D. Hobson, A. Lowe & P. Willis (eds.), *Culture, Media, Language*. London: Hutchinson, 157-162.

Hall, S., & Jefferson, T. (1976). *Resistance Through Rituals: Youth Subcultures in Post-War Britain*. London: Hutchinson.

Haraszti, M. (1987). *The Velvet Prison: Artists under State Socialism*. New York: Basic Books.

Harding, H. (1995). 'The Concept of "Greater China": Themes, Variations and Reservations', in D. Shambaugh (ed.), *Greater China: The Next Superpower?* Oxford: Oxford University Press.

Hardt, M. & Negri, A. (2000). *Empire*. Cambridge: Harvard University Press.

Hartley, J. (1987). 'Invisible Fictions: Television Audiences, Paedocracy, Pleasure', *Textual Practice 1, 2*, 121-138.

Hawkins, S. (1997). 'The Pet Shop Boys: Musicology, Masculinity and Banality', in S. Whiteley (ed.), *Sexing the Groove: Popular Music and Gender*. London: Routledge, 118-134.

He, L. (1997). 'Yaogun Gu'er (Rock'n'Roll Orphans)', *Jinri Xianfeng (Today's Avant-Garde)*, 5, 66-94.

Hebdige, D. (1979). *Subculture: The Meaning of Style*. London: Methuen.

Hebdige, D. (1988). *Hiding in the Light: On Images and Things*. London: Routledge.

Herman, A., & Sloop, J.M. (1998). 'The Politics of Authenticity in Postmodern Rock Culture: The Case of Negativland and The Letter "U" and the Numeral "2"', *Critical Studies of Mass Communication, 1*(15), 1-20.

Hermes, J. (1996). *Reading Women's Magazines: An Analysis of Everyday Media Use*. Cambridge: Polity Press.

Hermes, J. (2005). *Re-Reading Popular Culture*. Oxford: Blackwell.

Hershatter, G. (2004). 'State of the Field: Women in China's Long Twentieth Century', *Journal of Asian Studies, 63*(4), 991-1065.

Hesmondhalgh, D. (2005). 'Subcultures, Scenes or Tribes? None of the Above', *Journal of Youth Studies, 8*(1), 21-40.

Ho, W.C. (2000). 'The Political Meaning of Hong Kong Popular Music: A Review of Sociopolitical Relations between Hong Kong and the People's Republic of China since the 1980s', *Popular Music, 19*(3), 341-353.

Ho, W.-C. (2003). 'Between Globalisation and Localisation: A Study of Hong Kong Popular Music', *Popular Music, 22*(2), 143-157.

Hoagland, J. 'A Chinese Dissident's Faith', *Washington Post*, 28 May 2006.

Holt, F. (2007). *Genre in Popular Music*. Chicago: University of Chicago Press.

Hou, M. (1996). 'Jinzi Li de Zhang Chu' (Zhang Chu in the Mirror: A Music Life in Which One Waits and Complies), *Yuehai Daohang (Music Navigation), 10*, 2.

Hu, H. (1999). 'Lei Gang Yu Tiantang Yiban Yiban' (Review of Lei Gang and Paradise), *Modeng Tiankong (Modern Sky)*, 5, 21.

Hu, Y. (1997). 'Zhang Chu, Bei Renqun Ronghua de Haizi' (Zhang Chu: A Child that is Melted By the Crowd), *Zhongguo Bailaohui (Chinese Broadway)*, 8, 2-5.

Huang, C. (2007). 'Trace the Stones in Crossing the River: Media Structural Changes in Post-WTO China', *International Communication Gazette, 69*(5), 413-430.

Huang, H. (2001). 'Yaogun Yinyue: Rethinking Mainland Chinese Rock'n'Roll', *Popular Music, 20*(1), 1-11.

Huang, H. (2003). 'Voices from Chinese Rock, Past and Present Tense: Social Commentary and Construction of Identity in *Yaogun Yinyue* from Tiananmen to the Present', *Popular Music and Society, 26*(2), 183-202.

Hugenholtz, P. B. (1999). *Sleeping With the Enemy: Over de Verhouding Tussen Auteurs en Exploitanten in het Auteursrecht*. Amsterdam: Amsterdam University Press.

Huo, D. (2008). 'Tangchao: Huigui Zhuanti (Tang Dynasty: Return of the King)', *Zhongxing Yinyue (Heavy Metal), 30*, 7-9.

Huot, C. (2000). *China's New Cultural Scene: A Handbook of Changes*. Durham: Duke University Press.

IFPI. (1997). *The Recording Industry in Numbers 1997*. London: IFPI.

IFPI. (1998). *The Recording Industry in Numbers 1998*. London: IFPI.

IFPI. (1999). *The Recording Industry in Numbers 1999*. London: IFPI.

IFPI. (2000). *The Recording Industry in Numbers 2000*. London: IFPI.

IFPI. (2004). *The Recording Industry in Numbers: 2003*. London: IFPI.

IFPI. (2006). *2006: Global Recording Industry in Numbers*. London: IFPI.

Inglehart, R., Basanez, M., & Moreno, A. (1998). *Human Values and Beliefs: A Cross-Cultural Sourcebook*. Ann Arbor: University of Michigan Press.

Java. (2000). Review of CD "Cobra II". *Modeng Tiankong (Modern Sky)*, *8*, 29.
Jefford, S.M. (Writer) (2009). 'Beijing Punk', in N. Films (Producer). United States.
Jenkins, H. (1992). *Textual Poachers: Television Fans & Participatory Culture*. London: Routledge.
Jenkins, H. (2006). *Convergence Culture: Where Old and New Media Collide*. New York: New York University Press.
Jenson, J. (1992). 'Fandom As Pathology: The Consequence of Characterisation', in L.A. Lewis (ed.), *The Adoring Audience: Fan Culture and Popular Media*. London: Routledge, 9-29.
Johnson. (2004). 'Xiang Yongyou Gengduo De Qingxu – Muma Tan' (Want More Emotions – Interview with Mu Ma about 'Yellow Star'), *So Rock!*, *21*, 10.
Jones, A. F. (1992). *Like a Knife: Ideology and Genre in Contemporary Chinese Popular Music*: Cornell University.
Jones, A.F. (1994). 'The Politics of Popular Music in Post: Tiananmen China', in E.J. Perry & J.N. Wasserstrom (eds.), *Popular Protest & Political Culture in Modern China* (2nd ed.). Oxford: Westview Press, 148-165.

Kahn-Harris, K. (1999). *Darkthrone is Absolutely Not a Political Band: Difference and Reflexivity in the Global Extreme Metal Scene*. Paper presented at the IASPM, Sydney.
Kahn-Harris, K. (2004). 'The "Failure" of Youth Culture: Reflexivity, Music and Politics in the Black Metal Scene', *European Journal of Cultural Studies*, *7*(1), 95-111.
Kahn-Harris, K. (2007). *Extreme Metal: Music and Culture on the Edge*. Oxford: Berg.
Kamer, G. 'Loladamusica Struikelt Over Chinese Rockers'. *de Volkskrant*, 3 October 1997.
Keane, M. (2007). *Created in China: The Great New Leap Forward*. London: RoutledgeCurzon.
Khiun, L.K. (2003). 'Limited Pidgin-type Patois? Policy, Language, Technology, Identity and the Experience of Canto-pop in Singapore', *Popular Music*, *22*(2), 217-233.
de Kloet, J. (2000). 'Let Him Fuckin' See the Green Smoke Beneath My Groin: The Mythology of Chinese Rock', in A. Dirlik & X. Zhang (eds.), *Postmodernism and China*. Durham: Duke University Press, 239-274.
de Kloet, J. (2005a). 'Popular Music and Youth in Urban China: The Dakou Generation', *China Quarterly*, *183*, 609-626.
de Kloet, J. (2005b). 'Sonic Sturdiness: The Globalisation of "Chinese" Pop and Rock', *Critical Studies in Media Communication*, *22*(4), 321-338.
de Kloet, J. (2005c). Authenticating Geographies and Temporalities: Representations of Chinese Rock in China. *Visual Anthropology*, *18*(2-3), 229-256.
de Kloet, J. (2007). 'Cosmopatriot Contaminations', in J. De Kloet & E. Jurriëns (eds.), *Cosmopatriots: On Distant Belongings and Close Encounters*. Amsterdam: Rodopi, 133-154.
de Kloet, J. (2008). 'Media en Populaire Cultuur: Nieuwe Vormen van Cultureel Burgerschap?', in W.-L. Chong & T.-W. Ngo (eds.), *China in Verandering – Balans en Toekomst van de Hervormingen*. Almere: Parthenon, 120-142.
de Kloet, J. (2008). 'Gendering China Studies: Peripheral Perspectives, Central Questions', *China Information*, *XXII*(2), 195-220.
de Kloet, J. & Zoonen, L. v. (2007). 'Fan Culture: Performing Difference', in E. Devereux (ed.), *Media Studies: Key Issues and Debates*. London: Sage, 322-341.
Komlosy, A. (2008). 'Yunnanese Sounds: Creativity and Alterity in the Dance and Music Scenes of Urban Yunnan', *China: An International Journal*, *6*(1), 44-68.
Kooijman, J. (2008). *Fabricating the Absolute Fake: America in Contemporary Pop Culture*. Amsterdam: Amsterdam University Press.

Kovskaya, M. (1999). 'Thin Men: The Marketing of Authenticity and PRC Activist Rock Music'. Retrieved 20 March 2000, from www.chinanow.com

Kraus, R. (1989). *Pianos and Politics in China: Middle-Class Ambitions and the Struggle over Western Music*. New York: Oxford University Press.

Kraus, R. (2004). *The Party and the Arty*. New York: Rowan and Littlefield.

Kuipers, G. (2006). 'Television and Taste Hierarchy: The Case of Dutch Television Comedy', *Media, Culture & Society, 28*(3), 359-378.

La, L. (2004). 'Shouxin Li Jiaowang De Huaduo: Lengkuxianjing Yuedui Zhuchang' Fangtan (Interview with Miyadudu, the Lead Singer of Cold Fairyland), *So Rock!, 31*, 22-23.

Laing, D. (1985). *One Chord Wonders: Power and Meaning in Punk Rock*. Milton Keynes: Open University Press.

Laing, D. (1993). 'Copyright and the International Music Industry', in S. Frith (ed.), *Music and Copyright*. Edinburgh: Edinburgh University Press, 22-39.

Laing, D. (1998). 'Knocking on China's Door', in T. Mitsui (ed.), *Popular Music: Intercultural Interpretations*. Kanazawa: Kanazawa University, 337-342.

Laing, D. (2004). 'Copyright, Politics, and the International Music Industry', in S. Frith & L. Marshall (eds.), *Music and Copyright: Second Edition*. New York: Routledge, 70-88.

Lanning, G. (Writer) (1991). 'Voices of the World: Cui Jian'. London: BBC.

Lao, S. (2004). 'Chouda, Xueji, Jianjiao: Xingchoutiye Fangtan' (Interview with Pungent Liquid), *So Rock!, 28*, 22-23.

Lash, S. (1994). 'Reflexivity and its Doubles: Structure, Aesthetics, Community', in U. Beck, A. Giddens & S. Lash (eds.), *Reflexive Modernisation: Politics, Tradition and Aesthetics in the Modern Social Order*. Stanford: Stanford University Press, 110-173.

Lau, J.K.W. (ed.). (2003). *Multiple Modernities: Cinemas and Popular Media in Transcultural East Asia*. Philadelphia: Temple University Press.

Lee, G.B. (1996). *Troubadours, Trumpeters, Troubled Makers: Lyricism, Nationalism and Hybridity in China and Its Others*. London: Hurst & Company.

Lee, J.C.-Y. (1992). 'All For Freedom: The Rise of Patriotic/ Pro- Democratic Popular Music in Hong Kong in Response to the Chinese Student Movement', in R. Garofalo (ed.), *Rockin' the Boat: Mass Music and Mass Movements*. Boston: South End Press, 129-147.

Lessig, L. (2001). *The Future of Ideas: The Fate of the Commons in a Connected World*. New York: Vintage Books.

Leung, H.H.-S. (2001). 'Queerscapes in Contemporary Hong Kong Cinema'. *Positions, 9*(2), 423-448.

Leung, H.H.-S. (2008). *Undercurrents: Queer Culture and Postcolonial Hong Kong*. Vancouver: University of British Columbia Press.

Li, J. (1995). Wang Lei (Wang Lei). *Top Records Guangzhou*.

Li, M. (1999). *We Need Two Worlds: Chinese Immigrant Association in a Western Society*. Amsterdam: Amsterdam University Press.

Li, Y. 'Zhongguo Balinghou Zhi Zainan' (The Chinese 'Post-80s' in Disaster), *Guangming Daily*, 30 May 2008, 1.

Li, Y. (2008). 'Sanxiang Dajiang: Houhai Dashayu Chengwei Zuida Yingjia' (Three Big Awards, Queen Sea Big Shark Became the Biggest Winner), *Yinyue Shukong (In Music)*, May, 11.

Lim, S.H. (2007). 'Queering Chineseness: Searching for Roots and the Politics of Shame in (Post)Colonial Singapore', in J. De Kloet & E. Jurriëns (eds.), *Cosmopatriots: On Distant Belongings and Close Encounters*. Amsterdam: Rodopi, 75-92.

Lok, F. (1993). 'Daming Yipai Zhilu: Liuxing Yinyue De Shehui Yishi' (Trip of Tatming Pair: Social Consciousness in Pop Music), in P.K. Leung (ed.), *Popular Culture of Hong Kong*. Hong Kong: Joint Publishing, 35-57.

Long, H. (1999). 'Go West', *Modeng Tiankong (Modern Sky), 5*, 24-25.

Lu, S. (2008). 'Popular Culture and Body Politics: Beauty Writers in Contemporary China', *Modern Language Quarterly*, 69(1), 167-185.

Lyotard, J.F. (1984). *The Postmodern Condition: A Report on Knowledge*. Minneapolis: University of Minnesota Press.

Ma, E.K.-w. (2002). 'Emotional Energy and Sub-cultural Politics: Alternative Bands in Post-1997 Hong Kong', *Inter-Asia Cultural Studies*, 3(2), 187-200.

May, T. (2005). *Gilles Deleuze: An Introduction*. Cambridge: Cambridge University Press.

McCall, L. (2005). 'The Complexity of Intersectionality', *Signs: Journal of Women in Culture and Society*, 30(3), 1771-1800.

McGee, M. (2005). *Self-Help, Inc.: Makeover Culture in American Life*. Oxford: Oxford University Press.

McRobbie, A. (1991). *Feminism and Youth Culture: From "Jacky" to "Just Seventeen"* London: MacMillan Education.

Mertha, A.C. (2005). *The Politics of Piracy: Intellectual Property in Contemporary China*. Ithaca: Cornell University Press.

Messmer, S., & Lindt, G. (eds.). (2008). *Beijing Bubbles: Pop and Rock in China's Capital*. Berlin: Fly Fast Records.

Mian, M. (1999). *La La La*. Kunming: Kunming Renmin Chubanshe.

Mitchell, T. (1992). 'Mixing Pop and Politics: Rock Music in Czechoslovakia Before and After Revolution', *Popular Music*, 11(2), 187-204.

Mitchell, T. (2001). 'Another Root: Hip-Hop outside the USA', in T. Mitchell (ed.), *Global Noise: Rap and Hip-Hop Outside the USA*. Middletown: Wesleyan University Press, 1-38.

Mitchell, T. (2006). 'Tian Ci: Faye Wong and English Songs in the Cantopop and Mandapop Repertoire', in S. Homan (ed.), *Access All Eras: Tribute Bands and Global Pop Culture*. Berkshire: Open University Press, 215-228.

Morley, D. (1992). *Television, Audiences & Cultural Studies*. London: Routledge.

Morley, D. (2006). 'Unanswered Questions in Audience Research', *The Communication Review*, 9, 101-121.

Morris, M. (1988). 'Banality in Cultural Studies', *Discourse*, 10, 3-29.

Moskowitz, M.L. (2008). 'Message in a Bottle: Lyrical Laments and Emotional Expression in Mandopop', *China Quarterly*, 194, 365-379.

Muggleton, D., & Weinzielr, R. (eds.). (2003). *The Post-Subcultures Reader*. Oxford: Berg.

Mulder, J., ter Bogt, T., Eaaijmakers, Q., & Vollenbergh, W. (2007). 'Music Taste Groups and Problem Behavior', *Journal of Youth and Adolescence*, 36(3), 313-324.

Negus, K. (1992). *Producing Pop: Culture and Conflict in the Popular Music Industry*. London: Edward Arnold.

Negus, K. (1997). *Why Still Local in a Global World? National and International Dynamics in the Production of Popular Music*. Paper presented at the IASPM Conference.

Negus, K. (1998). 'Cultural Production and the Corporation: Musical Genres and the Strategic Management of Creativity in the US Recording Industry', *Media, Culture & Society 20*, 359-379.

Nightingale, V. (1996). *Studying Audiences: The Shock of the Real*. London: Routledge.

Ong, A. (1999). *Flexible Citizenship: The Cultural Logics of Transnationality*. Durham: Duke University Press.

Ong, A. (2006). *Neoliberalism as Exception, Exception to Neoliberalism*. Durham: Duke University Press.

Ong, A., & Zhang, L. (2008). 'Introduction: Privatising China: Powers of the Self, Socialism from Afar', in A. Ong & L. Zhang (eds.), *Privatising China: Socialism from Afar*. Ithaca: Cornell University Press, 1-20.

Osterhammel, J. (1989). *China und die Weltgesellschaft vom 18. Jahrhundert bis in unserer Zeit.* München: Beck.

Otake, A., & Shuhei, H. (2005). 'Karaoke in East Asia: Modernisation, Japanisation, or Asianisation?', in A. Abbas & J.N. Erni (eds.), *Internationalising Cultural Studies: An Anthology.* Oxford: Blackwell, 51-60.

Pang, L. (2006). *Cultural Control and Globalisation in Asia: Copyright, Piracy, and Cinema.* London: Routledge.

Pilkington, H., & Johnson, R. (2003). 'Peripheral Youth: Relations of Identity and Power in Global/local Context', *European Journal of Cultural Studies, 6*(3), 259-283.

Platt, K. (1998). 'China's Cutting-Edge Artists Join Global Village'. Retrieved 20 November 1999, from www.csmonitor.com/durable/1998/06/26/fp54s/-csm.htm

Punk, F. (2000). 'Shenzhen Yijiao Yuedui Yinxiang' (A Glimpse of Shenzhen Heathen Band), *Modeng Tiankong (Modern Sky), 7,* 12.

Qian, W. (2007). *The Declining Fortunes of Chinese Rock in the Mid-1990s: Weakness in Form or Weakness in Content?* Unpublished PhD Thesis, University of Liverpool, Liverpool.

Ramet, S. P. (1994). 'Rock: The Music of Revolution (and Political Conformity)', in S.P. Ramet (ed.), *Rocking the State: Rock Music and Politics in Eastern Europe and Russia.* Oxford: Westview Press, 1-14.

Rauhut, M. (1998). 'Looking East: The Socialist Rock Alternative in the 1970s', in T. Mitsui (ed.), *Popular Music: Intercultural Interpretations.* Kanazawa: Kanazawa University, 343-348.

Regev, M. (2007a). 'Cultural Uniqueness and Aesthetic Cosmopolitanism', *European Journal of Social Theory, 10*(1), 123-138.

Regev, M. (2007b). 'Ethno-National Pop-Rock Music: Aesthetic Cosmopolitanism Made From Within', *Cultural Sociology, 1*(3), 317-341.

Rofel, L. (2007). *Desiring China: Experiments in Neoliberalism, Sexuality, and Public Culture.* Durham: Duke University Press.

Rose, T. (1994). *Black Noise: Rap Music and Black Culture in Contemporary America.* Middletown: Wesleyan University Press.

Rosen, S. (2003). 'Chinese Media and Youth: Attitudes to Nationalism and Internationalism', in J. Li & C.-C. Lee (eds.), *Chinese Media, Global Contexts: Global Contexts.* London: Routledge, 97-118.

S&M. (1999). 'Asshole I Am Not Your Baby', *Modeng Tiankong (Modern Sky), 5,* 10.

Said, E. (1978). *Orientalism.* New York: Vintage Books.

Schein, L. (1997). 'Gender and Internal Orientalism in China', *Modern China, 23*(1), 69-98.

Schimmelpenninck, A. (1997). 'Chinese Folk Songs and Folk Singers. Shan'ge Traditions in Southern Jiangsu', *Chime Studies in East Asian Music, 1.*

Shang, G. (1997). 'He Laobai Xing Qian Yuande Zang Tianshuo' (Zang Tianshuo Contracted With Common People). *Zhongguo Bailaohui (Chinese Broadway),* October, 42, 14-15.

Shank, B. (1994). *Dissonant Identities: The Rock'n'Roll Scene in Austin, Texas.* Middletown: Wesleyan University Press.

Shih, S.-M. (2007). *Visuality and Identity. Sinophone Articulations across the Pacific.* Berkeley: University of California Press.

Shohat, E., & Stam, R. (1994). *Unthinking Eurocentrism: Multiculturalism and the Media.* London: Routledge.

Sisaro, B. 'For All the Rock in China [Electronic Version]', *New York Times.* Retrieved 25 November 2007 from www.nytimes.com/2007/11/25/arts/music/25sisa.html.

Sontag, S. (1964). Notes on "Camp". In S. Sontag (ed.), *Against Interpretation and Other Essays* (1967 ed., pp. 275-292). London Eyre & Spottiswoode.

Spivak, G.C. (1988). 'Can the Subaltern Speak?', in C. Nelson & L. Grossberg (eds.), *Marxism and the Interpretation of Culture*. Urbana: University of Illinois Press, 271-313.

Spivak, G. C., & Gunew, S. (1993). 'Questions of Multiculturalism', in S. During (ed.), *The Cultural Studies Reader*. London: Routledge, 194-202.

Stahl, G. (2004). '"It's Like Canada Reduced": Setting the Scene in Montreal', in A. Bennett & K. Kahn-Harris (eds.), *After Subculture: Critical Studies in Contemporary Youth Culture*. New York: Palgrave MacMillan, 51-64.

Steen, A. (1996). 'Der lange Marsch des Rock'n'Roll: Pop und Rockmusik in der Volksrepublik China', *Berliner China-Studien, 32*.

Steen, A. (1998). 'Buddhism & Rock music – A New Music Style?', *CHIME: Journal of the European Foundation for Chinese Music Research, 12/13,* 151-164.

Steen, A. (2000). 'Sounds, Protest and Business: Modern Sky Co. and The New Ideology of Chinese Rock', *Berliner China Hefte 19,* 40-64.

Steen, A. (2008). 'Post socialist Creativity and Confusion: CD-Covers and the Visual Presentation of Chinese Popular Music', *Berliner China Hefte, 34,* 27-52.

Steen, A., & de Kloet, J. (2005). 'Popular Music in Shanghai', in J. Shepherd, Horn & D. Laing (eds.), *The Encyclopaedia of Popular Music of the World*. London: Continuum International, 36-42.

Stokes, D.M. (2006). 'Reconstructing Rock Mythology: Constructions of Popular Music in the Chinese Print Media', *Perfect Beat, 7*(4), 82-108.

Stokes, M. (1994). *Ethnicity, Identity and Music: The Musical Construction of Place*. Oxford: Berg.

Straw, W. (1997). 'Communities and Scenes in Popular Music', in S.T. Ken Gelder (ed.), *The Subcultures Reader*. London: Routledge, 494-505.

Sun, M. (1999). 'Jujue, Chengshou yu Pangguande Yidai' (Refusal, Forebearing and a Generation of Onlookers), *Modeng Tiankong (Modern Sky)*, November, 5, 18-19.

Tao, R. (2000a). 'Chaos and Collusion: Contemporary Chinese Rock', *China Today*, June, 6.

Tao, R. (2000b). 'The Future Sound of Beijing', *Modeng Tiankong (Modern Sky)*, June, 6, 24-25.

Thornton, S. (1995). *Club Cultures: Music, Media and Subcultural Capital*. Cambridge: Polity Press.

Tianpigu. (1999). Review of CD *Zheng Jun, Modeng Tiankong (Modern Sky)*, February, 2, 17.

Tu, W. (ed.). (1994). *The Living Tree: The Changing Meaning of Being Chinese*. Stanford: Stanford University Press.

Tuan, Y.F. (1993). *Passing Strange and Wonderful, Aesthetics, Nature, and Culture*. New York: Kodansha International.

Vai, S. (1999). 'Guang Yao Bu Gun (Only Rock, But Not Roll)', *Yinxiang Shijie (Audio and Video World)*, 5, 31.

Vaidhyanathan, S. (2003). *Copyrights and Copywrongs: The Rise of Intellectual Property and How it Threatens Creativity*. New York: New York University Press.

Vincent. (1996). Review of 'Zhongguo Huo II' (China Fire II), *Yinyue Tiantang (Music Heaven)*, 11, 20.

Walser, R. (1993). *Running With the Devil: Power, Gender and Madness in Heavy Metal Music*. Middletown: Wesleyan University Press.

Wang, J. (1996). *High Culture Fever: Politics, Aesthetics, and Ideology in Deng's China*. Berkeley: University of California Press.

Wang, J. (2001). 'Culture as Leisure and Culture as Capital', *Positions, 9*(1), 69-104.

Wang, J. (2008). *Brand New China: Advertising, Media and Commercial Culture*. Cambridge: Harvard University Press.

Wang, L. (1999). 'Pengke Cuileidang: Xin Kuzi Fangtan' (Punk Tearjerker: Interview with New Pants), *Yinyue Tiantang (Music Heaven)*, 31, 22.

Wang, S. (2008). Review of Tang Dynasty, *Yinyue Shikong (In Music)*, August, 146.

Wang, X. (2003). 'China on the Brink of a "Momentous Era"', *Positions*, 11(3), 585-611.

Weber, I. (2002). 'Shanghai Baby: Negotiating Youth Self-Identity in Urban China', *Social Identities: Journal for the Study of Race, Nation and Culture*, 8(2), 347-368.

Weber, I. (2003). 'Localising the Global: Successful Strategies for Selling Television Programmes to China', *Gazette*, 65(3), 273-290.

Webster, J.G., & Phalen, P.F. (1997). *The Mass Audience: Rediscovering the Dominant Model*. New Jersey: Lawrence Erlbaum Associate.

Wen, C. (2004). 'SUBS: Cong Beijing Fachu De Shengyin' (SUBS: An independent voice from Beijing), *Tongse Gequ (Rock)*, 13.

Whiteley, S. (1997). 'Little Red Rooster V. The Honky Tonk Woman: Mick Jagger, Sexuality, Style and Image', in S. Whiteley (ed.), *Sexing the Groove: Popular Music and Gender*, 67-99.

Wicke, P. (1992). 'The Times They Are A-Changin': Rock Music and Political Change in East Germany', in R. Garofalo (ed.), *Rockin' the Boat: Mass Music and Mass Movements*. Boston: South End Press, 81-92.

Winfield, B. H., & Peng, Z. (2005). 'Market or Party Controls?', *International Communication Gazette*, 67(3), 255-270.

Witzleben, L. (1999). 'Cantopop and Mandapop in Pre-Postcolonial Hong Kong: Identity Negotiations in the Performances of Anita Mui Yim-Fong', *Popular Music 18, 2*, 241-528.

Wong, C. (1997). *Don't Tell Me How To Be: The Negotiation of Identity and Gender Difference on the Beijing Rock Scene*. Paper presented at the 1997 SEM Conference.

Wong, C. (2005). *Lost Lambs: Rock, Gender, Authenticity, and a Generational Response to Modernity in the People's Republic of China*. Unpublished PhD thesis, Columbia University, New York.

Xie, F. (2008). 'Jingdian Changpin Huigu Chi Zi Yue Yuedui Di Yici' (Classic Rock Review: The First Volume from Zi Yue), *Yinyue Shikong (In Music)*, 106-108.

Yan, J. (2002). *Didixia: Xin Yinyue Chanxingji (Underground: A Trip through New Music)*. Beijing: Wenhua Yishu Chubanshe.

Yan, J. (2004). 'Yongyuan Nianqing, Youngyuan Relei Ningkang – 2002 Midi Yinyuejie Jishi' (Forever Young, Forever Crying – Notes on Midi 2002 Music Festival), in G. Chen, W. Liao & J. Yan (eds.), *Boximiya Zhongguo (Bohemian China)*. Hong Kong: Hong Kong University Press, 176.

Yan, J., & Ou, N. (1999). *Beijing Xinsheng (New Sound of Beijing)*. Hunan: Wenyi Publishing.

Yi, S. (1996). 'Cui Jian, Shui Shi Bufu Zeren de Ren' (Cui Jian, Who Has Not Enough Responsibility?), *Yingyue Shenghuo (Music Life)* 15 September.

Yuen, C.C. (1999). 'Smells Like Teen Spirit: Beijing Punk-Pop Xinshengdai Tezi: Dixia Yin-g'er, Xin Kuzi, Hua'r '(Smells Like Teen Spirit: New Generation of Beijing Punk-Pop Special: Underground Babies, New Pants, Flowers), *Modeng Tiankong (Modern Sky)*, January, 1, 20-21.

Yurchak, A. (2005). *Everything Was Forever, Until It Was No More*. Princeton and Oxford: Princeton University Press.

Zhahuang, Z.X. (1999, January). Review of CD *HU Mage*, *Modeng Tiankong (Modern Sky)*, 1, 17.

Zhang, X. (1995). 'Wang Lei: Chumenren (Wang Lei: Wandering Man)'. *Top Records Guangzhou*, 8.

Zhang, X. (2000). 'New Music Guangzhou, Zai Guangzhou Zhao Le' (New Music Guangzhou, Looking For Fun in Guangzhou), *Modeng Tiankong (Modern Sky)*, July, 7, 16-17.

Zhang, X.D. (1997). *Chinese Modernism in the Era of Reforms: Cultural Fever, Avant-Garde Fiction and the New Chinese Cinema*. Durham and London: Duke University Press.

Zhang, X.D. (2008). *Postsocialism and Cultural Politics: China in the Last Decade of the Twentieth Century*. Durham: Duke University Press.

Zhang, Y. (2000). 'Hip Hop Yinyue Teji: Shuo He Chang' (Hip Hop Music Special: Speak and Sing), *Modeng Tiankong (Modern Sky)*, July, 7, 18-19.

Zhang, Y. (2008). 'Chen Danqing Han Han Duihua Lu' (A Talk Between Chen Danqing and Han Han), *Yinyue Shikong (In Music)*, 9 August, 389, 102-105.

Zhang, Z. (1997). 'Luo Qi Jiedu you Xiao You Xin Chongfan Getan' (Luo Qi Quit Using Drugs and Prepares to Sing Again), *Zhongguo Yanyuanbao (China Acting News)*, 10.

Zhang, Z. (2000). 'Mediating Time: The "Rice Bowl of Youth" in Fin de Siecle Urban China', *Public Culture*, 12(1), 93-113.

Zhao, K. (1999). 'Shijimo Yaogun: Yaogun Xintai Yijing Guoshile Ma?' (Rock By the End of the Century: Is Rock Mentality Outdated?), *Zhongguo Bailaohui (Chinese Broadway)*, March, 2-3, 14.

Zhao, Y. (2008). *Communication in China – Political Economy, Power, and Conflict*. Maryland: Rowan and Littlefield.

Zhong, X. (2006). 'Who is a Feminist? Understanding the Ambivalence towards Shanghai Baby, "Body Writing" and Feminism in Post-Women's Liberation China', *Gender & History*, 18(3), 635-660.

Zhu, D. (2006). *Liumangde Shengyang (The Festival of Liumang)*. Beijing: Xin Xing Chubanshe (New Star Press).

Zhu, T. (1996). 'Cui Jian Gongkai Xiang Zhang Chu Daoqian' (Cui Jian Apologises to Zhang Chu in Public), *Yinyue Shenghuo (Music Life)*, 15 September 1996, 14.

Zimmermann, B. (2007). 'Tracing the Action of Technical Objects in an Ethnography: Vinyls in Beijing', *Qualitative Sociology Review*, III(3), 22-45.

Zong, M. M. (2008). 'Wang Yue: Zai Meiyou Zheyang de Nuhai' (Wang Yue: There Can Never Be a Girl Like Her), *Popular Songs (Tongsu Gequ)*, September, 9, 8-9.

Index

 PUBLICATIONS SERIES

Josine Stremmelaar and Paul van der Velde (eds.)
What about Asia? Revisiting Asian Studies
2006 (ISBN 978 90 5356 959 7)

Monographs

Alex McKay
Their Footprints Remain. Biomedical Beginnings Across the Indo-Tibetan Frontier
Monographs 1
2007 (ISBN 978 90 5356 518 6)

Masae Kato
Women's Rights? The Politics of Eugenic Abortion in Modern Japan
Monographs 2
2009 (ISBN 978 90 5356 793 7)

Edited Volumes

Gijsbert Oonk (ed.)
Global Indian Diasporas. Exploring Trajectories of Migration and Theory
Edited Volumes 1
2007 (ISBN 978 90 5356 035 8)